◆ The Basic Writer's Book ◆

Third Edition

Anne Scrivener Agee
Anne Arundel Community College

Carolyn E. Phanstiel
Florida Community College at Jacksonville

PRENTICE HALL, Upper Saddle River, New Jersey 07458

Library of Congress Cataloging-in-Publication Data

Agee, Anne.
   The basic writer's book/Anne Agee, Carolyn E. Phanstiel.–3rd
ed.
        p.   cm.
   Includes index.
   ISBN   0-13-058637-4
   1. English language–Rhetoric.   2. Report writing.   I. Phanstiel,
Carolyn E.   II. Title.
PE1408.A42 1998   97-7220
808'.042–dc21   CIP
                                                          r97

Editorial Director: Charlyce Jones-Owen
Acquisitions Editor: Maggie Barbieri
Director of Production and Manufacturing: Barbara Kittle
Production Manager: Bonnie Biller
Production Editor
   and Interior Designer: Joan E. Foley
Copyeditor: Virginia Rubens
Editorial Assistant: Joan Polk
Manufacturing Manager: Nick Sklitsis
Prepress and Manufacturing Buyer: Mary Ann Gloriande
Line Art Coordinator: Michele Giusti

This book was set in 10/12 New Baskerville by The Clarinda Company
and was printed and bound by Hamilton Printing Company.
The cover was printed by Phoenix Color Company.

© 1998 by Prentice-Hall, Inc.
Simon & Schuster/A Viacom Company
Upper Saddle River, New Jersey 07458

For permission to use copyrighted material, grateful
acknowledgment is made to the copyright holders listed
on page 431, which is considered an extension of this
copyright page.

Printed in the United States of America
10 9 8 7 6 5 4 3 2 1

ISBN 0-13-058637-4

Prentice-Hall International (UK) Limited, *London*
Prentice-Hall of Australia Pty. Limited, *Sydney*
Prentice-Hall Canada Inc., *Toronto*
Prentice-Hall Hispanoamerica, S.A., *Mexico*
Prentice-Hall of India Private Limited, *New Delhi*
Prentice-Hall of Japan, Inc., *Tokyo*
Simon & Schuster Asia Pte. Ltd., *Singapore*
Editora Prentice-Hall do Brasil, Ltda., *Rio de Janeiro*

To the memory
of
Dr. Gary Dean Kline
(1943–1988)

◀ *Contents* ▶

◆ Part II ◆
Basic Paragraph Patterns, 258

◆ Part III ◆
The Writing Process, 309

◀ *Preface* ▶

Although the third edition of *The Basic Writer's Book* has been prepared with assistance from a new co-author, Carolyn E. Phanstiel, it maintains the same emphases that guided Gary Kline and me in the first two editions. Writing remains crucial to our students both for its practical value as a communication tool and for its humanistic value as a tool of independent and creative thinking.

As in the earlier editions, we continue to focus on writing as a process and to place grammatical, syntactic, lexical, and rhetorical choices in the context of that process. We try to familiarize student writers with the various options available to writers in any situation and to increase their ability to discriminate among these options. Likewise, we have emphasized throughout the book rhetorical considerations of audience and purpose as the operative standards for choosing effectively among alternative means of presenting an idea. We have not tried to be exhaustive in our coverage of the conventions of grammar and usage; nor have we unduly emphasized the terminology of these conventions. Rather, we have focused on those aspects of grammar and mechanics that can have an immediate impact on the effectiveness of a student's writing. We also continue to use sentence-combining extensively as a learning tool because it enables students to concentrate on effective presentation of ideas.

Thanks to many helpful comments from students and teachers who have used previous editions of *The Basic Writer's Book,* we have also made some changes that we hope will make the book even more useful:

- **The discussion of verbs has been moved to the beginning of the book to form the foundation for Part One: Basic Sentence Patterns.**

- Each chapter now begins with a preview of the major topics included in the chapter.

- Each chapter now includes a broader range of exercises that require different levels of knowledge and skill. Students not only identify techniques used in a sentence or paragraph, they also revise sentences and paragraphs to incorporate specific techniques and compose original sentences and paragraphs to practice the techniques presented in the chapter.

- Each chapter ends with a comprehensive revision exercise and two original writing assignments with suggestions for planning, drafting, and revising the writing.

- Each chapter focuses on a theme such as American History, Sports, or Science so that exercises have a more coherent intellectual content and students can relate writing to different contexts and cultures. In addition, the writing assignments at the end of the chapter relate in some way to the thematic contents of the chapter and often allow the writers to use information available in the chapter exercises to support the writing.

ACKNOWLEDGMENTS

We are especially grateful to our students who have shown us the strengths and weaknesses of *The Basic Writer's Book;* to our reviewers Linda Donahue, Naugatuck Valley College; Kate Gleason, Interboro Institute; Patrick Haas, Glendale Community College, who have read our manuscripts so carefully and made such thoughtful suggestions for change; to our colleagues, families, and friends, who have given us their generous support and encouragement over the years.

We hope this new edition of *The Basic Writer's Book* will help many students to share the challenge and the pleasure we feel as writers.

Anne Agee

Carolyn Phanstiel

The Basic Writer's Book

◆ Part I ◆

Basic Sentence Patterns

Ever since you sat in kindergarten and practiced ***The man ran***, you've been using sentences to communicate ideas in writing. After writing sentences for so long, you know a lot about them. This book will build on that knowledge to help you become a more skillful writer.

Being a good writer means knowing how to rework sentences to make them as effective as possible. A good writer can take the first draft of a sentence and expand or tighten it, make its parts more precise, shape and reshape it until it does exactly what is necessary for the situation.

Part One of this book will give you practice in working with the basic structure of sentences and in choosing alternative ways of expressing ideas.

The British statesman, orator, and writer Winston Churchill claimed that an outstanding part of his education was learning to understand the organization of sentences: "I got into my bones the essential structure of the ordinary English sentence—which is a noble thing." To grow as a writer is to appreciate this nobility.

◀ *Chapter 1* ▶

Verbs

• • • • • • • • • • • • • •

• • • • • • • • • • • • • •

Verbs are the heart of language. They show people or objects involved in action—physical (running, singing), mental (thinking, observing), or just the action of existence (being, feeling). Using verbs well can add a great deal to your flexibility as a writer. Verbs can do tremendous work for you if you know how to use them skillfully.

EXERCISE A

In the following list of words, which ones describe action? Put a check next to each word that could be used as a verb. If you are not sure of any word, test it by seeing if it will fit into the following blank: *Can you* _____? If the word makes sense in this slot, then it is almost certainly a verb.

✓ 1. sleep	✓ 11. send
✗ 2. car	✗ 12. Annette
✗ 3. beautiful	✗ 13. far
✓ 4. laugh	✓ 14. climb
✗ 5. it	✓ 15. attack
✗ 6. slowly	✓ 16. love
✓ 7. dive	✗ 17. point
✓ 8. feel	✗ 18. east
✗ 9. lip	✗ 19. badly
✗ 10. great	✓ 20. rise

▶ VERB FORMS

● Regular Verbs

To use verbs effectively, you first need to understand that they have several different forms. Every verb, in fact, has four basic forms: the **present** form, the **present participle** form, the **past** form, and the **past participle** form. Each of these forms is associated with a particular time frame for the action. These four forms are the basis of all the uses of verbs.

As an example, there are four forms of the verb *walk.*

Present	Present Participle	Past	Past Participle
(Every day I)	*(Right now I am)*	*(Yesterday I)*	*(For many years I have)*
walk	walking	walked	walked

All verbs form the present participle by adding *-ing* to the present form of the verb. The verb *walk* is one of a large category of verbs that have a regular pattern for forming the third and fourth principle parts, the past and the past participle. For regular verbs, both the past and the past participle are formed by adding *-d* or *-ed* to the present.

EXERCISE B

Using the pattern shown above, write out the four forms of the following verbs.

Present	Present Participle	Past	Past Participle
(Every day I)	*(Right now I am)*	*(Yesterday I)*	*(For many years I have)*
1. plant	planting	planted	planted
2. cook	cooking	cooked	cooked
3. discover	discovering	discovered	discovered
4. explore	exploring	explored	explored
5. start	starting	started	started
6. open	openning	opened	openned
7. watch	watching	watched	watched
8. play	playing	played	played
9. deliver	delivering	delivered	delivered
10. hypnotize	hypontizing	hypontized	hypnotized

Most English verbs are regular in the way they form their basic parts. They add *-d* or *-ed* to the present to create the past and the past participle forms.

■ *Spelling Changes with Regular Verbs*

Even with regular verbs, though, you do need to watch out for three kinds of spelling changes:

1. One-syllable verbs or verbs that end with an accented vowel–consonant pattern double the final consonant before adding *-ed* or *-ing*. Examples: plan → planning, planned; rub → rubbing, rubbed; permit → permitting, permitted
2. Verbs that end in a consonant followed by the letter *y* change the *y* to *i* before adding *-ed*, but not before adding *-ing*. Examples: carry → carrying, carried; try → trying, tried
3. Verbs that end in a long vowel followed by a consonant followed by the letter *e* drop the *e* before adding *-ing*. Examples: create → creating, created; hike → hiking, hiked

Spelling rules are discussed in more detail in Chapter 12. Any time you are not sure about the spelling of a verb form, you can consult a dictionary to find the correct spelling. Look up the present or base form of the verb, and the dictionary will show you the other forms of the verb, as the sample entry below indicates. If the dictionary doesn't show any other forms of the verb, that means the verb is regular with no spelling changes.

oc•cur (ə-kûr′) intr. v. –**curred**, –**curring**, –**curs**. 1. To take place; come about.

This dictionary entry indicates that the verb *occur* doubles its final *r* before adding *-ed* or *-ing*.

Exercise C

Write out the four principle parts of each of the following verbs. Apply the spelling rules shown above as necessary.

Present	Present Participle	Past	Past Participle
(Every day I)	*(Right now I am)*	*(Yesterday I)*	*(For many years I have)*
1. slip	_____	_____	_____
2. refer	_____	_____	_____
3. supply	_____	_____	_____
4. act	_____	_____	_____
5. worry	_____	_____	_____
6. control	_____	_____	_____

Present	Present Participle	Past	Past Participle
(Every day I)	*(Right now I am)*	*(Yesterday I)*	*(For many years I have)*
7. prepare	_____	_____	_____
8. cry	_____	_____	_____
9. drag	_____	_____	_____
10. pity	_____	_____	_____

● **Irregular Verbs**

Although most verbs are regular, some verbs have a different way of forming the past and the past participle. Because these verbs do not follow the *-ed* rule, they are called **irregular verbs.**

Here are some examples of irregular verbs:

IRREGULAR VERBS			
Present	Present Participle	Past	Past Participle
(Every day I)	*(Right now I am)*	*(Yesterday I)*	*(For many years I have)*
sing	singing	sang	sung
think	thinking	thought	thought
come	coming	came	come
go	going	went	gone
write	writing	wrote	written

As you can see from these examples, irregular verbs use a great many different patterns to form the past and past participle. The following pages list the most common irregular verbs. Since the present participle form of the verb is always formed in the same way—by adding *-ing* to the present form—the list does not show this form.

One way to tackle this list is simply to memorize it. This may not be as hard as you think because you probably know a great many of these verb forms, especially if you are a native speaker of English. Test yourself by covering up the second and third columns of the list. Check off the verbs you are not sure of and concentrate on memorizing those. It is often helpful to say the three parts out loud while you are memorizing them.

Present	Past	Past Participle
(Every day . . .)	*(Yesterday . . .)*	*(For many years . . .)*
(be) is, are, am	was, were	been
beat	beat	beaten
begin	began	begun
bite	bit	bitten
blow	blew	blown
break	broke	broken
bring	brought	brought
burst	burst	burst
buy	bought	bought
choose	chose	chosen
come	came	come
do	did	done
draw	drew	drawn
drink	drank	drunk
drive	drove	driven
eat	ate	eaten
fall	fell	fallen
fight	fought	fought
find	found	found
fly	flew	flown
forget	forgot	forgotten
freeze	froze	frozen
give	gave	given
go	went	gone
grow	grew	grown
hang (suspend)	hung	hung
have	had	had
hide	hid	hidden
hold	held	held
know	knew	known
lay	laid	laid
lie	lay	lain
lose	lost	lost
ride	rode	ridden
ring	rang	rung
rise	rose	risen
run	ran	run
see	saw	seen
send	sent	sent
set	set	set
shake	shook	shaken
shine	shone	shone
show	showed	shown
shrink	shrank	shrunk
sing	sang	sung
sink	sank	sunk
sit	sat	sat
slide	slid	slid
speak	spoke	spoken
spend	spent	spent

Present	Past	Past Participle
(Every day . . .)	*(Yesterday . . .)*	*(For many years . . .)*
spin	spun	spun
stand	stood	stood
steal	stole	stolen
stick	stuck	stuck
strike	struck	struck
swear	swore	sworn
swim	swam	swum
swing	swung	swung
take	took	taken
teach	taught	taught
tear	tore	torn
think	thought	thought
throw	threw	thrown
wear	wore	worn
weave	wove	woven
win	won	won
write	wrote	written

Another technique that may help you to remember the irregular verb forms is to group together verbs that follow a similar pattern. For example, *think → thought → thought* is similar to *hold → held → held* because these two verbs use the same form for the past and the past participle.

EXERCISE D

Using the example given below as a model, construct a chart showing at least five patterns that irregular verbs use to form the past and the past participle.

Pattern 1:   *Past and past participle the same* _____

Examples: *think/thought/thought* _____

  hold/held/held _____

  _____

  _____

  _____

Pattern 2:   _____

Examples: _____

  _____

Pattern 3: _____

Examples: _____

_____

_____

_____

Pattern 4: _____

Examples: _____

_____

_____

_____

Pattern 5: _____

Examples: _____

_____

_____

_____

■ *A Very Irregular Verb: Be*

Of all the irregular verbs, the one with the most variation is the verb *be*. The verb *be* indicates action only in the very broadest sense—it indicates the condition of existence. Because its meaning is so broad, it fits easily into a great many sentences. In fact, it is so easy to use that you have to take care not to overuse it. Because *be* conveys so little action, too many *be*-verbs can actually weaken a piece of writing. Nevertheless, this verb has numerous uses, and it is worth separate study to make sure you know all its parts.

As the box below shows, the verb *be* has four different forms of the present and two forms of the past as well as present and past participles.

FORMS OF THE VERB *BE*			
Present	**Present Participle**	**Past**	**Past Participle**
(Every day)	*(Right now)*	*(Yesterday)*	*(For many years)*
be am is are	being	was was/were	been

Later in this chapter, you will see how these forms of *be* are used.

■ *Especially Troublesome Irregular Verbs:* Lie/Lay, Sit/Set, Rise/Raise

Even if you know the correct forms of the irregular verbs, these three pairs of verbs—*lie/lay, sit/set, rise/raise*—may give you trouble if you can't distinguish the meaning of each verb. These pairs of verbs may need some extra attention. The box below shows the principle parts of these verbs.

FORMS OF *LIE/LAY, SIT/SET, RISE/RAISE*			
Present	**Present Participle**	**Past**	**Past Participle**
(Every day I)	*(Right now I am)*	*(Yesterday I)*	*(For many years I have)*
lie lay sit set rise raise	lying laying sitting setting rising raising	lay laid sat set rose raised	lain laid sat set risen raised

Actually, these three pairs of verbs have some things in common. One verb in each pair—*lie, sit,* and *rise*—indicates an action that is self-contained and self-initiated, an action that is done of one's own accord. The action is not done to anyone or anything else. Each of these is a kind of one-step action. *Sit* and *lie* have similar meanings. Both indicate remaining in a certain position. You might also link these verbs together in your mind by remembering that all three have types of *i* sounds in the present form.

EXAMPLES:

> Jill → *lies* in bed until her alarm goes off.
>
> Her cats → *lie* there next to her.
>
> Her dog → *sits* at the foot of the bed.
>
> The sun → *rises* over the horizon.
>
> Jill → finally *rises* from her bed.

The second verb in each pair—*lay, set,* and *raise*—indicates an action caused by an outside agent, an action done to or for someone or something else. Again, *lay* and *set* have similar meanings. Both indicate that something has been placed in a certain location by someone else. You might think of these as two-step actions.

EXAMPLES:

> Jill → *lays* → her book on the floor.
>
> Her dog → *lays* → its paw on her lap.
>
> She → *sets* → her glasses on the table.
>
> She → *sets* → a plate of cookies next to the glasses.
>
> The cat → *raises* → its head to look around.

EXERCISE E

In each of the following sentences, choose the appropriate verb. Consider whether the action is self-contained or whether it moves from the actor to something else. If it is a one-step action, use *lie, sit,* or *rise.* If it is a two-step action, use *lay, set,* or *raise.*

1. It is 10 March 1875. Alexander Graham Bell _____ at his workbench.
   sits/sets

2. Bell carefully _____ a strange-looking machine in front of him.
   sits/sets

3. A tall cone _____ from the center of the machine.
   rises/raises

4. He _____ his hand to begin the experiment.
   rises/raises

5. In his excitement, he knocks over the battery that _____ on the table.
   lies/lays

6. He _____ his tools aside and calls for his assistant.
   lies/lays

7. In another room, Thomas Watson _____ his head.
    rises/raises
8. In front of him _____ a machine similar to Bell's.
    sits/sets
9. Suddenly, Bell's voice _____ from the machine.
    rises/raises
10. The future of communication _____ in that strange machine—the
    telephone.   **lies/lays**

▶ VERB TENSE

One of the most important uses of the four different verb forms is the creation of
different tenses. **Tense** is the quality of a verb that shows *when* an action takes
place. English has six main verb tenses: three simple tenses—*present, past, future*—
and three perfect tenses—*present perfect, past perfect, future perfect.*

Some verb forms—such as *to cry* or *crying*—do not show time. When you are
constructing a sentence, you must include a verb that shows time. A verb that has
tense is one of the requirements for a complete sentence.

● The Simple Tenses

The three simple tenses place action within broad categories of time: the present,
the past, and the future. The simple tenses usually involve a single action contained in a single time frame. The sections that follow show the formation and
uses of the three simple tenses.

■ Present Tense

You use the **present tense** when you want to indicate that action is going on at the
present moment or that the action is habitual. The following sentences show verbs
in the present tense:

> A great inventor *imagines* new solutions to old problems.
>
> Today's inventors *build* on the work of their predecessors.

You also use the present tense in stating rules or general principles that
remain true at all times. For example:

> One hundred centimeters *equal* one meter.

The present tense is formed by using the first, or present, form of the verb.
A standard way of looking at verb tense is to show a verb with all its possible subjects. The table shows how the verb *write* looks in the present tense when it is set
up in this verb conjugation format.

WRITE		
	Singular	**Plural**
1st person	I **write**	we **write**
2nd person	you **write**	you **write**
3rd person	he/she/it **writes**	they **write**

In communication, the first person refers to the speaker or the writer—*I* or *we*. The second person refers to the audience or reader—*you*. The third person refers to the topic being spoken or written about—*he, she, it,* or *they*. These three—writer, audience, and topic—are the basic elements of communication. Thus, this table quickly shows all the possible subjects that a verb may have.

Notice that the present tense of the verb looks the same in five out of the six positions on the table. In the third person singular, however, when it is used with a *he, she* or *it* subject, the present tense verb adds an *-s*.

As you saw earlier in this chapter, the verb *be* has several different present tense forms. Here is how the verb *be* is conjugated in the present tense:

BE		
	Singular	**Plural**
1st person	I **am**	we **are**
2nd person	you **are**	you **are**
3rd person	he/she/it **is**	they **are**

You can use the verb *be* to construct another form of the present tense. When you want to show action currently in progress, you use the present participle or *-ing* form of the verb along with the appropriate form of *be*. For example, the verb *write* would form this progressive present tense as shown in the table below.

WRITE		
	Singular	**Plural**
1st person	I **am writing**	we **are writing**
2nd person	you **are writing**	you **are writing**
3rd person	he/she/it **is writing**	they **are writing**

Here are some sentences that show the two forms of the present tense.

The automotive industry *changes* constantly. *(habitual)*

The automotive industry *is changing* right now. *(in progress)*

The first example shows an action that happens regularly or habitually. In this case, the sentence indicates that changes occur in the automotive industry as a matter of course. This form of the present tense uses the present form of the verb with the *-s* ending in the third person singular. A habitual action is often accompanied by a word like *usually, always, often,* or *never* to emphasize the customary character of the action.

The second example uses the progressive form of the present tense. This sentence emphasizes that changes are happening in the automotive industry at this very moment. The progressive form of the present tense uses a form of the verb *be* plus the present participle of the action verb. The progressive form of the verb is often accompanied by a word like *now* or *today* to emphasize that the action is currently in progress.

EXERCISE F

Write out the present tense forms of each of the following verbs, filling in the chart to show how the verb would look with each of its possible subjects. Show both the habitual form of the present tense and the progressive form.

1.

GO		
	Singular	**Plural**
1st person	I	we
2nd person	you	you
3rd person	he/she/it	they

2.

BEGIN		
	Singular	**Plural**
1st person	I	we
2nd person	you	you
3rd person	he/she/it	they

3.

TALK		
	Singular	**Plural**
1st person	I	we
2nd person	you	you
3rd person	he/she/it	they

4.

LIE		
	Singular	**Plural**
1st person	I	we
2nd person	you	you
3rd person	he/she/it	they

5.

LAY		
	Singular	**Plural**
1st person	I	we
2nd person	you	you
3rd person	he/she/it	they

EXERCISE G

Write in a present tense verb for each subject below. If you use the habitual form, remember to add an *-s* to the verb if the subject is a *he,* a *she,* or an *it.* If you use the progressive form, remember to use the appropriate form of the verb *be.* Use some of each type in the exercise.

1. Modern inventors _go to the_ _____

2. Guglielmo Marconi _____

3. The American public _____

4. You and Mr. Franklin _____

5. That automobile _____

6. Horses _____

7. Wilbur and Orville Wright _____

8. The average television viewer _____

9. Marie Curie_____

10. George Washington Carver and I _____

11. Thomas Edison's electric light bulb _____

12. Benjamin Banneker _____

13. A clock _____

14. Photographs _____

15. Many experiments _____

EXERCISE H

On a separate sheet of paper, write a short summary (10 to 12 sentences) of the plot of a television show or movie you have seen recently. Tell the story in the present tense. Underline all the present tense verbs in your story.

EXAMPLE:

It is a dark and stormy night. The mad scientist stands at the window of her laboratory. She shakes her fist at the crowd below. "I am not finished yet," she screams. Her assistant grabs her from behind and pushes her out the window. "You are finished now," he says. He rubs his hands together gleefully. The crowd runs away.

■ Past Tense

You use the **past tense** to indicate that an action was completed at some time before the present moment. For example, the following sentences contain verbs in the past tense.

Elizabeth Keckley, a slave, *developed* a unique system of cutting and fitting women's clothing.

She *taught* her method to other seamstresses.

She *bought* her freedom with her earnings.

The past tense uses the third, or past, form of the verb. For instance, the verb *write* looks like this in the past tense:

WRITE		
	Singular	**Plural**
1st person	I **wrote**	we **wrote**
2nd person	you **wrote**	you **wrote**
3rd person	he/she/it **wrote**	they **wrote**

Notice that the form of the verb stays the same for all subjects in the past tense.

The verb *be* is an exception to this general principle, since it has two different forms in the past tense. The table below shows the verb *be* with all its subjects in the past tense. The first person singular subject—*I*—and the third person singular subjects—*he/she/it*—use *was* in the past tense. All the other subjects use *were*.

BE		
	Singular	**Plural**
1st person	I **was**	we **were**
2nd person	you **were**	you **were**
3rd person	he/she/it **was**	they **were**

EXERCISE I

Write out the past tense forms of each of the following verbs, filling in the table to show how the verb would look with each of its possible subjects.

1.

GO		
	Singular	**Plural**
1st person	I	we
2nd person	you	you
3rd person	he/she/it	they

2.

BEGIN		
	Singular	**Plural**
1st person	I	we
2nd person	you	you
3rd person	he/she/it	they

3.

TALK		
	Singular	**Plural**
1st person	I	we
2nd person	you	you
3rd person	he/she/it	they

4.

LIE		
	Singular	**Plural**
1st person	I	we
2nd person	you	you
3rd person	he/she/it	they

5.

LAY		
	Singular	**Plural**
1st person	I	we
2nd person	you	you
3rd person	he/she/it	they

EXERCISE J

Underline all the verbs in the following paragraph. Then, rewrite the paragraph changing the verbs from the present tense to the past tense. The first sentence has been done for you as an example.

America's love affair with gadgets really grows up in the late nineteenth century. In the thirty years after the Civil War, the U.S. Patent Office does a booming business. It issues 440,000 patents. In the twentieth century, the number rises even higher. Many of the inventions are useless, but the numbers indicate America's fascination with "building a better mousetrap." Throughout the century, Americans speak in awestruck tones about the wonders of such newfangled contraptions as vacuum cleaners, automobiles, and wireless telegraphs. When the great age of invention comes, they think they see the ultimate in human achievement. They have no idea what awaits them in the future.

America's love affair with gadgets really grew up in the late nineteenth

century.

_____

_____

_____

_____

_____

_____

_____

_____

_____

_____

_____

_____

_____

_____

EXERCISE K

Underline all the verbs in the following paragraph. Then, rewrite the paragraph changing the verbs from the past tense to the present tense. Remember to use the *-s* form of the verb for *he, she,* or *it* subjects. The first sentence has been done for you as an example.

Although eyeglasses were invented in the thirteenth century, it took 350 years to figure out how to keep them on. At first, someone put lenses in leather or metal frames and riveted them together in an inverted V-shape. The lenses sat precariously on the bridge of the nose. These rivet spectacles pinched the nose, and the wearer held his head at an odd angle. Even so, the contraption often fell off. By the fifteenth century, the Italians rigged a wire hat where the glasses dangled down over the forehead. The Spanish later experimented with silk ribbons that tied behind the wearer's ears. The Chinese attached small weights to strings that ran behind the ears. Around 1730, Edward Scarlett, a London optician, perfected the use of rigid sidepieces. Finally, vision was enhanced in relative comfort.

Although eyeglasses are invented in the thirteenth century, it takes 350 years

*to figure out how to keep them on.*_____

_____

_____

_____

_____

_____

_____

_____

_____

_____

_____

_____

_____

_____

_____

_____

_____

EXERCISE L

Choose any ten irregular verbs from the list on pages 7 to 8. List the present forms of those verbs in the blanks below:

1. _____   6. _____

2. _____   7. _____

3. _____   8. _____

4. _____   9. _____

5. _____   10. _____

Using the verbs you have just chosen, write a short story about a real or imagined event. Your story should be written in the past tense, and you should use each of your chosen verbs at least once in your story. Use your own paper to write this story. When you have finished the story, circle all the past tense verbs.

■ *Future Tense*

You use the **future tense** of a verb to indicate that an action is going to take place at some time after the present moment: next hour, next day, next week, next year, and so on. The sentences below show verbs in the future tense.

No one *will* ever *forget* their contributions to research.

The college *will plan* a celebration in their honor.

They *will hold* the celebration on their twentieth wedding anniversary.

To form the future tense, you start with the first, or present, form of the verb and add the helping verb *will*. The table below shows the verb *write* in the future tense. Notice that the form of the verb stays the same for all subjects in the future tense.

WRITE		
	Singular	**Plural**
1st person	I **will write**	we **will write**
2nd person	you **will write**	you **will write**
3rd person	he/she/it **will write**	they **will write**

The verb *be* forms its future tense in the same way as other verbs. It uses the present form *be* with the helping verb *will*. All its forms stay the same in the future tense, as shown in the table below.

BE		
	Singular	**Plural**
1st person	I **will be**	we **will be**
2nd person	you **will be**	you **will be**
3rd person	he/she/it **will be**	they **will be**

EXERCISE M

Write out the future tense forms of each of the following verbs, filling in the table to show how the verb would look with each of its possible subjects.

1.

GO		
	Singular	**Plural**
1st person	I	we
2nd person	you	you
3rd person	he/she/it	they

2.

BEGIN		
	Singular	**Plural**
1st person	I	we
2nd person	you	you
3rd person	he/she/it	they

3.

TALK		
	Singular	**Plural**
1st person	I	we
2nd person	you	you
3rd person	he/she/it	they

4.

LIE		
	Singular	**Plural**
1st person	I	we
2nd person	you	you
3rd person	he/she/it	they

5.

LAY		
	Singular	**Plural**
1st person	I	we
2nd person	you	you
3rd person	he/she/it	they

EXERCISE N

The following paragraph is a report by a twenty-second-century historian. Underline all the verbs in the paragraph. Then, rewrite the paragraph changing the verbs from the past tense to the future tense so that it reads as a prediction about the future instead of a report on the past. The first sentence has been done for you as an example.

About the middle of the twenty-first century, the first colonists settled on Mars. The settlement was made possible by a very simple invention, the carbon dioxide converter. Scientists in California developed the first converter in 2025. The converter allowed people to continue living in the smog-filled Los Angeles–San Francisco metropolitan area that covered more than half the state. In fact, it significantly improved the city's environment within a few years. The device proved equally effective in the thin Martian atmosphere. Robot-driven spaceprobes demonstrated the device in a series of landmark field tests. Soon, the cumbersome device shrank to a manageable size, thanks to new miniaturization circuits. Then, all the Martian colonists implanted the converters in their noses. Thus the colonists went about their everyday life with no need to worry about the breathability of the air. The carbon dioxide converter removed the last obstacle to the Martian settlement plan.

About the middle of the twenty-first century, the first colonists will settle

on Mars.

_____

_____

_____

_____

_____

_____

_____

_____

_____

_____

_____

_____

_____

_____

_____

_____

■ *Review: The Three Simple Tenses*

THE THREE SIMPLE TENSES		
Past	Present	Future
← He called	He calls He is calling	He will call →
Before the present time	In the present time	After the present time

As the box above suggests, the three simple tenses—the past, the present, and the future—place action in three broad categories of time. Action that happens habitually or happens in the present time is shown by the present tense. Action that was completed before the present is shown by the past tense. Action that will occur at some time after the present is shown by the future tense.

EXERCISE O

Underline the verb or verbs in each of the following sentences and indicate the tenses. Then rewrite the sentence in the tense shown. Be prepared to show how the meaning of the sentence changes when you change the tense of the verb.

<u>EXAMPLE:</u>

Garrett Morgan's invention of the automated three-way traffic light <u>saved</u> many lives _____*past*_____

(future) *Garrett Morgan's invention of the automated three-way traffic light*

will save many lives.

1. Hypatia, a Greek woman, invents the astrolabe in the fourth century. _____

   (past) _____

2. The computer will revolutionize everyday life. _____

   (past) _____

3. Edward Hunt will create the safety pin to pay off a $15 debt. _____

   (present) _____

4. Isaac Singer's sewing machines made thousands of military uniforms. _____

   (future) _____

5. Sixteenth-century Spanish explorers learn about rubber from the natives of

   South America. _____

   (past) _____

6. Laser beams carry most telephone communication. _____

   (future) _____

7. Levi Strauss started the American passion for "jeans" during the California

   gold rush. _____

   (present) _____

8. Chester Greenwood's invention of earmuffs in 1877 at the age of eighteen will

   make him famous. _____

   (past) _____

9. Will and John Kellogg's wheat flakes started out as a health food for hospital

   patients. _____

   (present) _____

10. The first ballpoint pens sell in 1945 for $12.50 each. _____

    (past) _____

EXERCISE P

Supply the correct form of the verb in each sentence below. Study the context of the sentence to determine whether the verb should be in the past, present, or future tense. Be prepared to explain your choice.

(stretch)   1. The use of the sun as a source of energy _____ far back into human history.

(trap)   2. Desert dwellers in ancient Egypt _____ the sun's heat in the thick walls of their houses to warm them at night.

(build)   3. Cliff dwellers at Mesa Verde in southwestern Colorado likewise

                    _____ houses to absorb the sun's energy.

(consider)   4. Many people today _____ solar energy the perfect power source.

(be)   5. Solar energy _____ abundant and nonpolluting.

(become)   6. With the increasing price of fossil fuels, solar energy

                    _____ even more popular in the decades ahead.

(lag)   7. Until the middle of the twentieth century, the United States

                    _____ behind other countries in solar energy research.

(experiment)   8. In 1939, scientists at the Massachusetts Institute of Technology

                    _____ with a rooftop solar collector to heat a house.

(design)   9. In 1948, architect Eleanor Raymond and engineer Maria Telkes

                       _____ a successful solar-heated house.

(include)   10. Solar energy currently _____ a variety of technologies.

(make)   11. A solar-powered aircraft _____ aviation history by flying
                       across the English Channel in 1981.

(see)   12. For the rest of this century, however, people probably

                       _____ the most extensive applications of solar energy in
                       the design of home heating systems.

(go)   13. About one fourth of America's energy now _____ to heat
                       water and living and working spaces.

(offset)   14. Over time, according to experts, the savings from solar heating

                       _____ the initial cost of installing a solar heater.

(create)   15. More research and experimentation _____ many more
                       practical applications of solar energy for the next century.

● The Perfect Tenses

The perfect tenses are not called "perfect" because they are better than the simple
tenses. "Perfect" in this context means complete. All three of the **perfect tenses**
indicate that an action occurred prior to some fixed time in the past, present, or
future.

   All three of the perfect tenses use the fourth principle part of the verb, the
past participle, which is, in fact, sometimes called the "perfect" form of the verb.
Along with the past participle, each of the perfect tenses uses a helping verb, some
form of the verb *have.* Since the form of the past participle never changes, the helping verb distinguishes the three perfect tenses. The present perfect tense uses the

present form of the helping verb. The past perfect tense uses the past form of the helping verb. The future perfect tense uses the future form of the helping verb.

The sections that follow show the formation and uses of the three perfect tenses.

■ *Present Perfect Tense*

The following sentence uses a verb in the past tense—*studied:*

1. Dr. Gwynn *studied* the problem for three years.

This sentence indicates that Dr. Gwynn's three-year study of the problem is finished. The study took place at some time in the past, but you can't tell exactly when in the past. Suppose, however, that you wrote the sentence this way:

2. Dr. Gwynn *has studied* the problem for three years.

What would this sentence say about the state of Dr. Gwynn's study? By using the verb *has studied,* this sentence tells you that Dr. Gwynn's study started three years ago and continues up to the present. *Has studied* is the present perfect tense of the verb. The present perfect tense indicates that an action started in the past and continues into the present. The timeline below illustrates the difference between the past tense and the present perfect tense.

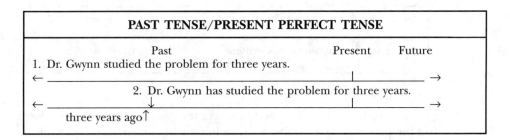

Here are two more sentences that show the difference between the past tense and the present perfect tense.

Dr. Gwynn *won* a Nobel Prize in chemistry.

Dr. Gwynn *has won* a Nobel Prize in chemistry.

What is the difference in meaning between these two sentences? The first sentence tells the reader that Dr. Gwynn's winning of the prize took place at some time in the past. The second sentence, using the present perfect tense, could indicate that the winning of the prize has just taken place in the very recent past, so close to the present that it may almost seem to continue into the present.

The present perfect tense, then, sets up a relationship between the past and the present. The present perfect tense indicates present actions that have a connection to the past or past actions that are completed in the present. Either the action began in the past and continues right up to the present, or it has been completed so recently in the past that it might almost be considered as a present action. While the past tense usually considers action as a single completed event, the present perfect tense usually considers action as a continuing series of events covering a span of time from the past to the present.

The first example above—*Dr. Gwynn studied the problem for three years.*—considers the action of studying as a single event that is now finished.

The second example—*Dr. Gwynn has studied the problem for three years.*—emphasizes that the action of studying occurred continuously over a period of three years.

The present perfect tense is formed by combining the fourth principle part of the verb, the past participle, with the present tense of the verb *have*. The table below shows the verb *write* in the present perfect tense. Notice that the form of the verb stays the same except in the third person singular. There *have* changes to *has*, following the *s* rule for the present tense.

WRITE		
	Singular	**Plural**
1st person	I **have written**	we **have written**
2nd person	you **have written**	you **have written**
3rd person	he/she/it **has written**	they **have written**

The verb *be* forms its present perfect tense in the same way as other verbs. It uses the past participle *been* with the helping verb *have* or *has*. All its forms stay the same in the present perfect tense, except, as noted above, that *have* changes to *has* in the third person singular form. The table below shows the verb *be* in the present perfect tense.

BE		
	Singular	**Plural**
1st person	I **have been**	we **have been**
2nd person	you **have been**	you **have been**
3rd person	he/she/it **has been**	they **have been**

EXERCISE Q
Write out the present perfect tense forms of each of the following verbs, filling in the table to show how the verb would look with each of its possible subjects.

1.

GO		
	Singular	**Plural**
1st person	I	we
2nd person	you	you
3rd person	he/she/it	they

2.

BEGIN		
	Singular	**Plural**
1st person	I	we
2nd person	you	you
3rd person	he/she/it	they

3.

TALK		
	Singular	**Plural**
1st person	I	we
2nd person	you	you
3rd person	he/she/it	they

4.

LIE		
	Singular	**Plural**
1st person	I	we
2nd person	you	you
3rd person	he/she/it	they

5.

	LAY	
	Singular	**Plural**
1st person	I	we
2nd person	you	you
3rd person	he/she/it	they

EXERCISE R

In each of the following sentences, supply the appropriate form of the verb, either past tense or present perfect tense. Look carefully at the context of the sentence to determine which tense best fits the meaning of the sentence. Be prepared to explain your choice.

(identify)   1. Scholars over the years _____ the development of written language as the first mark of a civilized society.

(write)   2. For centuries, people _____ all their documents by hand, one at a time.

(suggest)   3. In various discussions of the origin of printing, historians

                     _____ several sources.

(devise)   4. Both the ancient Romans and the Chinese _____ methods of stamping words with wood or clay blocks.

(lay)   5. In addition, the Chinese _____ a solid claim to the invention of movable type.

(conceive)   6. A Chinese printer named Bi Sheng _____ the idea of printing with individual clay characters in the middle of the eleventh century.

(begin)   7. In Europe, however, printing with movable type _____ only in the fifteenth century.

(show)   8. To date, no one _____ exactly how the Chinese developments influenced the Europeans.

(develop)   9. Johann Gutenberg, a German goldsmith, _____ the first printing works in Europe.

(design)   10. Besides using movable type, Gutenberg also _____ a printing press.

(provide)   11. Gutenberg's design _____ a model for printing presses ever since.

(see)   12. Before Gutenberg, ordinary people seldom _____ a book.

(sweep)   13. After Gutenberg, the printed word _____ through Europe like a hurricane.

(print)   14. In 1455, Gutenberg announces that he _____ two hundred copies of the Bible, more than a monk could hand-copy in a lifetime of work.

(estimate)   15. Scholars _____ that more than 40,000 separate works were in print by 1500.

(benefit)   16. Since the fifteenth century, the world _____ enormously from the easy availability of books.

(reap)   17. Unfortunately, Gutenberg himself _____ no benefit from his cleverness.

(seize)   18. His creditors _____ his business.

(die)   19. Gutenberg _____, poor and forgotten, in 1468.

(transform)   20. Arguably, no invention _____ the world more than Johann Gutenberg's.

EXERCISE S

The following paragraph is an award nomination for Elijah McCoy, an inventor who died in 1929. The paragraph is written in the past tense since McCoy's accomplishments are now completed. Underline all the verbs in the paragraph and then rewrite it using the present perfect tense, as if it had been written during McCoy's lifetime, when his accomplishments were still in progress. The first sentence has been rewritten for you as an example.

Present-day version:

    Elijah McCoy, the son of two fugitive slaves, built a worldwide reputation as the "father of machine lubrication." The expression "the real McCoy" entered the English language because of his creative genius. McCoy changed the time-consuming system of stopping machinery periodically to oil the parts. He provided a system of continuous lubrication built into the machine. Because of his invention, factories increased their efficiency and railroads improved their service. Machine buyers began to ask, "Is this the real McCoy?" to make sure their equipment was fitted with the automatic lubricator. Further, McCoy's genius did not stop with a single invention. He patented more than fifty devices in the United States and in many foreign countries. He was often called to advise large industrial corporations. In addition, he volunteered many hours to counsel teenage boys in Detroit. He stayed active well into his eighties. Because of Elijah McCoy's many contributions to American society, the American Association of Engineers chose to honor him this year with a Lifetime Achievement Award.

1920 Version:

Elijah McCoy, the son of two fugitive slaves, has built a worldwide reputation as the "father of machine lubrication."

_____

_____

_____

_____

_____

_____

_____

_____

■ *Past Perfect Tense*

Here is a sentence using a verb in the past tense, the example used in the previous section:

Dr. Gwynn *studied* the problem for three years.

As the previous discussion indicated, the past tense verb indicates that the action of studying was completed in the past. The past tense, however, does not locate the action at any specific time in the past.

Now look at this sentence:

Before she *proposed* a solution, Dr. Gwynn *had studied* the problem for three years.

How does this sentence differ from the previous example? The action of studying still took place in the past, but this sentence presents the action in reference to another action that also took place in the past—the proposing of a solution. Both actions—studying and proposing—took place in the past. The use of the past perfect tense—*had studied*—calls attention to the sequence of the actions. Studying the problem occurred before proposing a solution.

Here is another illustration of the use of the past perfect tense:

Dr. Gwynn *began* the experiment when her students *arrived*.

Dr. Gwynn *had begun* the experiment when her students *arrived*.

Each of these two sentences presents the same actions—beginning and arriving. The different verb tenses create a different sequence for the actions. In the first example, Dr. Gwynn's beginning the experiment and the students' arrival both happened at the same time in the past. In the second example, which uses the past perfect tense, Dr. Gwynn's beginning the experiment happened before the arrival of her students.

The past perfect tense, then, identifies which of two past actions happened first. The timeline below illustrates this point:

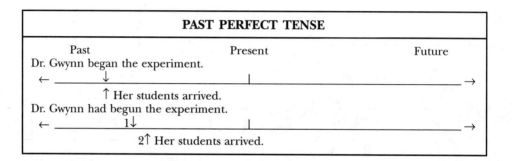

You don't always need to use the past perfect tense to show the sequence of actions. Sometimes the sequence is clear from the way the actions are presented in the sentence. If the sentence presents two actions in the order in which they occurred, you may not need to further emphasize the order by using the past perfect tense. For example, the two sentences below show two correct options for presenting a sequence of actions. Both sentences show the actions in the order in which they happened. Using the past perfect tense here simply emphasizes the sequence.

1   2
Dr. Gwynn *left* the lab and *returned* an hour later.

1   2
Dr. Gwynn *had left* the lab and *returned* an hour later.

However, if the sentence does not show the actions in the order in which they occurred, it is usually a good idea to use the past perfect tense to make the sequence perfectly clear for your reader.

2   1
Dr. Gwynn *returned* to the lab an hour after she *had left.*

It is also important to use the past perfect tense when you want to emphasize that one action was completely finished before a second action started, as the following examples show:

As Dr. Gwynn *performed* the test, sparks *shot* out of the machine.

After Dr. Gwynn *had performed* the test, sparks *shot* out of the machine.

In the first sentence, the sparks shoot out at the same time as Dr. Gwynn performs the test. In the second example, Dr. Gwynn has completed her test before the sparks appear. The past perfect tense helps to make this sequence of actions clear.

While the simple past tense indicates a single completed action, the past perfect tense places a past action in reference to another past action. The past perfect tense emphasizes the earlier of two past actions.

The past perfect tense is formed by combining the fourth principle part of the verb, the past participle, with the past tense of the verb *have*. The table below shows the verb *write* in the past perfect tense. Notice that the form of the verb stays the same all the way through.

WRITE		
	Singular	**Plural**
1st person	I **had written**	we **had written**
2nd person	you **had written**	you **had written**
3rd person	he/she/it **had written**	they **had written**

The verb *be* forms its past perfect tense in the same way as other verbs. It uses the past participle *been* with the helping verb *had*. All its forms stay the same in the past perfect tense. The table below shows the verb *be* in the past perfect tense.

BE		
	Singular	**Plural**
1st person	I **had been**	we **had been**
2nd person	you **had been**	you **had been**
3rd person	he/she/it **had been**	they **had been**

EXERCISE T
Write out the past perfect tense forms of each of the following verbs, filling in the table to show how the verb would look with each of its possible subjects.

1.

GO		
	Singular	**Plural**
1st person	I	we
2nd person	you	you
3rd person	he/she/it	they

2.

BEGIN		
	Singular	**Plural**
1st person	I	we
2nd person	you	you
3rd person	he/she/it	they

3.

TALK		
	Singular	**Plural**
1st person	I	we
2nd person	you	you
3rd person	he/she/it	they

4.

LIE		
	Singular	**Plural**
1st person	I	we
2nd person	you	you
3rd person	he/she/it	they

5.

LAY		
	Singular	**Plural**
1st person	I	we
2nd person	you	you
3rd person	he/she/it	they

EXERCISE U

In each of the following sentences, fill in the appropriate form of the verb, either the past tense or the past perfect tense. In making your choice, consider the sequence of actions involved. Be prepared to explain your choice.

(change)   1. Beginning in the mid-nineteenth century, technological advances

_____ the whole fabric of domestic life.

(come)   2. Before the development of steam engines, a community's water supply

_____ straight from the local stream or well.

(make)   3. Steam engines and cast iron pipes _____ it possible to move water over great distances to serve cities.

(supply)   4. Where once a single standpipe _____ a whole community, now each house could have its own water piped in.

(provide)   5. Similarly, wood and coal, which _____ heat for most of human history, were gradually replaced with gas and electricity.

(do)   6. In 1810, the first food preserving factory opened near Paris, France, thus taking over some of the kitchen work that individual housewives

_____ for centuries.

(allow)   7. The canning process _____ food to be kept in the cupboard for months without spoiling.

(provide)   8. By the end of the nineteenth century, the canning industry

_____ a great range of meats, milk, fruit, and vegetables cheaply in most parts of the world.

(appear)   9. This was a great benefit since no home refrigerators _____ on the scene as yet.

(see)   10. The latter part of the nineteenth century also _____ the mechanization of domestic work, like laundry and housecleaning.

(sew)   11. Isaac Singer's sewing machine enabled home seamstresses to produce clothes ten times faster than they _____ them previously.

(introduce)   12. Singer also _____ the convenient but expensive system of buying the machine on the installment plan with a small down payment and a succession of monthly payments.

(wash)   13. Traditionally, women _____ the family's clothes by hand, a task that might occupy an entire day or two a week.

(offer)   14. By the mid-nineteenth century, domestic washing machines and public laundries _____ women some less time-consuming alternatives.

(become)   15. As carpets _____ more popular, cleaning them was a considerable chore.

(beat)   16. About 1901, H. C. Booth introduced a mobile suction machine that would remove the dust that housewives formerly _____ out of the carpets by hand.

(take)   17. At first, traveling contractors _____ the machines from house to house; later, individually owned vacuum cleaners began to appear in wealthier households.

(buy)   18. While previous generations _____ their goods from small individual merchants or made them at home, America's consumer palaces—the department stores—set all these mechanical marvels out on counters for everyone to see and buy.

(lead)   19. Department stores, in turn, _____ to the development of such conveniences as the paper bag and the cash register.

(deny)   20. For those whose rural locations previously _____ them access to department stores, Montgomery Ward created the mail order catalog in 1872.

EXERCISE V

In each pair of sentences below, supply the correct sequence of verbs. Use the present tense with the present perfect tense and the past tense with the past perfect tense. Then create your own pair of sentences imitating the pattern of the sample sentences.

EXAMPLE:

(believe, solve)

Nowadays, many people ___*believe*___ that technology ___*has solved*___ their problems.

Fifty years ago, many people ___*believed*___ that technology ___*had solved*___ their problems.

Nowadays, many families think that education has improved their lives.

Fifty years ago, many families thought that education had improved their lives.

1. (develop, imagine)

Every day, someone _____ an idea that no one _____ before.

Yesterday, someone _____ an idea that no one _____ before.

_____

_____

_____

_____

2. (feel, visit)

As an adult, seeing a new place, I often _____ that _____ it before.

As a child, seeing a new place, I often _____ that _____ it before.

_____

_____

_____

_____

3. (win, plan)

When he was in high school, John's designs frequently _____ the

top awards because he _____ them so well.

Now that he is a respected architect, John's designs frequently _____

the top awards because he _____ them so carefully.

_____

_____

_____

_____

_____

4. (teach, be)

Up until now, no one _____ Margaret how to operate the system

because she _____ too inexperienced.

Up until last year, no one _____ Margaret how to operate the system

because she _____ too inexperienced.

_____

_____

_____

_____

_____

5. (make, be, leave)

If our new research team _____ a mistake, it _____ usually

because they _____ some information out of their calculations.

If our old research team _____ a mistake, it _____ usually

because they _____ some information out of their calculations.

_____

_____

_____

_____

_____

EXERCISE **W**

The paragraph below is a discussion of changes in medicine that have occurred during the twentieth century. It is written in the present perfect tense from the perspective of someone living in the twentieth century. Underline all the verbs in this paragraph. Then, rewrite it in the past perfect tense so that it becomes a record of changes in medicine that occurred in the twentieth century from the perspective of someone living in a later time period and looking back on the twentieth century. The first sentence has been rewritten for you as an example.

In the twentieth century, medicine has rapidly become more of a science than an art. The whole nature of medical practice has been transformed by advances in technology. Surgeons, for example, have always had to cope with two major problems: the ability of the patient to withstand an operation and the likelihood of infection. In the twentieth century, sophisticated anesthesia has 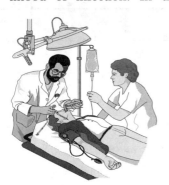 replaced brute force as a means of keeping the patient quiet during surgery. Surgeons have also universally adopted sterilization procedures that have drastically reduced the incidence of postoperative infections. Vaccination has virtually eliminated diseases such as smallpox and polio that have plagued people for centuries. This century has also seen the development of powerful antibiotics such as penicillin, discovered by Alexander Fleming in 1928. X-rays and their later cousins, nuclear scanners, have vastly improved the medical profession's capabilities. Organ transplants, almost unheard of before the twentieth century, have opened up many new possibilities for dealing with disease. Finally, preventive medicine has assumed new importance as people have realized that promoting health has produced even greater benefits than treating disease after it has appeared.

By the end of the twentieth century, medicine had rapidly become more of a science than an art.

_____

_____

_____

_____

_____

_____

_____

_____

_____

_____

_____

_____

_____

_____

■ Future Perfect Tense

Here is a sentence with its verb in the future tense:

Dr. Gwynn *will study* the problem for three years.

The future tense, as explained earlier in this chapter, indicates that an action is expected to occur at some time after the present moment. The simple future tense covers the whole range of future time.

The future perfect tense, on the other hand, is used when a specific point in the future is specified for the completion of the action. The sentence below illustrates this use:

By the year 2000, Dr. Gwynn *will have studied* the problem for three years.

This sentence specifies a completion date in the future for Dr. Gwynn's study—*by the year 2000.*

The future perfect tense is also used to show that one action in the future will have been completed before another action in the future is begun. The future perfect tense indicates the earlier of two future actions. In dealing with two future actions, one of the actions is often treated as a present action, as the sentences below illustrate. Instead of using the future tense, one of the two actions is shown in the present tense.

                  1   2

1. After Dr. Gwynn (will agree) *agrees* to study the problem, the project *will be* funded.

                  2   1

2. Before Dr. Gwynn (will agree) *agrees* to study the problem, the project *will have been* funded.

In the first example, Dr. Gwynn's agreement comes before the funding of the project. In the second example, it comes after the funding of the project. The future perfect tense helps to clarify the sequence of the actions.

The timeline below illustrates the difference between the future and the future perfect.

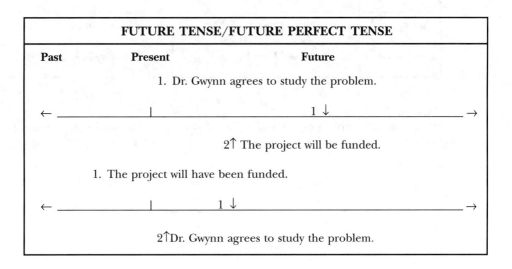

The future perfect tense is formed by combining the fourth principle part of the verb, the past participle, with the future tense of the verb *have.* The next table shows the verb *write* in the future perfect tense. Notice that the form of the verb stays the same throughout.

WRITE		
	Singular	**Plural**
1st person	I **will have written**	we **will have written**
2nd person	you **will have written**	you **will have written**
3rd person	he/she/it **will have written**	they **will have written**

The verb *be* forms its future perfect tense in the same way as other verbs. It uses the past participle *been* with the helping verb *will have*. All its forms stay the same in the future perfect tense. The table below shows the verb *be* in the future perfect tense.

BE		
	Singular	**Plural**
1st person	I **will have been**	we **will have been**
2nd person	you **will have been**	you **will have been**
3rd person	he/she/it **will have been**	they **will have been**

EXERCISE X

Write out the future perfect tense forms of each of the following verbs, filling in the table to show how the verb would look with each of its possible subjects.

1.

GO		
	Singular	**Plural**
1st person	I	we
2nd person	you	you
3rd person	he/she/it	they

2.

BEGIN		
	Singular	**Plural**
1st person	I	we
2nd person	you	you
3rd person	he/she/it	they

3.

TALK		
	Singular	**Plural**
1st person	I	we
2nd person	you	you
3rd person	he/she/it	they

4.

LIE		
	Singular	**Plural**
1st person	I	we
2nd person	you	you
3rd person	he/she/it	they

5.

LAY		
	Singular	**Plural**
1st person	I	we
2nd person	you	you
3rd person	he/she/it	they

EXERCISE Y

Supply the appropriate forms of the verbs—future tense or future perfect tense—for each sentence below. Then write a pair of sentences of your own imitating the pattern shown.

EXAMPLE:
(direct)
After her retirement, Dr. Gwynn *will direct* the project.

By the time she is sixty-five, Dr. Gwynn *will have directed* the project for twenty years.

Next year, I will go to graduate school.

By the time I am thirty, I will have gone to school for twenty-five years.

1. (test)

The company _____ the product extensively after receiving preliminary approval.

The company _____ the product for three years by the time it is finally approved.

_____

_____

_____

_____

2. (perfect)

The scientists are determined that they _____ the solar heating unit.

The scientists are determined that they _____ the solar heating unit before the application deadline arrives.

_____

_____

_____

_____

3. (change)

Everyone is sure that computer technology _____ soon

_____ dramatically.

Everyone is sure that computer technology _____ dramatically by the end of this century.

_____

_____

_____

_____

4. (write)

Because she is so talented, Professor Ramirez _____ certainly

_____ many successful grant proposals.

Because she is so talented, Professor Ramirez _____ certainly

_____ many successful grant proposals by the time she is promoted.

_____

_____

_____

_____

5. (revise)

When he takes over the project, Mr. Bajor _____ the project's goals and objectives.

By the time he has been here for a year, Mr. Bajor _____ the project's goals and objectives.

_____

_____

_____

_____

EXERCISE Z

Supply the appropriate form of the verb—future tense or future perfect tense—for each of the sentences below. In making your choice, consider the time sequence suggested by the sentence. Be prepared to explain your choice.

You are seeing Marie Curie's life in a crystal ball.

(enter)   1. Marie Sklodovska _____ this world in 1867 in Warsaw, Poland.

(gaze)   2. As a child, Marie _____ at her father's scientific instruments and dream of becoming a scientist herself.

(come)   3. By the time she reaches adulthood, her dream

_____ true, but only after much hard work on her part.

(struggle) 4. Marie and her sister Bronya _____ to obtain scientific training.

(refuse)   5. Warsaw University _____ to admit them because they are women.

(work)   6. By the time Marie begins her own studies, she

_____ for six years as a governess to pay for her sister's education.

(begin)   7. At the age of twenty-four, Marie _____ her own studies at the Sorbonne in Paris supported by Bronya and her husband.

(be)   8. Marie _____ the first woman ever admitted to the Sorbonne.

(earn)   9. Upon graduation, she _____ two degrees—one in physics and one in mathematics.

(marry)   10. In 1895, Marie _____ Pierre Curie, a teacher of physics and chemistry.

(create)   11. By the time of Pierre's death in 1906, they

_____ one of the most remarkable partnerships in the history of science.

(study)   12. To complete her doctorate in physical science, Marie Curie

_____ with Henri Becquerel, conducting experiments in heat radiation.

(discover) 13. The Curies _____ that radiation can destroy some cancerous tumors.

(patent)   14. The Curies _____ not

_____ their process for producing radium because they do not wish to take personal advantage of their discovery.

(share)   15. In 1903, Becquerel and the Curies _____ a Nobel Prize in physics for their work on radioactivity.

(exceed)   16. By the end of her life, however, Marie Curie's achievements

_____ by far those of her colleagues.

(immerse) 17. Heartbroken at her husband's death, Marie

_____ herself in research on the medical uses of radium.

(receive) 18. In 1911, she _____ a second Nobel Prize, this time in chemistry, becoming the first person ever to receive two Nobel Prizes.

(assist)   19. Marie's daughter, Irene, _____ her mother in her research and eventually receive a Nobel Prize of her own.

(fall)   20. By the time of her death from leukemia caused by her constant

exposure to radiation, Marie Curie _____ victim to her own discovery.

EXERCISE AA

Underline all the verbs in the following paragraph. Then, rewrite the paragraph changing the verbs from the future tense to the future perfect tense. The first sentence has been rewritten for you as an example.

In the coming years, you will see some exciting developments in the field of transportation. First of all, computer-controlled cars will replace driver-operated vehicles. The car's computer will receive information about the other cars on the road and will automatically choose the safest and fastest route to your destination. Because of increasing concern about air pollution, manufacturers will build more cars powered by electricity, alcohol, or other alternative fuels. Trains will become increasingly popular. Rail travel will become as fast and quiet as flying is now. Engineers will design trains to move at a steady 250 miles per hour, automatically banking for curves. Rail systems will convert to magnetic levitation. They will replace their clattering wheels with quiet, powerful magnetic cushions. Perhaps the most amazing development of all will be the intercontinental spaceplane. The spaceplane will link America with Europe by a thirty-minute ride at speeds of more than 6,000 miles per hour. All in all, you will see transportation change in some amazing ways.

By the end of the decade, you will have seen some exciting developments in the field of transportation.

_____

_____

_____

■ *Review of Simple Tenses and Perfect Tenses*

While the simple tenses show broad categories of time—the past, the present, and the future—the perfect tenses help to place actions more specifically within those time periods. The past perfect shows a definite time in relation to the past. The present perfect shows a definite time in relation to the present. The future perfect shows a definite time in relation to the future. The timeline below illustrates the time relationships of the six tenses.

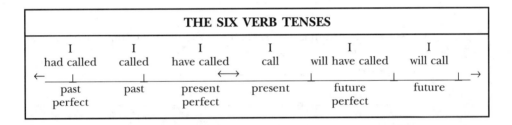

THE SIX VERB TENSES					
I had called	I called	I have called	I call	I will have called	I will call
past perfect	past	present perfect	present	future perfect	future

EXERCISE **BB**

Underline the verb and identify the tense of the verb in each of the following sentences. Then rewrite the sentence changing the verb tense as indicated. Be prepared to explain how the meaning of the sentence changes when you change the tense of the verb. Make any other changes in wording that you think are necessary to go along with the changed meaning.

<u>EXAMPLE:</u>

From the earliest times, birds <u>have demonstrated</u> the feasibility of flight. *present perfect*

(past perfect) *From the earliest times, birds had demonstrated the feasibility of*

flight. _____

1. The Montgolfier brothers were almost certainly the first to achieve free flight,

   remaining aloft in a hot-air balloon for half an hour. _____

   (present) _____

   _____

2. From 1783 on, there is a continuous history of ballooning up to the present

    day, partly for pleasure and partly for transport. _____

    (present perfect) _____

    _____

3. By the twentieth century, however, the future of flight will rest with heavier-

    than-air machines. _____

    (future perfect) _____

    _____

4. The great disadvantage of the balloon was its lack of maneuverability. _____

    (past perfect) _____

    _____

5. Count Ferdinand von Zeppelin will change all that with the launch of his first

    airship. _____

    (present) _____

    _____

6. The internal combustion engine really makes manned flight possible. _____

    (past) _____

    _____

7. Wilbur and Orville Wright had worked for many
    years before producing their famous biplane.

    _____

    (past) _____

    _____

8. France, the early home of ballooning, has actually shown more enthusiasm for aviation than the United States. _____

(past perfect) _____

9. At first, military leaders view airplanes with distrust. _____

(future) _____

10. By the beginning of World War I, though, the military will have taken over the field of aviation. _____

(present perfect) _____

11. By 1914, only about 5,000 airplanes had existed. _____

(present) _____

12. By 1918, the major combatants have built over 200,000 flying machines. _____

(future perfect) _____

13. Aircraft with welded steel bodies gradually replaced the wooden-framed biplane. _____

(future) _____

14. After the war, the military had accumulated quite a surplus of aircraft. _____

    (present perfect) _____

    _____

15. Civilians will quickly convert these surplus machines to commercial use. _____

    (past) _____

    _____

EXERCISE CC

Supply the correct form of the verb in each sentence below. Study the context of the sentence to determine which verb tense is appropriate. Indicate on the line at the right which verb tense you have chosen. Be prepared to explain your choices.

EXAMPLE:

(tell)   Sometimes, there is more to history than the history books

              _____*tell.*_____   ___*present*___

(top)   1. Eli Whitney (1765–1825) usually _____ _____
              the list of examples of American ingenuity.

(plague)   2. Before Whitney, the problem of separating cotton   _____

              seeds from cotton fibers _____
              southern farmers for years.

(solve)   3. Eli Whitney, as everyone knows, _____ _____
              the problem by inventing the cotton gin in 1793.

(believe) 4. Everybody _____ this because it says so   _____
              right in the sixth-grade history book.

(spend)   5. Before inventing the cotton gin, Eli Whitney   _____

              _____ his whole life in New England,
              far from any cotton plantations.

(go)   6. As a young man, Whitney _____ south   _____
              to tutor the children of a plantation owner.

(stay) 7. The job didn't materialize, but he _____

_____in Georgia as the guest of Catherine Greene, the widow of General Nathaniel Greene.

(hear) 8. While he is staying at Mrs. Greene's, Whitney _____

_____the planters describe the problem of cleaning cotton.

(become) 9. Within a few weeks of his arrival in Georgia, Whitney had invented the machine for which he _____

_____ famous in future history books.

(give) 10. For almost two hundred years, history books _____

_____ Whitney full credit for inventing the cotton gin.

(take) 11. And, until recently, everyone _____ _____ these facts for granted.

(borrow) 12. Now, however, some people think that Whitney _____

may _____ the idea.

(suggest) 13. One current theory _____ that _____ Whitney saw a slave using a comblike tool to loosen seeds from the cotton.

(improve) 14. In this version, Whitney _____ _____ the slave's invention and secures a patent for it.

(rule) 15. Earlier, the attorney general _____ _____ that slaves could not hold patents.

(know) 16. As a result, future generations _____

_____ never _____ what inventions were devised by slaves.

(present) 17. Some people believe that Catherine Greene _____

_____ Whitney with a complete set of drawings for her invention.

(install)   18. At the least, Catherine Greene probably   _____
                      improved Whitney's idea by substituting wire
                      teeth for the wooden ones Whitney

                      _____ on the trial version of his
                      machine.

(finance)   19. Catherine Greene also _____ the   _____
                      penniless Whitney through the entire
                      development of the machine and the
                      subsequent battle to secure his patent rights.

(earn)   20. Thus, some historians now suggest, Catherine   _____

                      Greene's contributions _____ her at
                      least partial credit for the invention of the
                      cotton gin.

(make)   21. Ironically, Eli Whitney never _____   _____
                      much money from the cotton gin because so
                      many planters simply borrowed his idea and
                      made their own machines.

(change)   22. In any case, within a few years of its invention, _____

                      the cotton gin _____ the course of
                      American history.

(jump)   23. By 1807, the South's cotton crop _____ _____
                      from 8 million to 80 million pounds.

(become)   24. Because of the gin, cotton and slavery   _____

                      _____ the economic mainstays of
                      the South.

(find out)   25. Probably, no one ever _____ the   _____
                      whole story of the invention of the cotton gin.

▶ VERB MOOD: HELPING VERBS

In looking at how verbs form their different tenses, you have already seen how some tenses require helping verbs. The present progressive form, for example, requires a form of the verb *be* as a helping verb. The perfect tenses all use some form of *have* as a helping verb.

Besides putting an action in a time frame through the use of tense, verbs can also help your reader interpret the meaning of an action. You create these shades of meaning by using another set of helping verbs. These helping verbs may appear along with such tense indicators as *be* or *have*. A particular helping verb can show such attitudes as certainty, expectation, or possibility, as the examples below illustrate.

The invention did fail. *(emphasizes certainty)*

The invention should fail. *(emphasizes expectation)*

The invention may have failed. *(emphasizes possibility)*

Each of these sentences expresses a slightly different understanding of the action of failing.

The box below shows the most common helping verbs.

COMMON HELPING VERBS	
can, could	(shows ability, power, or skill to act)
do, does, did	(shows intensity or certainty of action)
may, might	(shows possibility or potential for action)
must	(shows compulsion or obligation to act)
shall, should	(shows expectation of action, obligation to act)
will, would	(shows likelihood of action, willingness to act)

These helping verbs are always used with the present or base form of the verb. For example, here is the verb *speak* used with various helping verbs:

can speak	could speak	could have spoken
does speak	may speak	may have spoken
might speak	must speak	must have spoken
should speak	would speak	would have spoken

EXERCISE DD

Each of the sentences below contains a verb used with a helping verb to express a particular attitude or tone in the action. Underline the helping verb and the main verb in each sentence. Sometimes there may be words in between the helping verb and the main verb. Be prepared to explain how the helping verb affects the interpretation of the action.

EXAMPLE:

Patenting an invention does not guarantee success.

1. Inventors may see the merit of their ideas very clearly.
2. The public, however, can prove difficult to convince.
3. Indeed, some patents might generate more laughter than revenue for the inventor.

4. Chicken goggles (to prevent chickens from pecking each other's eyes) should have excited farmers, but the idea failed.
5. Someone must have believed in the parachute hat as a means for escaping from burning buildings.
6. Not many people would pay handsomely for a locket in which to save their used chewing gum.
7. A life-size horse attached to the front of a car may have been a brilliant idea, but drivers refused to buy it.
8. Apparently, many hunters could resist a hunter's blind disguised as a grazing cow.
9. John Fitch's noisy steam-powered oars did not please sailors.
10. Sometimes the world may fail to appreciate an inventor's brilliance.

Exercise EE

Underline the verb in each sentence below. Then, rewrite each sentence using a helping verb to change the time or mood of the action. Sometimes you may have to change the form of the main verb to fit with a helping verb. Be prepared to explain the difference in meaning between your sentence and the original sentence.

<u>Example:</u>

The search for a cheaper billiard ball <u>led</u> to the invention of plastics.

The search for a cheaper billiard ball may have led to the invention of plastics.

_____

1. Billiards, a popular game in the nineteenth century, used balls carved from ivory.

_____

_____

2. The balls cost a lot of money.

_____

_____

3. Billiard ball makers offered a prize for creating an ivory substitute.

_____

_____

4. The prize inspired John Wesley Hyatt, a printer in Albany, New York.

   _____

   _____

5. He worked for years to find a substitute.

   _____

   _____

6. He tried mixing sawdust and glue.

   _____

   _____

7. Finally, he developed celluloid, a moldable plastic.

   _____

   _____

8. Unfortunately, he never won the prize.

   _____

   _____

9. The offer had expired.

   _____

   _____

10. Nevertheless, his invention eventually opened up a whole new industry in plastics.

    _____

    _____

WRITING PRACTICE:

1. In a recent magazine, find a picture that shows a scene filled with activity. On a separate sheet of paper, write six to ten sentences describing the activities going on in the picture. Try to use at least two different verb tenses in describing the activities. To use different verb tenses in your description, you may need to include what happened before the activities started or what you think will happen next.

PLANNING:
Study the picture and make a list of activities that you observe. You might want to work with a partner to generate a list of activities.

DRAFTING:
From your list, choose the activities you find most interesting and write a sentence or two describing each activity. Make sure each sentence contains a verb.

REVISING/EDITING:
Circle the verbs you used in your draft. Have you used more than one verb tense? See how many forms of the verb *be* you have used. Remember that too many *be* verbs can make your writing seem weak. If you have used more than three *be* verbs, try to change some of them to stronger, more action-filled verbs. If you have trouble thinking of stronger verbs, your teacher or a classmate may be able to give you some suggestions.

2. Many of the exercises in this chapter have given information about inventors and inventions. Using this material as well as your own knowledge, write a paragraph of six to ten sentences explaining what you think is the greatest invention of all time. Try to convince your classmates to agree with you by providing several reasons to support your choice. Emphasize what the invention *does* that makes it so important.

PLANNING:
Use the table below to help generate some ideas about the greatest invention of all time. Choose three possible candidates for the greatest invention of all time and see how many reasons you can give for each choice.

GREATEST INVENTION OF ALL TIME			
?	**Possibility #1**	**Possibility #2**	**Possibility #3**
Reason #1			
Reason #2			

GREATEST INVENTION OF ALL TIME			
?	**Possibility #1**	**Possibility #2**	**Possibility #3**
Reason #3			
Reason #4			

DRAFTING:

From the table you just completed, choose the candidate for which you have the best support. Write one or two sentences explaining each reason for your choice. Emphasize what this invention *does*. Make sure each sentence contains a verb.

REVISING/EDITING:

Circle the verbs you used in your draft. See how many forms of the verb *be* you have used. Remember that too many *be* verbs can make your writing seem weak. If you have used more than three *be* verbs, try to change some of them to stronger, more action-filled verbs. If you have trouble thinking of stronger verbs, your teacher or a classmate may be able to give you some suggestions.

Chapter 2

Basic Sentence Structure

• • • • • • • • • • • • • •

• • • • • • • • • • • • • •

If you have ever taken piano or guitar lessons or lived in the same house with someone who has, you know that beginning musicians spend a lot of time practicing patterns of notes known as scales and chords. Because every composition they may play or create is built on these patterns, students play them over and over again until their hands and ears have "memorized" the relationships among these sets of sounds.

Until these patterns become almost automatic, every new piece of music must be learned one note at a time. But once the musician has mastered these forms, he or she can recognize them easily in a new piece and can even create variations that will add interest to the music or allow the music to be adapted for special circumstances.

In fact, almost every profession—from marine biologist to shortstop—involves certain patterns of thought and action that beginners must absorb before they can advance in that field.

As a writer, you also need to become very familiar with the basic patterns of your trade—sentences. All your written and spoken compositions are built from these basic sets of relationships among words. Once you have mastered the patterns of the sentence, you can control the shape and direction of your writing more easily.

To exercise that control, you have to become consciously aware of information about sentences that you have unconsciously absorbed over the years. Also, since you and your classmates and your teacher will be discussing the effects of various sentences, it is important that you all be able to use the same terms for the parts of the sentence.

In Chapter 1, you learned how to use verbs, which are a vital part of every sentence. In this chapter, you will be looking at the other elements necessary to create the basic pattern of a sentence.

▶ SENTENCE DEFINITION

EXERCISE A

Look at the word groups below. Which ones do you recognize as sentences? Put a check next to each group of words that you think is a sentence.

_____ 1. Near Naples in Italy.

_____ 2. Stretches back 12,000 years.

_____ 3. The prosperous commercial center.

_____ 4. The people experiencing tremors.

_____ 5. The people experienced tremors.

_____ 6. The people who experienced tremors.

_____ 7. A volcanic eruption in 79 A.D.

_____ 8. Witnessed the event.

_____ 9. Pliny the Younger to witness the event.

_____10. Pliny the Younger witnessed the event.

_____11. Since Pliny the Younger witnessed the event.

_____12. Pliny wrote letters to a historian.

_____13. A firsthand account of Mount Vesuvius.

_____14. A huge dark cloud rising from Mount Vesuvius.

_____15. During the first force of the blast.

_____16. Hot ash rains on Pompeii.

_____17. Poisonous gas filling the air.

_____18. Buried alive.

_____19. Buildings collapsed.

_____20. When Pliny the Elder sailed toward Pompeii.

_____21. The shoreline strewn with fallen rock.

_____22. The entire city lay beneath a gray snow.

_____23. Under an avalanche of volcanic mud.

_____24. Pompeii was rediscovered in 1748.

_____25. Perfectly preserved under the ash.

On the lines below, copy all of the word groups from Exercise A that you and your teacher agree are sentences.

_____

_____

_____

_____

_____

_____

_____

_____

_____

_____

_____

_____

What do these word groups have in common that makes you know they are sentences?

First, you probably noticed that each of these sentences contains a verb that shows action in past, present, or future time. For instance, one of the sentences is

The people experienced tremors.

However, the group of words right above that one is not a sentence:

The people experiencing tremors.

These two word groups are alike except that in one case—*experienced*—the verb shows tense; in the other case—*experiencing*—it does not. So, having a verb that shows tense is one crucial requirement for a sentence.

Another basic requirement for a sentence is that the verb has to be related to a subject. Some person or thing must be involved in the action of a sentence. For example, this group of words is not a sentence:

Witnessed the event.

However, this group of words is a sentence:

Pliny the Younger witnessed the event.

Although both groups of words contain a verb that shows tense—*witnessed*—only the second example shows who did the witnessing—*Pliny the Younger.* A sentence sets up a special relationship between the verb and a subject who performs or receives the action. This subject–verb relationship is another crucial element of a sentence.

Finally, every sentence must have a subject–verb unit that is capable of expressing an idea independently. For example, the word group below has the same subject and verb as the previous example, but in this case they don't convey a complete idea:

Since Pliny the Younger witnessed the event.

In this example, the word *since* in front of the subject–verb unit gives the reader a sense of incompleteness about the idea. The reader of this group of words is left waiting for additional information to complete the thought. *Since* is a subordination signal, one of a whole group of words used to distinguish secondary ideas from primary ideas in a sentence. (Also see page 87.)

The box below summarizes the basic requirements for a sentence.

A SENTENCE EXPRESSES A COMPLETE THOUGHT BY PRESENTING
A SUBJECT–VERB UNIT (INCLUDING A VERB THAT SHOWS TIME)
NOT INTRODUCED BY A SUBORDINATION SIGNAL.

▶ PARTS OF A SENTENCE

● Subjects

Every group of words that is a sentence names the person or thing that is the focus of attention in the sentence. In other words, every sentence has a **subject.** Look at the sentence below:

Modern Ghana takes its name from an ancient empire.

In this sentence, *Modern Ghana* is what the writer wants the sentence to focus on. *Modern Ghana* is the subject.

EXERCISE B

Underline the subject in each of the following sentences. Who or what is each sentence about?

1. Modern Ghana was formerly the African Gold Coast.
2. Ancient Ghana lay many miles to the north.
3. The Maga dynasty ruled Ghana at that time.
4. The Soninke tribes then ousted the Maga.
5. In 790 they expanded the empire.

6. The empire had a reputation for gold.
7. Its greatest glory was attained in the 900s.
8. These accomplishments attracted the attention of the Arabs.
9. A war ensued.
10. Eventually, the empire, its political structures, and its culture collapsed.

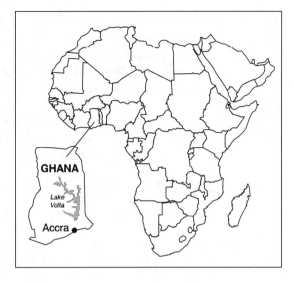

In Exercise B, you can observe some of the common characteristics of subjects. Subjects are ordinarily nouns—words that name a person, place, or thing—such as *Ghana, war,* or *empire.* Pronouns—words that take the place of nouns—can also be subjects. *I, we, you, he, she, it,* and *they* are all examples of pronouns that can function as subjects. You might remember that you used these subject pronouns throughout Chapter 1 when you conjugated verbs.

All of the sentences in Exercise B place the subject in its most common position—right at the beginning of the sentence, just before the verb. In general, then, your readers will expect to find the subject at the beginning of the sentence. However, not all sentences follow this pattern. There are some circumstances where you may put the subject in a different position. The discussion that follows shows some of the most common variations.

■ Subjects in a Question

A question sentence often places the subject in the middle of the verb. Notice what happens to the position of the subject in the following example.

In the fifteenth century, <u>*the Aztecs*</u> *built* a great empire.

↓

When *did* <u>*the Aztecs*</u> *build* a great empire?

In the question sentence, the verb becomes a two-part verb and the subject appears in between the two parts of the verb. Here is another example of that pattern:

In the fifteenth century, <u>*Joan of Arc*</u> *led* the French armies to victory.

↓

Which armies *did* <u>*Joan of Arc*</u> *lead* to victory?

■ Subjects with *Here* and *There*

Another common sentence pattern uses the words *here* or *there* as the sentence opener. Even though these words hold the opening position in such sentences, they are not really the focus of attention in the sentence. In this kind of sentence, the subject comes after the verb. The following examples illustrate this pattern.

> There were *many explorers* in America before Columbus.
>
> Here was *an opportunity for adventure.*
>
> In the fifteenth century, there was *a great desire* to find a shorter route to Asia.

■ Inverted Subjects

In some situations, you may wish to put the subject at the end of a sentence to call special attention to it. Using this technique too frequently can weaken its effect, so you should choose carefully the sentences where you want to give the subject a little extra impact by placing it out of its normal position. The examples below illustrate this pattern.

> *Ivan IV* waited outside Moscow.
>
> Outside Moscow waited *Ivan IV.*
>
> *The wind* raged wildly.
>
> Wildly raged *the wind.*
>
> *Ivan the Terrible* was beginning his reign of tyranny.
>
> Beginning his reign of tyranny was *Ivan the Terrible.*

■ Subjects in a Command

One final instance where the subject may take a different position is in a command sentence. In fact, the subject usually goes unexpressed in a command. The subject of a sentence that gives an order is understood to be *you,* even if the word *you* is not written as part of the sentence. The sentences below illustrate this pattern.

> Leave Rome at once.
>
> (You) leave Rome at once.
>
> Take two legions of soldiers.
>
> (You) take two legions of soldiers.
>
> Come back with your shield or on it.
>
> (You) come back with your shield or on it.

Exercise C

Keeping in mind the variations you have just seen, underline the subject in each of the following sentences.

1. On the throne sat Harun al-Raschid.
2. Here was the caliph of Baghdad.
3. Does everyone know about the mighty caliph?
4. Emerging as the center of Islamic culture was the court of Baghdad.
5. The powerful eighth-century ruler supported the arts generously.
6. He figures prominently in the stories of the *Thousand and One Nights.*
7. There lies the secret of Harun al-Raschid's fame.
8. Harun's empire included all of southwest Asia and the northern part of Africa.
9. How did Harun become so powerful?
10. Do not miss reading about Harun al-Raschid.

EXERCISE D
Add a logical subject to each of the following sentences.

1. There are many _____ to study other cultures.

2. Do _____ understand the importance of history?

3. _____ provided extensive information about that time period.

4. Appearing from the pages of legend was _____.

5. Here is a _____.

6. When can _____ begin the project?

7. _____ begin the project now.

8. Around the room stood _____.

9. _____ will want to see the results.

10. Why do _____ prefer that location?

● **Verbs**

As you have already seen from Chapter 1, verbs present the action in a sentence and place that action in present, past, or future time. In a sentence, the verb normally follows the subject. However, as you saw in the discussion of subjects, there are some situations where the sentence may not follow that pattern. For example, a question sentence may put the verb in front of the subject:

Why *did* the Mayan civilization *disappear*?

Likewise, a sentence with the subject at the end may have split the verb into two parts:

> *Emerging* in the lowland jungles of Central America *was* an interesting civilization.

A command sentence may begin with the verb and not express the subject at all:

> *Concentrate* on the details of their ceremonies.

EXERCISE E
Underline the verb in each of the following sentences and identify its tense on the blank to the left. Don't forget that helping verbs should be identified as part of the verb.

Tense

_____ 1. Observe Mayan civilization carefully.

_____ 2. The Maya built few cities.

_____ 3. There were four political centers.

_____ 4. Will their culture survive the Spanish invasion?

_____ 5. For centuries, the Maya had used an incredibly accurate calendar.

_____ 6. Here are their predictions of solar eclipses.

_____ 7. Remember also their exquisite jade carvings.

_____ 8. After the Spanish conquest, the Mayan communities collapsed.

_____ 9. Maya in Mexico and Guatemala today have retained many elements of their culture.

_____ 10. Will archaeologists have learned even more about Mayan culture by the end of the century?

EXERCISE F
Add a verb to show the action each of the following subjects is involved in. Try to vary the verb tenses through the exercise.

1. Shoguns or supreme commanders _____ in Japan for several centuries.

2. Yoritomo _____ a system of military government.

3. _____ the emperor _____?

4. The power of the shoguns _____ rapidly.

5. Shoguns _____ elaborate costumes.

6. _____ a traditional shogun's costume for me.

7. The title of shogun _____ great respect.

8. The last shogun _____.

9. A revolution _____ in the nineteenth century.

10. _____ modern Japan _____ the shogunate?

● Objects

Every verb functions in relationship to a subject. That is a basic requirement of all sentences. However, some verbs may also direct action from a subject to another person or thing. For example, a sentence like the one below—even though it is technically a complete sentence—would probably raise some questions for a reader:

King Edward produced.

Looking at this sentence, a reader might wonder what it was that King Edward produced. You might supply the information by adding a second sentence:

No heirs were produced.

Most likely, though, you would combine these two sentences to form one sentence that indicated both the origination of the action and its completion:

King Edward produced no heirs.

In this sentence, the action in the verb *produced* is completed by the words *no heirs*. *No heirs* is the object of the verb *produced*. The **object** of a verb shows the goal, result, or conclusion of the verb's action. The object shows toward what or whom the action is directed. The sentences below illustrate the way an object relates to a verb. You might think of a sentence with an object as having a two-part action. Notice how in each sentence the action originates with the subject but moves on toward someone or something else.

Edward → supported → *the Normans* in England. *(Whom did Edward support?)*

An English council → elected → *Harold* as their king. *(Whom did the council elect?)*

William of Normandy → also claimed → *the throne*. *(What did William claim?)*

Sometimes a verb may have more than one object, as the following example shows. In this sentence, the action has three parts. The action of giving is initiated by the council, directed toward the throne, and received by Harold.

Object 1   Object 2
The council → gave → Harold → the throne. *(What did the council give? Who received what the council gave?)*

When sentences contain an object, the object answers the question *what* or *whom*. Of course, not every verb has an object. Some actions are self-contained; they do not move on from the subject to something else. The following sentence, for example, shows an action that is self-contained:

Edward died in 1066.

Exercise G
In the sentences below, underline the words that show the goal, result, or conclusion of the verb's action. Remember that not all verbs have objects.

1. King Edward the Confessor of England left no children.
2. Harold, the Earl of Wessex, was chosen.
3. William of Normandy immediately invaded England.
4. Harold fought with inexperienced troops.
5. William killed Harold at the Battle of Hastings.
6. William the Conqueror ruled from 1066 to 1087.
7. They crowned William the Conqueror in Westminster Abbey on Christmas Day.
8. He gave his followers large estates.
9. William's census of England helped in assessing taxes.
10. The Domesday Book contains information about England in the Middle Ages.

Exercise H
Combine each of the following pairs of sentences to produce one sentence that uses an object to show the completion of the verb's action.

1. Queen Hatshepsut ruled.
    The Eighteenth Dynasty of ancient Egypt was ruled.

    _____

    _____

2. The queen assumed.
    The double crown of Upper and Lower Egypt was assumed.

    _____

    _____

3. In art, Queen Hatshepsut wears.
    Male attire and a ceremonial beard are worn.

    _____

    _____

4. During her reign, Hatshepsut bars.
    Military undertakings are barred.

    _____

    _____

5. She built.
    A splendid temple at Deir el-Bahri was built.

    _____

    _____

6. Hatshepsut gave.
    Two decades of peace and prosperity were given to Egypt.

    _____

    _____

7. Her building projects enhanced.
    Her popularity was enhanced.

    _____

    _____

8. Hatshepsut changed.
    The roles assigned to royal women were changed.

    _____

    _____

9. Many Egyptians revered.
    Hatshepsut was revered as a god.

    _____

    _____

10. Hatshepsut's successor erased.
    Her name was erased from her monuments and from the list of kings.

    _____

    _____

Exercise 1

Write five sentences of your own that use the subject–verb–object pattern. Identify each part of the sentence.

<u>Example:</u>
S   V   O
I love food from other cultures. _____

1. _____

   _____

2. _____

   _____

3. _____

_____

4. _____

_____

5. _____

_____

▶ SUBJECT–VERB RELATIONSHIPS

The subject of a sentence, as you saw earlier, establishes the focus of attention in a sentence. In many cases, you may have several different ways to focus the sentence. For example, look at the information given below.

Solomon built.

A magnificent temple was built.

This information could be combined to produce a sentence with *Solomon* as the subject and *temple* as the object, a pattern you have practiced earlier in this chapter. This sentence emphasizes *Solomon* by making him the subject of the sentence:

Solomon built a magnificent temple.

On the other hand, you could combine the same information to produce a sentence that emphasizes *temple* by making it the subject:

A magnificent temple was built by Solomon.

Here is another example of these two different ways to focus a sentence:

King David captured.

Jerusalem was captured.

With the emphasis on *King David,* the sentence would look like this:

King David captured Jerusalem.

With the emphasis on *Jerusalem,* the sentence would look like this:

Jerusalem was captured by King David.

Which version of the sentence you would choose to write would depend on which idea was more important in a particular writing situation. If the writing focused on David's accomplishments, then the first version might be more appropriate. If the writing focused on the history of Jerusalem, then the second version might be better. You can exercise control over a sentence by deciding which idea you want your reader to focus on and making that idea the subject.

Exercise J

Practice controlling the focus of a sentence by combining each of the following pairs of sentences in two different ways, each version emphasizing a different idea.

1. Scholars will always remember.
   The classical civilization of fifth-century Greece will be remembered.

   (emphasize scholars)

   _____

   _____

   (emphasize civilization)

   _____

   _____

2. Pericles' name symbolizes.
   The achievements of the Athenian Golden Age are symbolized.

   (emphasize Pericles' name)

   _____

   _____

   (emphasize achievements)

   _____

   _____

3. Pericles championed.
   Democracy was championed.

   (emphasize Pericles)

   _____

   _____

(emphasize democracy)

_____

_____

4. The Athenians completely rebuilt.
   The Acropolis was completely rebuilt.

   (emphasize Athenians)

_____

_____

   (emphasize Acropolis)

_____

_____

5. Ancient people praised.
   The beauty of the Acropolis was praised.

   (emphasize ancient people)

_____

_____

   (emphasize beauty)

_____

_____

6. Great Athenian playwrights wrote.
   Tragedies and comedies were written.

   (emphasize playwrights)

_____

_____

   (emphasize tragedies and comedies)

_____

_____

7. Greek philosophers discovered.
   Basic truths about science and medicine were discovered.

   (emphasize Greek philosophers)

   _____

   _____

   (emphasize truths)

   _____

   _____

8. In 429 B.C. , bubonic plague took.
   The life of Pericles was taken.

   (emphasize plague)

   _____

   _____

   (emphasize life)

   _____

   _____

9. No successor could win.
   The support of a majority of citizens could not be won.

   (emphasize successor)

   _____

   _____

   (emphasize support)

   _____

   _____

10. The Spartans conquered.
    Athens was conquered soon thereafter.

(emphasize the Spartans)

_____

_____

(emphasize Athens)

_____

_____

Every sentence sets up a relationship between a subject and a verb. The exercise above illustrates two basic ways that subjects and verbs relate in sentences. One pattern, the most common one, is the **active sentence.** The other is the **passive sentence.**

● Active Sentences

In an **active sentence,** the subject of the sentence performs the action shown in the verb. This is an active sentence since the subject is the actor. The sentence below is an active sentence:

Solomon built a magnificent temple in Jerusalem about 950 B.C.

Here, the subject of the sentence—*Solomon*—is performing the action of building. This sentence emphasizes *Solomon* as the doer of the action. This is the essence of the active sentence; the subject performs the action.

In most cases, the doer of an action is the most appropriate focus for a sentence. That is why active sentences are the most common relationship between subjects and verbs.

● Passive Sentences

However, you may not always know who performed a certain action, or you may have reason to emphasize something other than the doer of the action. In these circumstances, you may choose a different kind of subject-verb relationship—the passive sentence.

In a **passive sentence,** the emphasis falls on the receiver of the action rather than the doer of the action. In the following sentence, the subject is the receiver of the action:

A magnificent temple was built by Solomon.

In this sentence, the subject—*temple*—is not performing any action. Instead, it is being acted on by someone else—*Solomon.* Sometimes, a passive sentence does not indicate the doer of the action at all:

> **A magnificent temple was built.**

The passive relationship can be used in situations where you do not know the specific doer of an action. For example, in writing about Solomon's temple, you might use a sentence like this:

> **Someone destroyed Solomon's temple in the sixth century B.C.**

However, this sentence emphasizes what you don't know. In most cases, it's better to emphasize what you do know, so a passive sentence might work better for presenting this information:

> **Solomon's temple was destroyed in the sixth century B.C.**

■ *Passive Verbs*

Passive sentences use a particular verb form—the **passive verb.** For example, the verb in the sentence above is *was destroyed. Was destroyed* is a passive verb. Here are some other examples of sentences with passive verbs:

> **The temple *was rebuilt* later.**
>
> **Its site *is occupied* now by the Wailing Wall.**
>
> **Slave labor *was used* in building the temple.**
>
> **Gold, silver, and ivory *were brought* to Jerusalem.**
>
> **Jerusalem *has been excavated* by many archaeologists.**
>
> **Its archaeological riches *will* never *be exhausted.***

What are the characteristics of a passive verb? As you may notice in the examples above, a passive verb always uses a form of the verb *be.* It is this part of the verb that indicates the tense. A passive verb also includes the past participle. The box below shows you some examples of the active and passive forms of a verb.

	Active	**Passive**
present	rules	is ruled
past	conquered	were conquered
future	will lead	will be led
present perfect	have finished	have been finished
past perfect	had written	had been written
future perfect	will have drawn	will have been drawn

EXERCISE K

Identify the subject–verb relationship in each sentence below as active or passive. Then rewrite the sentence to show a different subject–verb relationship. Remember that in order to write an active sentence, you must know the doer of an action.

EXAMPLE:

The Chinese invented paper in the first century A.D. *active*

Paper was invented by the Chinese in the first century A.D.

The first book was printed in 868 by the Chinese. *passive*

The Chinese printed the first book in 868.

1. A system of block printing was devised by the Chinese. _____

_____

_____

2. Carved wood was stamped on a piece of paper. _____

_____

_____

3. The Arabs in southern Spain manufactured paper. _____

_____

_____

4. Gutenberg invented movable type. _____

_____

_____

5. Thousands of books were circulated in Europe. _____

_____

_____

6. Previously monks had copied books. _____

_____

_____

7. Widespread information increased literacy. _____

_____

_____

8. Pope Alexander VI introduced censorship. _____

_____

_____

9. Religious leaders debate the new technology. _____

_____

_____

10. Prosperous businessmen educate their children. _____

_____

_____

11. They developed a textbook market. _____

_____

_____

12. Law books were sought by students. _____

_____

_____

13. Professors will no longer hand down information. _____

_____

_____

14. Individuals are guided by no religious authority. _____

_____

_____

15. Readers will make their own interpretations. _____

_____

_____

EXERCISE L

Using the verbs shown in the box on page 82 or your own pairs of verbs, write five sets of sentences showing the difference between an active sentence and a passive sentence.

EXAMPLE:

Active:

A good leader makes sound judgments. _____

Passive:

Sound judgments are made by good leaders. _____

1. Active:

_____

_____

Passive:

_____

_____

2. Active:

_____

_____

    Passive:

_____

_____

3. Active:

_____

_____

    Passive:

_____

_____

4. Active:

_____

_____

    Passive:

_____

_____

5. Active:

_____

_____

    Passive:

_____

_____

▶ SUBORDINATION SIGNALS

The basic pattern of meaning in a sentence is established by the subject–verb unit. However, not every subject–verb group is a sentence. For example, look at the following group of words:

Even though London had a population of nearly half a million.

There is a subject–verb unit here—*London had*—but this group of words is not a sentence. The subordination signal *even though* tells you that this idea is incomplete. *Even though* is one of a whole group of subordination signals. Writers use these signal words to show that a given group of words is not a complete idea.

The group of words below also uses a subordination signal—*who*—to indicate an idea that is not complete. Notice that the subordination signal *who* functions as the subject of the verb *were crowded*.

People _who_ were crowded into decaying houses.

The box below shows some of the most important subordination signals.

SUBORDINATION SIGNALS		
after	if	when
although	since	which
as if	so that	while
because	that	who
before	though	whom
even though	unless	whose
	until	

Subordination signals are explained in detail in Chapter 5.

The main idea of a sentence—the base sentence—is expressed as an unsubordinated subject–verb unit. Subordinate subject–verb groups cannot function as sentences. In order to convey meaning, they must be attached to a base sentence. In your writing, then, you must be sure that each sentence is built on the base of an unsubordinated subject–verb unit.

EXERCISE M

Underline the subject–verb units in each of the following groups of words. Indicate which ones are base sentences and which ones are subordinated.

EXAMPLES:

    subordinate   When *Akbar ruled* India in the sixteenth century.

    base sentence   The *name* "Akbar" *means* "very great."

1. _____   Literature flourished during Akbar's reign.

2. _____   People who never learned to read.

3. _____   Because the Mogul emperor was a fearless hunter.

4. _____   Akbar's law forbade child marriage.

5. _____   It also allowed freedom of religion.

6. _____   While Akbar directed the construction of the famous fort at
                          Agra.

7. _____   The fort which was later torn down.

8. _____   Akbar held a conference for representatives of all religions in
                          his empire.

9. _____   After Akbar's kingdom declined.

10. _____   The system depended on Akbar's superior qualities.

Exercise N

Underline the subject–verb units in each of the following sentences. Indicate with labels which subject–verb units are part of the base sentence (BS) and which are subordinate ideas (SI).

Example:

                    SI   BS
Even though London had a population of nearly half a million, many people were packed into decaying wooden houses in narrow streets.

                    BS   SI
Christopher Wren began work on the new St. Paul's Cathedral, which still dominates London's skyline.

1. The upper stories of buildings almost touched because they were built so close together.
2. When the fire began on a Sunday in 1666, buckets of water were useless.
3. Since London had had a dry summer, the whole street was ablaze.
4. Samuel Pepys, who had heard about the fire, took a boat on the river to see for himself.
5. Since it was fanned by strong east winds, the fire raged on.
6. While attempts were made to tear down buildings in its path, the fire leapt the ruined buildings.

7. The fiery red sky that marked London could be seen forty miles away by Monday night.
8. As soon as the winds dropped, the fire was brought under control.
9. Though only a handful of people died in the fire, hundreds of thousands had no roof over their heads.
10. Once the old city had burned, a safer and healthier city could be built.

SUMMARY

A SENTENCE EXPRESSES A COMPLETE THOUGHT BY PRESENTING
AN UNSUBORDINATED SUBJECT–VERB UNIT
THAT SHOWS PAST, PRESENT, OR FUTURE TIME.

▶ PUNCTUATING SENTENCES

As you have seen in this chapter, a sentence generally focuses on one main idea—an unsubordinated subject–verb group. The base sentence may also have subordinate word groups attached to it.

When writing was first invented, it did not use punctuation and capitalization. Readers had to figure out for themselves how the ideas were supposed to be grouped together.

> **so an ancient reader might have seen sentences something like this without punctuation or capitalization to guide him he might have had difficulty following the ideas and the thoughts of the writer could have been misinterpreted**

Over the centuries, people developed various conventions about writing, including the use of a capital letter at the beginning of a sentence and a period at the end. These conventions for beginning and ending sentences help readers to know when one idea is complete and another one is being introduced. Writers who don't follow these conventions run the risk of confusing their readers.

In the first example on page 90, two sentences have been run together without punctuation. This kind of **fused sentence** or **run-on sentence** makes it more difficult for readers to distinguish the main ideas. Every sentence should focus on one main idea as stated in the subject and verb. Correct punctuation helps readers to distinguish ideas clearly.

A comma is not enough punctuation to separate two sentences. The second example shows two sentences incorrectly "spliced" together with just a comma. In some circumstances a semicolon may separate one main idea from another; however, the general rule is that you need a period, an exclamation point, or a question mark at the end of every sentence.

Fused or run-on sentence **Genghis Khan united the Mongol tribes he conquered most of northern China.**

Comma splice **Genghis Khan united the Mongol tribes, he conquered most of northern China.**

Correctly punctuated sentences **Genghis Khan united the Mongol tribes. He conquered most of northern China.**

EXERCISE O

Some of the following groups of sentences are incorrectly punctuated. Identify which groups contain fused sentences, which contain comma splices, and which are correctly punctuated. Add appropriate punctuation where it is needed to separate one sentence from another.

EXAMPLE:

comma splice	Kublai Khan expanded his grandfather's empire, he defeated the Sung dynasty of China. ↑
correct	Kublai Khan built a magnificent capital at Cambuluc. The city is now called Beijing.
fused sentence	Marco Polo reached Kublai Khan's court in 1275 he returned to Venice twenty years later. ↑

1. Joan of Arc was born to a poor farming family, she became a national heroine in France.

2. At a young age, Joan heard voices. She claimed that three saints spoke to her.

3. A war had left France under English control the voices inspired Joan to help her country.

4. Joan dressed in soldier's clothes, she led an army against the English.

5. The girl drove the English army from Orleans, the city had been under siege.

6. A new French king was crowned at Rheims Cathedral. Joan had saved her country.

7. Joan was captured the Burgundians sold her to the English.

_____ 8. The Maid of Orleans was convicted of witchcraft for her supposed heresy she was burned at the stake.

_____ 9. Twenty-five years later, her conviction was annulled, five hundred years later, she was named a saint of the Catholic Church.

_____ 10. Many legends surround Joan of Arc's career. Many artists have depicted her heroic deeds.

▶ FRAGMENTS

Any group of words that does not meet the three requirements for a sentence is a **fragment** or incomplete sentence. Fragments can occur in several ways depending on which sentence requirement has not been met.

● No Verb or No Verb with Tense

The first way of checking for a sentence fragment is to look for the verb in the group of words. If the group of words does not contain a verb that shows tense, then it is a fragment. The examples below show sentences that are incomplete because they lack verbs or they lack verbs that show tense.

> *Fragment* The Renaissance a transition from the Middle Ages to the modern period. (The word group does not contain a verb.)
>
> *Sentence* The Renaissance *formed* a transition from the Middle Ages to the modern period.
>
> *Fragment* The Renaissance *marking* the rich development of Western civilization. (The verb in this word group doesn't show tense.)
>
> *Sentence* The Renaissance *marked* the rich development of Western civilization.

● No Subject

The second test of a sentence is to look for the subject that goes with the verb. Except in the case of a command, a sentence must show the person or thing involved in the action of the verb. The examples below show sentences that are incomplete because they lack subjects.

> *Fragment* Provided a background for a new view of the world. (The word group is not a command and does not show a subject for the verb *provided*.)
>
> *Sentence* The Italian cities provided a background for a new view of the world.
>
> *Fragment* And supported the arts lavishly. (The word group is not a command and does not show a subject for the verb *supported*.)
>
> *Sentence* Wealthy patrons supported the arts lavishly.

● Subject–Verb Group with a Subordination Signal

The third test of a sentence is to look for a subordination signal. A complete sentence must be based on an unsubordinated subject–verb unit. The examples below show sentences that are incomplete because they are marked by subordination signals.

Fragment When the Renaissance reached its height in the sixteenth century. (The only subject–verb unit in this word group is introduced by the subordination signal *when*.)

Sentence The *Renaissance reached* its height in the sixteenth century.

Sentence When the Renaissance reached its height in the sixteenth century, *it brought* new importance to individual expression.

Fragment Universities that flourished throughout Europe. (The verb *flourished* is connected with the subordination signal *that*. The subject *universities* has no verb.)

Sentence *Universities flourished* throughout Europe.

Sentence *Universities* that flourished throughout Europe *became* centers for new growth in scholarship.

Exercise P

Identify each group of words below as a sentence (S) or a fragment (F). For any fragment, be prepared to explain why it is not a sentence, and write a complete sentence below, making whatever changes are necessary to correct the fragment.

_____ 1. The beginning of the modern period.

_____ 2. *Renaissance* means rebirth.

_____ 3. A rebirth of learning following the darkness.

_____ 4. A great increase in learning and practice of the arts.

_____

_____

_____ 5. As with all changes and movements.

_____

_____

_____ 6. The exact beginning is hard to establish.

_____

_____

_____ 7. When Constantinople fell to the Ottoman Turks.

_____

_____

_____ 8. Scholars fled for safety.

_____

_____

_____ 9. Questioning accepted ideas.

_____

_____

_____10. The well-rounded individual became an ideal.

_____

_____

_____11. Since Leonardo da Vinci is a perfect example of the Renaissance man.

_____

_____

_____12. Fresh ideas encouraged explorers.

_____

_____

_____13. Christopher opened new lands and trade routes.

_____

_____

_____14. The human rather than the divine.

_____

_____

_____15. To set in motion the Reformation.

_____

_____

EXERCISE Q
Rewrite the paragraph below to correct any sentence fragments.

Although the mighty Inca empire of Peru was well-organized and well-governed. It was conquered by fewer than two hundred Spaniards. The Spanish adventurers being led by Pizarro, his three brothers, and Diego de Almagro. Sailing to Peru in 1531 and having a difficult journey. While the Incas had a large army. The Spaniards had guns. When Pizarro arrived. A civil war was raging among the Incas. Pizarro seized the Inca emperor, Atahualpa. Holding him for ransom. When the ransom was paid. Atahualpa was strangled. Within three years, the Spaniards were masters of Peru. Though it was thirty years before the last Inca rebellion was stamped out.

_____

_____

_____

_____

_____

_____

_____

_____

_____

_____

EDITING PRACTICE:

Rewrite the following paragraphs to correct any errors in sentence completion or sentence punctuation. Look for fragments, spliced sentences, or fused sentences.

1. The Indian mausoleum. Designed to reflect the pleasures of this world and to foreshadow the pleasures of the world to come. The mausoleums were set in elaborate gardens with flowers and fountains, they were used by their owners as places of entertainment when they could enjoy them no longer, they became the solemn resting places of their remains. One of the loveliest buildings on earth, the Taj Mahal at Agra which was built for two purposes. Erected between 1630 and 1648 by Shah Jahan for a wife who died while she was still young. The Taj Mahal was intended as a tomb for Mumtaz Mahal, it was also a pleasure garden for the Shah who loved her. The Taj emerged as a new work of art it was a totally original work. Its uniqueness and dual purpose are often lost. To those who have never visited the Taj Mahal.

_____

_____

_____

_____

_____

_____

_____

_____

_____

_____

_____

2. Elizabeth I, who lived from 1533 to 1603. Established her court as a center of art and learning. Although the influence of Italian art was not strong in England. The new humanism is reflected in many Elizabethan writers. After the invention of the printing press, William Claxton introduced the printing press to England books became increasingly plentiful and cheap. The new readers were eager for more. In addition, the English theater flourishing. With Shakespeare and Marlowe as the contributing giants. Peace reigned within England's borders, Queen Elizabeth I had challenges to face on other fronts. The Spanish had taken over the Netherlands, Elizabeth sensed the threat of a Spanish invasion of England she sent 6,000 troops to fight alongside the Netherlanders. Spain took its anger to the sea by using its Armada. The largest fleet the world had ever seen. Sir Francis Drake had lighter, faster ships. But a huge storm defeated the Spanish fleet. The Elizabethan Age ended with tales of English valor and daring.

_____

_____

_____

_____

_____

_____

_____

_____

_____

WRITING PRACTICE:

1. The exercises in this chapter of the text have dealt with various people who have made an impact on history. If you were part of a time-travel experiment, which period in history would you most like to visit? Write a short proposal to the time-travel project board in which you present your choice of a destination and the reasons for your choice. Remember that time travel is very expensive, so the board will only endorse projects that meet its criteria. The time trip must be relatively safe; it must have a high educational value; and it must focus on a person who has had great influence on modern society.

PLANNING:

One way to choose a destination for the time-travel project is to think about the criteria for the project. Try using the chart below to help find a destination that will win the board's approval. You may consider some of the destinations shown and add others of your choice. Give each destination from 1 to 10 points for each criterion. In this system, 30 points would be an ideal destination, very safe, very educational, and very focused.

Destination	Safety	Educational Value	Focus-Person	Total Points
Court of Elizabeth I				
Genghis Khan's camp				
Johann Gutenberg's workshop				

DRAFTING:

In writing your proposal, be sure to show the project board how your destination meets the three criteria. Use one or two sentences to address each criterion.

REVISING/EDITING:

When you have written a draft of your proposal, go back and make sure that all your sentences are complete and correctly punctuated. Perhaps another student would be willing to double-check your sentences.

2. The board has approved your time-travel project. As the second phase of the project, you are encouraged to bring a guest back for a short visit to your century. Write a one-page letter to the person you have chosen to visit, inviting him or her for a return visit and explaining why you think he or she would be interested in seeing your society.

PLANNING:

To persuade your guest to visit your society, you need to consider what your guest is interested in and how your society might appeal to those interests. The chart below might help to match your guest's interests with things in your society that might appeal to those interests.

Guest's Interests		Appeal to Interest
1. _____	→	A. _____
_____	→	B. _____
_____	→	C. _____
2. _____	→	A. _____
_____	→	B. _____
_____	→	C. _____
3. _____	→	A. _____
_____	→	B. _____
_____	→	C. _____

DRAFTING:

In writing your letter, call your guest's attention to various people, places, or activities in your society that might arouse his or her interest. Use one or two sentences to address each of your guest's major interests.

REVISING/EDITING:

When you have written a draft of your letter, go back and make sure that all your sentences are complete and correctly punctuated. Perhaps another student would be willing to double-check your sentences.

◀ Chapter 3 ▶

Adding Detail to the Basic Sentence

• • • • • • • • • • • • • •

• • • • • • • • • • • • • •

The subject–verb unit, as you saw in Chapter 2, presents the basic information needed to communicate an idea in writing. However, writing would be a slow and frustrating process if you wrote only in simple subject–verb sentences, and the resulting communication would probably lack coherence.

Making sure that your reader has the basic subject–verb information is only the first step in writing an effective sentence. Once you have shown the center of attention in the sentence and the action involved, you need to fine-tune the sentence so it presents your idea to your reader as accurately as possible. You can use a special sentence pattern to emphasize a certain quality of your subject, or you can make additions to the basic sentence to describe the subject and the action more precisely.

▶ LINKING VERB SENTENCES

The subject of a sentence, as you saw in the previous chapter, names the person or thing on which the sentence focuses attention. One possible way of adding descriptive detail about the subject of your sentence is to use a special sentence pattern called the **linking verb sentence.** The sentence below shows this pattern:

Explorers are brave.

This sentence emphasizes one particular quality of explorers—their bravery.

The Phoenicians were curious.

This sentence emphasizes one quality of the Phoenicians—their curiosity.

Notice how the verbs in these descriptive sentences relate the subject to one particular quality. *Explorers* is linked to *brave. The Phoenicians* is linked to *curious.* The word used to describe the subject in each of these sentences is called the **subject complement** because it identifies one particular aspect of the subject.

In an active sentence, as presented in the previous chapter, a verb might be followed by an object that showed the goal or result of an action. In the descriptive sentences shown here, the verb does not really convey any action. Instead, the verb merely defines a condition of existence. The verb serves as a link between the subject and a descriptive word about the subject. Because of this function, these verbs are called linking verbs. The linking verb works almost like an equal sign (=) between the subject and the subject complement.

The Mediterranean Sea was treacherous.
The Mediterranean Sea = treacherous.

The Greeks had been the first map makers.
The Greeks = the first map makers.

Early maps were inaccurate.
Early maps = inaccurate.

The most common linking verb is the verb *be*. You may remember that the verb *be* can work with a past participle to create a passive verb or with a present participle to show action in progress. In the linking verb sentence, however, a form of *be* stands alone as the main verb. Some other verbs can sometimes function as linking verbs, as the examples below indicate. Like the *be* verbs, these other linking verbs also serve to identify one particular aspect of the subject.

Early maps seem strange.

Early maps = strange.

Venice had grown rich and powerful.

Venice = rich and powerful.

Marco Polo felt excited.

Marco Polo = excited.

Verbs like *grow* and *feel* may function as linking verbs sometimes and as action verbs at other times. If they are linking verbs, you should be able to substitute a form of *be* in the sentence, as the following examples show:

Marco Polo *felt* excited.

Marco Polo *was* excited.

Venice *had grown* rich and powerful.

Venice *was* rich and powerful.

If these verbs are not linking verbs, you will not be able to make the substitution.

Marco Polo felt the sea slapping the side of the boat. (Here Marco Polo does not equal the sea. You cannot write that Marco Polo *was* the sea. Therefore, *felt* is not a linking verb in this sentence.)

The box below shows the most common linking verbs.

LINKING VERBS
be, am, is, are, was, were
have been, has been, had been, will have been
appear, become, feel, grow, look
prove, remain, seem, smell, sound, taste, turn

EXERCISE A

Identify with labels the subject (S), linking verb (LV), and subject complement (SC) in each of the following sentences. Notice how each of these sentences focuses on one quality or one aspect of the subject. The subject complement names that quality or aspect of the subject.

1. The search for the sunken ship was difficult.
2. The legend of the *Titanic* remains fascinating.
3. The ship was "unsinkable."
4. Every detail of the ship appeared perfect.
5. The damage from the iceberg seemed minor at first.
6. Nevertheless, the iceberg's blow proved fatal.
7. The captain grew worried.
8. The passengers felt secure.
9. Many lifeboats were half-empty.
10. The *Titanic*'s story has become more intriguing every year.

EXERCISE B

Identify the pattern in each of the following sentences.

A: The sentence shows a self-contained action, no object, no subject complement.

B: The sentence shows the completion of an action in the object of the verb.

C: The sentence uses a subject complement to refer back to and describe the subject.

___C___ 1. Pytheus was a Greek mathematician and astronomer.

___A___ 2. Pytheus lived in the fourth century B.C.

___B___ 3. Pytheus sailed the Atlantic Ocean.

_____ 4. He became one of the greatest explorers of all time.

_____ 5. His journey was dangerous.

_____ 6. He explored England.

_____ 7. The country seemed very wild.

_____ 8. His journey did not end in England.

_____ 9. Pytheus also crossed the Arctic Circle.

_____ 10. This crossing was a historic first for human explorers.

_____11. After his journey, Pytheus wrote a book.

_____12. His book, *The Ocean,* proved highly popular.

_____13. Later, opinion shifted.

_____14. People no longer believed Pytheus.

_____15. The polar lands must be a myth.

_____16. Pytheus was a fake.

_____17. A thousand years later, other explorers followed his path.

_____18. Pytheus' descriptions were accurate after all.

_____19. No copies of Pytheus' book have survived.

_____20. The disappearance of the book is a great loss to scholars.

EXERCISE C

Emphasize one quality of each subject below by adding a linking verb and a subject complement. Use forms of *be* for half of your sentences and other linking verbs for the other half of your sentences.

EXAMPLE:

    The ships

    The ships looked fragile.

    The ships were sturdy.

1. The desert

_____

_____

2. Jungles

_____

_____

3. Hunters

_____

_____

4. Mount Everest

_____

_____

5. A volcano

_____

_____

6. Sonar equipment

_____

_____

7. The Pacific Ocean

_____

_____

8. The African continent

_____

_____

9. Cities

_____

_____

10. The Vikings

_____

_____

▶ KINDS OF MODIFIERS

The linking verb sentence is a useful tool if the main point of your sentence is to describe some quality of the subject. Most of the time, however, sentences try to show the subject involved in some action. Then, the qualities of the subject are important, but not the main point of the sentence. You can include modifiers in a sentence to show important qualities without making them the focus of the whole sentence.

Modifiers change the subject, verb, or object of a sentence by adding detail about its specific qualities or conditions. Modifiers make it easier for your readers to visualize exactly what you are writing about. Modifiers fall into two categories: adjectives and adverbs. In general, adjectives describe nouns and adverbs describe verbs and other modifiers.

● Adjectives

Adjectives tell readers more about a noun in the sentence. They help to limit and define nouns so that readers will understand your ideas more clearly. For instance, suppose you had this base sentence:

The explorer told a tale.

You might want to influence your reader's attitude toward the explorer by providing some additional detail. Perhaps the explorer was hesitant, in which case the reader might be suspicious of his story. Or perhaps he was very confident, in which case the reader might accept his story more readily.

You could present this description of the explorer and his tale by using linking verb sentences:

The explorer told a tale.

The explorer was confident.

The tale was remarkable.

Or you could combine these sentences to produce one sentence that contains all the descriptive language:

The *confident* explorer told a *remarkable* tale.

Using linking verb sentences puts a great deal of emphasis on the confidence of the explorer and on the remarkableness of his tale. The second version presents the information much more efficiently by including all the detail in a single sentence. When you use words or phrases to give more precise information about some person or thing in a sentence, you are using **adjectives.** *Confident* and *remarkable* in the sentence above are both adjectives.

Carefully chosen adjectives can make a great difference in the effect of a sentence. For example, *Roget's Thesaurus* lists all of the following adjectives related to the idea of confident: *bold, cocksure, intrepid, fearless, puffed up, pushy, self-satisfied, uppity, valiant.* Each of these adjectives could create a different impression of the explorer in a reader's mind.

Adjectives usually answer the questions *which one?* or *what kind?*

For example:

> The *powerful* ruler welcomed the travelers. *(What kind of ruler?)*
>
> The travelers *from Venice* greeted Kublai Khan. *(Which travelers?)*
>
> A band *of Saracens* attacked the caravan. *(What kind of band?)*
>
> The caravan crossed the *hot and endless* desert. *(What kind of desert?)*

Notice that adjectives may be single words or they may be phrases introduced by a preposition like *in, of, to, from,* or *with.* An adjective is closely tied to the word that it modifies. Normally, a single-word adjective comes immediately before the noun it describes. A phrase adjective normally comes immediately after the word it describes.

The box below shows the most common prepositions used to introduce modifiers.

PREPOSITIONS USED TO INTRODUCE MODIFIER PHRASES

about	because of	despite	into	to
above	before	down	near	toward
across	behind	during	next to	under
after	below	except	of	until
against	beneath	for	on	up
along	beside	from	over	upon
among	between	in	since	with
around	beyond	inside	through	within
as	by	in spite of	throughout	without
at				

EXERCISE D

Fill in the blanks next to each sentence, identifying each adjective in the sentence and the word the adjective describes. Remember that adjectives may be a single word or a phrase introduced by a preposition.

	Adjective	Word Described by the Adjective

<u>EXAMPLE:</u>

	Adjective	Word Described by the Adjective
1. The young man and his father and uncle left Venice in 1271.	*young*	*man*

2. The Venetian caravan traveled in heavy, two-wheeled carts. _____ _____

3. Three years later, the exhausted adventurers reached the fabulous palace of Kublai Khan. _____ _____

4. The ruler of the Mongol Empire received his honored guests with lavish ceremonies. _____ _____

5. Marco Polo wrote a popular book about his fascinating years in China. _____ _____

6. Marco Polo's marvelous stories described curious creatures and incredible places. _____ _____

7. Of course, the learned scholars of Europe doubted the truth of Polo's exotic tales. _____ _____

8. The large and rich island of Zipangu (Japan) must be fictional. _____ _____

9. Uninformed criticism of his book did not disturb the wise Marco Polo. _____ _____

10. The old man treasured his pleasant memories of distant places and strange people. _____ _____

EXERCISE E

Combine each of the following sets of sentences to create one sentence that uses adjectives to describe the nouns in the sentence.

EXAMPLE:

Ibn Batuta set off for Mecca
Ibn Batuta was of Tangier.
He was twenty-one years old.

Twenty-one-year-old Ibn Batuta of Tangier set off for Mecca.

1. This pilgrim traveled throughout the world.
   It was the Muslim world.
   It was the world of the fourteenth century.

_____

_____

2. Ibn Batuta followed a trail.
   The trail was hazardous.
   The trail went through deserts.
   The deserts were unpopulated.

   _____

   _____

3. Ibn Batuta crossed continents.
   The continents were African.
   The continents were European.
   The continents were Asian.
   Ibn Batuta was intrepid.

   _____

   _____

4. Batuta tripled the record.
   Batuta was determined.
   The record was for travels.
   The record was Marco Polo's.

   _____

   _____

5. His story is told in a manuscript.
   The manuscript is brittle.
   The manuscript is Arabic.

   _____

   _____

6. Paintings of Batuta show a scholar.
   The paintings are modern.
   The scholar is bearded.
   The scholar has eyes.
   The eyes are penetrating.

_____

_____

7. Batuta wears a robe.
   Batuta is scholarly.
   The robe is hooded.
   The robe is Moroccan.

_____

_____

8. Ibn Batuta sought out Muslims.
   The Muslims were educated.
   The Muslims were pious.
   The Muslims were powerful.

_____

_____

9. He told them tales.
   The tales were of wisdom.
   The wisdom was Koranic.
   The tales were from lands.
   The lands were distant.

_____

_____

10. Batuta is still considered a source.
    The source is reliable.
    The source is for geography.
    The geography is medieval.
    The source is for culture.
    The culture is Islamic.

_____

_____

EXERCISE F

In the following sentences, add adjectives to show specific detail about the subject or another noun. At least half of your adjectives should be phrases introduced by prepositions.

1. The oceanographer stood by the hatch. (What kind of oceanographer?)

_____

_____

2. She had designed the vessel. (Which vessel?)

_____

_____

3. The team descended. (Which team?)

_____

_____

4. Sediment clouded their masks. (What kind of masks?)

_____

5. With a motion, she signaled them to stop. (What kind of motion?)

_____

_____

6. The area was filled with chunks of minerals. (Which area? What kind of chunks?)

_____

_____

7. A rumbling came from beneath the ocean floor. (What kind of rumbling?)

_____

_____

8. The group was astonished. (What kind of group?)

_____

_____

9. Cheryl had received a gift from the sea. (What kind of gift?)

_____

_____

10. Years of research had paid off. (What kind of research?)

_____

_____

EXERCISE G

Expand each of the following sentences by using one or more adjectives to make the nouns more specific and concrete. You may want to use a thesaurus to help you select interesting and vivid adjectives.

EXAMPLES:
    The group packed up early.
    The weary group packed up early.

1. The group departed from the village.

_____

_____

2. The leaders followed the road.

_____

_____

3.   The fever captured their imaginations.

_____

_____

4.   The survivors conquered the heat.

_____

_____

5.   People still tell the tale.

_____

_____

● Adverbs

   ■ *Adverbs Modifying Verbs*

Adverbs help you control the effect of a verb by showing the conditions of the action. **Adverbs** are words or groups of words that show when, where, why, how, or to what degree some action is done.

For example, look at how the sentences below use adverbs:

> Vikings *frequently* sailed the North Atlantic. (*When* did the Vikings sail?)
>
> Their influence was felt *throughout Europe*. (*Where* was their influence felt?)
>
> The Vikings succeeded *because of their ships*. (*Why* did they succeed?)
>
> Their ships were *cunningly* built. (*How* were the ships built?)
>
> The Norse sagas have *completely* documented the Vikings' adventures. (*To what degree* have the sagas documented the adventures?)

Like adjectives, adverbs can be either single words or phrases introduced by prepositions. As you can see in the examples above, many single-word adverbs—such as *frequently, cunningly,* and *completely*—end in *-ly.* Not all adverbs end in *-ly,* and not all *-ly* words are adverbs. Nevertheless, the *-ly* ending is one clue to recognizing adverbs.

Unlike adjectives, adverbs can take different positions in a sentence. Even though an adverb describes the circumstances of action, it does not necessarily appear right next to the verb it modifies. For example, the following set of sentences illustrates several different positions for the adverb:

> *Five hundred years before Columbus,* Vikings reached North America.
>
> Vikings reached North America *five hundred years before Columbus.*
>
> Vikings, *five hundred years before Columbus,* reached North America.

EXERCISE H

Fill in the table below, identifying each adverb in the following sentences and the verb that the adverb describes. Remember that adverbs may be a single word or a phrase introduced by a preposition.

1. By the eighth century, Scandinavia could not adequately support its population.
2. The people constantly roamed the sea because of the scarcity of farmland.
3. In Old Norse, *Viking* literally means *sea raiders*.
4. Vikings violently raided the coasts of Europe for about two hundred and fifty years.
5. In 800 A.D., one Norse tribe, the Russ, brazenly established a colony around Kiev.
6. By the tenth century, the Vikings had effectively colonized Iceland and Greenland.
7. One spring, Viking Leif Ericson sailed west from Greenland.
8. After an exhausting voyage, Leif the Lucky eventually sighted a land of trees and grapevines.
9. This Vinland was probably located somewhere in present-day Newfoundland.
10. Because of constant hostility with the natives, the Viking colony never took root and was soon forgotten.

Adverb	Verb Described by the Adverb
EXAMPLE:	
By the eighth century	*could support*
not	*could support*
adequately	*could support*
1. _____	_____
2. _____	_____
3. _____	_____
4. _____	_____

5. _____   _____

6. _____   _____

7. _____   _____

8. _____   _____

9. _____   _____

10. _____   _____

EXERCISE 1

Combine each set of sentences below into one sentence in which an adverb describes the action of the verb.

EXAMPLE:

> Ferdinand Magellan's father enrolled him.
> The enrollment was in the Royal School for Pages.
> The enrollment took place in Ferdinand's twelfth year.

In Ferdinand's twelfth year, Magellan's father enrolled him in the Royal

School for Pages.

1. Magellan studied astronomy.
   His study was diligent.
   His study took place in Queen Leonora's court.

_____

_____

2. Portugal was famous.
   Portugal's fame extended around the world.
   Portugal's fame was because of Vasco da Gama's exploits.

   _____

   _____

3. Magellan served Portugal.
   His service took place in the Far East.
   His service lasted for ten years.
   His service was brave.

   _____

   _____

4. The Portuguese king refused to reward Magellan.
   The reward was for his services.
   The refusal was after Magellan's return to Portugal.
   The refusal was callous.

   _____

   _____

5. Magellan developed a plan to circumnavigate the globe.
   He developed it after King Manuel's dismissal of him.
   The development of the plan took many months.

   _____

   _____

6. Magellan believed he could sail his ship.
   Magellan's belief was confident.
   The sailing would be from the Atlantic Ocean to the Pacific.
   The sailing would be through a water passage in the far south.

   _____

   _____

7. Charles I, the young king of Spain, supported Magellan's plan.
His support was eager.
He showed his support by outfitting five ships.

_____

_____

8. Magellan found the southern passage and crossed it.
He found it finally.
He found it after more than a year of storms, mutinies, and deaths.
He crossed it with difficulty.

_____

_____

9. Magellan himself died.
He died before reaching home again.
He died in the Philippines.

_____

_____

10. Magellan's ship had circled the globe.
The circling took place by the end of its voyage.
The circling was complete.
The circling took three years.

_____

_____

■ Adverbs with Other Modifiers

Besides describing the circumstances of an action—when, where, why, how, to what degree—adverbs may also describe an adjective or another adverb. The sentences below illustrate this use of adverbs.

> David Livingstone became an *internationally* famous explorer. *(Here the adverb* internationally *describes the adjective* famous: *How was Livingstone famous?)*

Livingstone was *extremely* disturbed by the slave trade's devastation of Africa. *(How disturbed was he?)*

Livingstone searched *very* diligently for the source of the Nile. *(How diligently did he search?)*

The box below shows some adverbs that often modify adjectives or other adverbs.

ADVERBS COMMONLY USED WITH OTHER MODIFIERS			
almost	more	really	too
extremely	much	so	very
just	quite	somewhat	

EXERCISE J
Underline the adverbs in the following sentences and indicate with an arrow whether they describe the action of a verb or show some quality of another modifier.

EXAMPLE:

Several civilizations <u>quickly</u> reached high levels of development.

1. Why could the Europeans conquer other civilizations so easily?
2. At times, they used gunpowder in their conquests.
3. The often-attacked Tupinamba of Brazil barely resisted.
4. The extremely resourceful Iroquoian Indians were primarily hunters.
5. They could resist more adequately.
6. The Maya of Guatemala, however, had much more primitive weapons.
7. Frequently, they had also been weakened by civil wars.
8. The Aztecs and the Incas were the most vulnerable.
9. The fiercely determined Spanish quickly took over their intricately designed administrative systems.
10. The indigenous people had always respected a strictly defined social order and had unquestioningly obeyed their spiritually powerful leaders.

EXERCISE K
Add adverbs to the following sentences as indicated.

1. The adventurous group left. (Why?)

_____

_____

2. The adventurous group left. (How?)

_____

_____

3. They journeyed. (Where?)

_____

_____

4. They were tired. (To what degree?)

_____

_____

5. The excited group arrived. (When?)

_____

_____

6. They had gone. (Why?)

_____

_____

7. Their spirits rose. (To what degree?)

_____

_____

8. The disappointed members left. (Where and when?)

_____

_____

9. The leader complained. (When and how?)

_____

_____

10. The group rejoiced. (How and where?)

_____

_____

Exercise L

Expand each of the following sentences using adverbs to show the circumstances of the action or a quality of the modifier.

1. Explorers face the unknown.

_____

_____

2. They rely on their innate skill and courage.

_____

_____

3. Men and women will challenge themselves to "push the envelope."

_____

_____

4. Explorers possess intense curiosity.

_____

_____

5. Some adventurers explore the uncharted territory within themselves.

_____

_____

● Distinguishing Between Adjectives and Adverbs

Many descriptive words have both an adjective and an adverb form. For example, the adjective *recent* also has an adverb form—*recently*. The adjective *bitter* also has an adverb form—*bitterly*. However, you can't always tell whether a word is an adjective or an adverb just by looking at it. While it is true that many adverbs end in *-ly*, some *-ly* words, like *early* or *friendly,* can be adjectives as well as adverbs. Words like *better* and *fast* can also be either adjectives or adverbs.

When you add modifiers to a sentence, therefore, you need to understand how the modifier will function in order to be sure you've chosen the correct form—adjective or adverb. This can be particularly tricky when an adjective acts as a subject complement after a linking verb. For example, look at the two sentences below:

> The native tribes are *independent.*
>
> They respond *independently.*

In the first sentence, the modifier describes the noun *tribes* and is therefore an adjective. *Independent* shows *what kind* of people the tribes are. In the second sentence, *independently* describes the verb *respond.* It tells *how* the action of responding took place and is therefore an adverb.

Can you tell which of the following sentences contains an adverb?

> The animal growled weakly.
>
> She seemed weak.

Remember that adverbs can also modify other modifiers, as the following examples show:

> The captain looked thoughtfully out the window. *(Here the adverb thoughtfully describes the circumstances under which the action of looking took place.)*
>
> The captain looked especially thoughtful. *(Here the adjective thoughtful indicates a certain quality of the captain. The adverb especially describes the degree of that quality.)*
>
> The deadline arrived unbelievably quickly. *(Here the adverb quickly describes the circumstances of the action of arriving. The adverb unbelievably shows the degree of quickness involved.)*

Exercise M

For each modifier shown below, decide whether it could describe a noun or a verb or both and identify it as an adjective or an adverb. If it is an adjective, write out the corresponding adverb form. If it is an adverb, write out the corresponding adjective form. Consult your dictionary if you need help.

<u>EXAMPLE:</u>

	Adjective	**Adverb**
quaint	*X*	*quaintly*
1. weakly		
2. heroic		
3. adventurously		
4. dauntless		
5. vastly		
6. uncanny		
7. barefoot		
8. blunt		
9. accidental		
10. stubbornly		

EXERCISE N

Following the examples shown below, rewrite each of the following sentences so that the underlined adjective becomes an adverb.

<u>EXAMPLES:</u>

Because of the <u>unceasing</u> demand, many explorers looked for a route to the spice countries.

Spices were unceasingly demanded, so many explorers looked for a route to the spice countries.

Many naturalists explored the world with the <u>sole</u> aim of gathering scientific information.

Many naturalists explored solely to gather scientific information.

1. Nineteenth-century studies brought a <u>great</u> increase in knowledge of the natural world.

_____

_____

2. Henry Bates kept <u>meticulous</u> records of the new insect
   species he discovered in the Amazon rain forest.

   _____

   _____

3. Naturalists were <u>delicate</u> when using nets to capture
   insects.

   _____

   _____

4. Mary Kingsley's <u>determined</u> search for new species of fish took her into the
   wildest parts of West Africa.

   _____

   _____

5. During his voyage on the *Beagle,* Charles Darwin's <u>industrious</u> accumulation of
   specimens helped him develop his theory of evolution.

   _____

   _____

6. The 1850s saw the <u>independent</u> development of theories of evolution by
   Darwin and Alfred Wallace.

   _____

   _____

7. <u>Simultaneous</u> publication of the two theories occurred in 1858.

   _____

   _____

8. Naturalist explorers engage in a <u>constant</u> search for new plants.

   _____

   _____

9. Aimé Bonpland's <u>fortuitous</u> discovery of the cinchona plant has helped to prevent many deaths from malaria.

_____

_____

10.   The naturalist's work brings more <u>scientific</u> than <u>monetary</u> rewards.

_____

_____

EXERCISE O

For each pair of adjectives and adverbs shown in Exercise M, above, write a pair of sentences illustrating the difference between the adjective and the adverb. Use your own paper for this exercise.

<u>EXAMPLE:</u>
quaint, quaintly

The village elders' <u>quaint</u> dress seemed to come from another time.

The village elders dressed <u>quaintly</u>, seeming to come from another time.

EXERCISE P

Supply the correct adjective or adverb form in each of the following sentences.

(painful)   1. As a young woman, Margaret Mead was _____ rejected by the sorority system at her college.

(sensitive)   2. This event caused the _____ Margaret to switch colleges and to meet people who would change her life.

(inconspicuous)   3. In 1929, Margaret Mead _____ became the first American woman to earn a Ph.D. in anthropology.

(inconspicuous)   4. Earning her degree may have been the last

                         _____ thing Margaret Mead ever did.

(extraordinary)   5. Mead's career was characterized by _____ controversy.

(candid)   6. She spoke _____ on almost every national issue of her time.

(enduring)   7. She achieved _____ fame as an anthropologist
                    for her studies of nonliterate cultures.

(wide)   8. Her most _____ acclaimed works include
                    Coming of Age in Samoa, published in 1928, and *Growing Up in New
                    Guinea,* published in 1930.

(clear)   9. Margaret Mead's studies _____ show that
                    culture molds personalities more than biology does.

(virtual)   10. She earned a reputation as a _____ tireless
                    researcher.

(fluent)   11. To do research, Mead became _____ in seven
                    primitive languages.

(extensive)   12. She pioneered the _____ use of photography
                    for anthropological research.

(free)   13. Mead _____ adapted her findings to
                    contemporary life.

(eager)   14. For instance, she wrote a book explaining to

                    _____ American soldiers how to get along with
                    British girls.

(posthumous)   15. In recognition of her achievements, she was

                    _____ awarded the Presidential Medal of
                    Freedom in 1979.

▶ FORMS OF MODIFIERS

● Simple, Comparative, and Superlative Forms

Adjectives and adverbs can appear in three forms, indicating different degrees of
the quality they describe. The **simple** or base form is used to describe a single
object or action. It describes without making any comparison:

> **The team demonstrated the *new* equipment.**
> **The demonstration went *smoothly*.**

The **comparative** form indicates that one object or action shows a greater
degree of the particular quality than another. The comparative compares the
object or action to one other thing. The comparative form frequently uses the
word *than* to indicate a comparison:

The Beta Team tested a *newer* version of the equipment.

The trial proceeded *more smoothly* than their previous efforts.

The **superlative** form indicates that one object or action displays the greatest degree of the particular quality out of a whole group. The superlative form compares the object or action with two or more others:

The *newest* equipment outperformed all the others.

This demonstration went the *most smoothly* of all six of the trials.

Adjectives and adverbs form the comparative and superlative forms in one of three ways.

1. Almost all one-syllable adjectives and adverbs and many two-syllable adjectives form the comparative by adding *-er* to the base form. They form the superlative by adding *-est* to the simple form.

Simple	Comparative	Superlative
tall	taller	tallest
long	longer	longest
fast	faster	fastest
*big	bigger	biggest
*hot	hotter	hottest
*funny	funnier	funniest
*steady	steadier	steadiest

*Note the spelling changes: one-syllable words with a single vowel followed by a consonant double the consonant before adding *-er* or *-est*. Words ending in *-y* change the *y* to *i* before adding *-er* or *-est*.

2. Many adjectives with two or more syllables and almost all adverbs with two or more syllables form the comparative by adding *more* to the base form. They form the superlative by adding *most* to the base form.

Simple	Comparative	Superlative
isolated	more isolated	most isolated
exciting	more exciting	most exciting
deeply	more deeply	most deeply
forcefully	more forcefully	most forcefully

3. A few adjectives and adverbs have their own distinctive form of the comparative and superlative. These need to be memorized.

Simple	Comparative	Superlative
good	better	best
well	better	best
bad	worse	worst
badly	worse	worst
little	less	least

Note that adjectives and adverbs never use both the *-er* and the *more* form at the same time. Likewise, adjectives and adverbs never use both the *-est* and the *most* form at the same time. Comparative or superlative forms like *more sillier* or *most silliest* are incorrect.

Exercise Q

Write the comparative and superlative forms for each of the modifiers shown below. If you are not sure about the correct form, look up the modifier in the dictionary.

Simple	Comparative	Superlative
1. heavy	_____	_____
2. sad	_____	_____
3. early	_____	_____
4. accurately	_____	_____
5. agile	_____	_____
6. giddy	_____	_____
7. roguishly	_____	_____
8. morose	_____	_____
9. biased	_____	_____
10. rebelliously	_____	_____
11. rowdy	_____	_____
12. sarcastically	_____	_____
13. stale	_____	_____
14. tedious	_____	_____
15. vividly	_____	_____

EXERCISE R

Choose any ten of the modifiers shown in Exercise Q, above. For each one, write a series of sentences using the simple, comparative, and superlative form. Use your own paper for this exercise.

EXAMPLE:
accurately

simple: This map accurately locates all the mineral deposits.

comparative: My map locates the mineral deposits more accurately than the one you provided.

superlative: The 1990 map locates the mineral deposits the most accurately of all the ones I have seen.

EXERCISE S

In each of the following sentences, supply the appropriate form of the adjective or adverb: simple, comparative, or superlative.

(preeminent)   1. The Leakey family has established a _____ reputation in archaeology and anthropology.

(famous)   2. It is hard to decide who is _____: Louis S. B. Leakey, his wife Mary Douglas Leakey, or their son Richard Leakey.

(commonly)   3. One of the _____ held beliefs prior to the Leakeys' work was that human beings appeared on earth only about 100,000 years ago.

(old)   4. However, the Leakeys' discoveries suggested that humans are

far _____ than that.

(conclusively)   5. In addition, the Leakeys demonstrated _____ than any other researchers that human life originated in Africa, not Asia.

(important)   6. In 1942, Mary Leakey discovered what was considered the

_____ collection of Stone Age hand axes ever found.

(late)   7. Six years _____, she uncovered one of the

(spectacular)   _____ archaeological finds of the century.

(ancient)   8. Her 25-million-year-old skull of *Proconsul africanus* was the

_____ skull of its kind.

(possibly)   9. *Proconsul* was an apelike creature who was

_____ an ancestor of both apes and
humans.

(controversial)   10. In the 1960s, the Leakeys made a discovery that was

perhaps _____ than their previous
ones—fossil remains of *Homo habilis.*

(early)   11. The Leakeys argued that *Homo habilis* was the

_____ direct ancestor of human beings.

(far)   12. Mary Leakey's later discoveries indicated the existence of humanlike
creatures about four million years ago,

_____ back in time than scientists had previously
thought.

(thoroughly)   13. After many years of research, the Leakeys had documented

their theories _____ than any other researchers had.

(broad)   14. Each new piece of evidence has led to a _____ picture
of human and primate development than was possible before.

(influential)   15. The Leakeys have been among the _____ scientists of
this century.

▶ PLACEMENT OF MODIFIERS

● Misplaced Modifiers

When you use modifiers, you have to place them carefully so that it is absolutely
clear what they describe. Misplaced modifiers can confuse your reader.

For example, suppose you received the following message:

Dr. Livingstone said on Thursday we would leave for Africa.

The modifier *on Thursday* might go with the verb *said,* meaning that Dr. Livingstone made the announcement on Thursday. On the other hand, it might be
describing the verb *leave,* meaning that departure is scheduled for Thursday. The
difference here could be crucial to your future as a member of Dr. Livingstone's
team. But because *on Thursday* appears between two verbs, you can't be exactly
sure which one it is intended to modify.

To make the intended meaning clear, the modifier would need to be placed
closer to one verb or the other:

On Thursday, Dr. Livingstone said we would leave for Africa.

Dr. Livingstone said we would leave for Africa on Thursday.

Here, the first version shows when Dr. Livingstone made the announcement. The second version shows when the departure is scheduled.

In general, modifiers should be placed as close as possible to the word they describe.

EXERCISE T

Rewrite each sentence below, inserting the modifier to create the indicated meaning.

1. In 1889, Roald Amundsen stood on the docks of Christiana and cheered the return of Norway's famous explorer, Fridtjof Nansen. (seventeen-year-old)

   Show Amundsen's age:

   _____

   _____

   Show the age of the docks:

   _____

   _____

2. Roald promised himself he would be a polar explorer. (that afternoon)

   Show when he made the promise:

   _____

   _____

Show when he would be a polar explorer:

_____

_____

3. However, Amundsen's mother insisted that he should speak to the professor about studying medicine.   (emphatically)

   Show how she insisted:

   _____

   _____

   Show how he should speak:

   _____

   _____

4. Since he failed his medical exams, Amundsen left the university.   (after his mother's death)

   Show when he failed:

   _____

   _____

   Show when he left:

   _____

   _____

5. Nicknamed "The Last of the Vikings," the young Amundsen was a man with a long, lean face and blue eyes.   (intense)

   Describe what kind of man he was:

   _____

   _____

   Describe his eyes:

   _____

   _____

6. Roald Amundsen of Norway responded to the challenge of the unknown. (remote)

   Describe Amundsen:

   _____

   _____

   Describe Norway:

   _____

   _____

7. In 1906, Amundsen had sailed the Northwest Passage among the Arctic islands of Canada.   (only)

   Describe Amundsen:

   _____

   _____

   Describe where he had sailed:

   _____

   _____

8. In 1911, Amundsen and British explorer Robert Scott engaged in a race to be the first at the South Pole.   (well-publicized)

   Describe the British explorer:

   _____

   _____

   Describe the race:

   _____

   _____

9. Scott, ill-prepared for the rigors of polar exploration, lost the race and his life. (tragically)

   Show how ill-prepared Scott was:

   _____

   _____

Show how he lost the race:

_____

_____

10. In 1913, Amundsen had an idea to explore the North and South Poles by air. (strange and exciting)

    Describe his idea:

    _____

    _____

    Describe the poles:

    _____

    _____

11. Amundsen went into partnership with an American, Lincoln Ellsworth. (well-funded)

    Describe Ellsworth:

    _____

    _____

    Describe Amundsen:

    _____

    _____

12. In their first attempt, their two planes went down 150 miles from the North Pole.   (ice-covered)

    Describe the planes:

    _____

    _____

Describe the North Pole:

_____

_____

13. The two teams of explorers thought they would not see each other.   (for a few days)

    Describe when they thought this:

_____

_____

    Describe when they would not see each other:

_____

_____

14. Later, Amundsen flew a dirigible over the North Pole and became the first person to reach both poles.   (with an Italian pilot)

    Show how he flew the dirigible:

_____

_____

    Show how he reached both poles:

_____

_____

15. Roald Amundsen was seen in 1928 when he headed out over Arctic waters in search of a downed pilot.   (for the last time)

    Show when he was seen:

_____

_____

    Show when he headed out:

_____

_____

● **Dangling Modifiers**

Misplaced modifiers may cause some confusion, but the confusion can be cleared up by moving the modifier to its proper position. A dangling modifier, on the other hand, sits in a sentence with nothing to attach itself to. Modifiers don't have any meaning unless your reader knows what they are supposed to describe. Look carefully at the sentence below:

As a young man, the life of an explorer seemed exciting.

What does the modifier *as a young man* describe? This sentence puts it next to *the life of an explorer.* However, that connection isn't logical. The sentence really has no place to attach that modifier, so the confusion can't be fixed simply by moving the modifier to another position. To correct the problem with this modifier, you would need to rewrite the sentence and put in something that the modifier can logically describe. For example:

As a young man, **Matthew Henson found the life of an explorer exciting.**

Now the modifier *as a young man* describes Matthew Henson.

Here is another example of a dangling modifier and a suggested revision:

DANGLING   **With an expression of triumph, an American flag was planted at the North Pole.**

REVISED   **With an expression of triumph, Henson planted an American flag at the North Pole.**

EXERCISE U

Rewrite the following sentences to correct any dangling or misplaced modifiers.

1. Amelia Earhart developed her interest in flying first during World War I.

   _____

   _____

2. As a military nurse, aviation became a consuming passion.

   _____

   _____

3. Although she was only a passenger, Amelia Earhart became the first woman to cross the Atlantic by air in 1928.

4. Fearless, the crossing was repeated in 1932, this time with Earhart flying solo.

5. With a dwindling fuel supply, an Irish cow pasture became her landing field.

6. Longer than the distance between the United States and Europe, she later made the hazardous crossing from Hawaii to California.

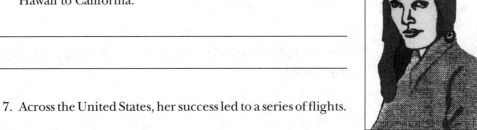

7. Across the United States, her success led to a series of flights.

8. In the new profession of aviation, Earhart actively encouraged women to work.

9. Still in existence, Earhart helped found the "Ninety-Nines," a female pilots' organization.

10. Around the world, Earhart set out in 1937 for a flight from Miami.

_____

_____

11. Earhart and her navigator over the Pacific disappeared.

_____

_____

12. Earhart, Noonan, and the plane they were flying mysteriously vanished near Howland Island.

_____

_____

13. Searchers could find no trace of Earhart's Lockheed Electra with the most sophisticated equipment.

_____

_____

14. From spy missions to secret romances, people never get tired of trying to explain the disappearance.

_____

_____

15. After all these years, still the fate of the celebrated aviator remains unknown.

_____

_____

▶ REVIEW OF MODIFIERS

MODIFIERS

ADJECTIVES	ADVERBS
Adjectives describe persons, places, things. Adjectives show *which one? what kind?* Single-word adjectives precede the noun. Phrase adjectives follow the noun.	Adverbs describe circumstances of action. Adverbs describe the quality of modifiers. Adverbs show *when, where, why, how, to what degree.* Adverbs may precede or follow.

EXERCISE V

Combine each of the following sets of sentences into one sentence in which modifiers provide details about the main elements of the sentence.

EXAMPLE:

The attempt occurred on March 3, 1972.
    The attempt was serious.
    The attempt was the first.
    The first serious attempt occurred on March 3, 1972.

1. The attempt was to communicate.
    The communication was with civilizations.
    The civilizations were extraterrestrial.

2. A space age started with the launching.
    The space age was more mature.
    The launching was successful.

The launching was of the *Pioneer 10* spacecraft.
The launching was from Cape Kennedy.

_____

_____

3. A message was drawn.
    The message was for other civilizations.
    The message was significant.
    The drawing was on a plaque.
    The plaque was gold.
    The plaque was six inches by nine inches.

_____

_____

4. The message shows the origins.
    The message is on the plaque.
    The showing is graphic.
    The origins are of the spacecraft.
    The spacecraft is human-made.

_____

_____

5. Figures portray beings.
    The portrayal is on the plaque.
    The figures are human.
    The beings are intelligent.
    The beings are next to a model.
    The model is of the spacecraft.

_____

_____

6. The silhouettes maintain neutrality.
    The silhouettes are of a man and a woman.
    The maintaining is tasteful.
    The neutrality is ethnic.
    The neutrality is for the culture.
    The culture is alien.

7. The hand is raised.
    The hand is of the man.
    The hand is his right one.
    The raising is as a gesture.
    The gesture is of goodwill.
    The gesture is symbolic.

8. Other symbols represent a language.
    The symbols are common.
    The symbols are on the plaque.
    The representation is hopeful.
    The language is general.
    The language is galactic.

9. This drawing is a card.
    That card is golden.
    The card is of greeting.
    The card is for the future.
    The future is distant.

10. We are engaged in a discourse.
    The discourse is cosmic.
    The discourse is with a civilization.
    The civilization is superior.
    The superiority is possible.

EXERCISE W

Expand each of the following sentences by adding one or more modifiers that will help readers understand the sentence more clearly.

1. Exploration can be an adventure.

_____

_____

2. Everyone can experiment with styles.

_____

_____

3. People can explore relationships.

_____

_____

4. Relationships can celebrate diversity.

_____

_____

5. Studying cultures opens up possibilities.

_____

_____

6. Music shows the spirit.

_____

_____

7. Food offers a taste.

_____

_____

8. Exploration begins.

_____

_____

9. The adventure is free.

_____

_____

10. Curiosity is the requirement.

_____

_____

EDITING PRACTICE:

Read the following paragraphs carefully, checking them for these kinds of problems:

1. Fragments
2. Fused sentences
3. Spliced sentences
4. Incorrect form of adjectives or adverbs
5. Incorrect placement of adjectives or adverbs

Then, write a corrected version in the blanks below.

    1. Many ordinary women have become the most wonderfulest explorers by pushing through their limitations. While the better physicians looked down on her methods for years, Sister Elizabeth Kenny obtained amazing results by massaging and manipulating the muscles of polio victims. Another woman who became an explorer. Junko Tabei becoming the first woman to reach the top of Mount Everest only 4′11″ tall. She claimed to be "just an ordinary housewife, I only like climbing." Another ordinary woman, Soviet cosmonaut Valentina Tereshkova. She was a former cotton mill worker Tereshkova first went skyward as a parachute jumper. In

1963, during her three-day nearly mission, she completed forty-eight orbits in space thus she became the first woman. Ordinary women have done extraordinary deeds.

_____

_____

_____

_____

_____

_____

_____

_____

_____

2. Being a person with a disability doesn't necessary mean having an unadventurous life. Even though he is confined to a wheelchair. Stephen Hawking is called the "new Einstein." But he be unable to speak. So he communicates through a computer and a voice synthesizer. Suffering from Lou Gehrig's disease with just two fingers, Hawking controls his computer. Hawking's major scientific insight concerns the collapse of black holes. He joking explains that his most best known discovery essentially says that "black holes ain't black." Hawking may have physical limits, his mind goes where none has gone before.

_____

_____

_____

_____

_____

_____

_____

_____

_____

_____

WRITING PRACTICE:

1. As a set designer for a television series based on space exploration, you are often called upon to represent exotic locations on strange planets. In one upcoming show, the cast meets the rulers of the planet Trenax. To help the actors understand the mood of the scene, write a brief description of the location on Trenax where this meeting will take place. Be as specific and concrete as possible in your description.

PLANNING:
One way to generate concrete detail for a description is to use your five senses as cues. Under the headings of *sight, sound, smell, taste,* and *touch,* list as many details as you can for each sense. Exactly what would the actors expect to see, hear, smell, taste, or touch on the planet Trenax?

DRAFTING:
Organizing your description spatially will help the actors visualize the set more clearly. For example, start at the right side of the set and move across to the left side. Include as much sensory detail as you can, using adjectives and adverbs that will really help the actors get a sense of the planet Trenax.

REVISING/EDITING:
When you have written a draft of your set description, go back and look carefully at the adjectives and adverbs you have used. Work with a dictionary and/or a thesaurus to make sure you have chosen the most vivid and precise modifiers you can find. Share your draft with a classmate to see if he or she can suggest any places where your description could be more concrete.

2. You have acquired a pen pal of your own age in another country. The sponsoring organization has asked participants to introduce themselves and the way they live by describing their favorite way to spend a free day. Write a letter of about one page describing your ideal day off.

PLANNING:
Make a list of several activities you really enjoy. Of the activities on your list, consider which one might be the most informative for a person who wants to know more about you and your lifestyle. You might want to use a graphic organizer like

the one shown below to help you generate details about when, where, why, and how you enjoy your favorite activity.

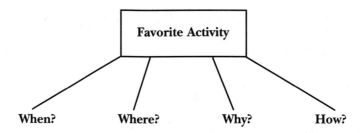

DRAFTING:

Organizing your description of an ideal day by using a time order—morning, afternoon, evening—may help your pen pal follow your discussion more easily. Try to include modifiers that will help your pen pal visualize your experience concretely.

REVISING/EDITING:

When you have written a draft of your description, go back and look carefully at the adjectives and adverbs you have used. Work with a dictionary and/or a thesaurus to make sure you have chosen the most vivid and precise modifiers you can find. Share your draft with a classmate to see if he or she can suggest any places where your description could be more concrete.

◀ *Chapter 4* ▶

Coordination

• • • • • • • • • • • • • •

• • • • • • • • • • • • • •

So far you have concentrated on creating sentences that present one idea completely and precisely. However, you can make a sentence do even more than that. You can use a sentence to show a relationship between two or more ideas. One of the basic relationships you can show is coordination.

Coordination shows that two ideas are equally important. The word *coordination* comes from two Latin roots—*co-*, meaning together or jointly, and *ordinare*, meaning to arrange in order. Coordination, then, means arranging ideas together, on the same level.

This chapter will explain three methods of coordinating ideas: by using a coordination signal, by using an explaining noun, and by using a linking adverb.

COORDINATE IDEAS BY:

1. USING A COORDINATION SIGNAL

2. USING AN EXPLAINING NOUN

3. USING A LINKING ADVERB

► USING COORDINATION SIGNALS

Coordination signals are special words used to call your reader's attention to a coordinate relationship between ideas. These seven words—*but, or, yet, for, and, nor, so*—can be used to coordinate parts of a sentence or even two complete sentences.

Here are some examples of sentences using these coordination signals:

coordinate subjects
The League of Five Nations or the Iroquois Confederacy brought a form of democracy to the Iroquois tribes.

The Constitution and government of the United States may have used the Iroquois Confederacy as a model.

coordinate verbs
Native Americans *respected but did* not *"own"* the land they lived on.
Most northern tribes *formed* few intertribal bonds *and created* no empires.

coordinate modifiers
In some tribes, the chief was *both a political and a religious* leader.
In others, a separate priesthood handled *religious or ceremonial* duties.

coordinate sentences

Men represented each clan at the Iroquois tribal councils, <u>*but*</u> Iroquois women chose the male representatives.

Native Americans believed that animals and plants possessed powerful spirits, <u>*so*</u> the tribes regularly made sacrifices to these spirits.

The box below shows the seven coordination signals arranged so that their first letters spell out the two words BOY FANS. This acronym may help you remember the coordination signals. The box also shows the paired coordination signals that may be used for additional emphasis.

COORDINATION SIGNALS

B∪T

Oʀ

Yᴇᴛ

Fᴏʀ

Aɴᴅ

Nᴏʀ

Sᴏ

EITHER . . . OR

NEITHER . . . NOR

BOTH . . . AND

NOT . . . BUT

Exercise A

Identify the coordinate elements in each of the following sentences. Circle the coordination signal and underline the two coordinate ideas being linked by the coordination signal.

1. Women's chief roles in colonial America were homemaker and mother.

2. These roles gave women some security but also many restrictions.

3. Both the laws and the customs of eighteenth-century America reinforced

   women's place in society.

4. Women could neither sign contracts nor bring lawsuits.

5. A wife's property and earnings technically belonged to her husband.

6. As a result, a woman might work hard yet see none of the profits.

7. Most women lived in isolated rural areas, so they had little access to books.

8. Most women were pregnant or nursing during much of their adult lives.

9. Divorce was rare, for most colonies prohibited divorce.

10. Some women broke out of the established patterns, but most of them

    accepted the relatively secure yet restricted roles society had defined for them.

● Coordinating Subjects

■ *Coordinating Subjects with* and

The subject of a sentence, as you remember from Chapter 2, tells a reader who or what is the focus of attention in a sentence. If you want your sentence to focus on two subjects equally, you coordinate them. For example, the two sentences shown below both focus on explorations of America before Columbus:

> **Chinese monks may have reached the American continent hundreds of years before Columbus.**
>
> **Vikings may have reached the American continent hundreds of years before Columbus.**

By using the coordination signal *and,* you can create a single sentence that gives these two sets of explorers equal emphasis:

> ***Chinese monks* <u>*and*</u> *Vikings* may have reached the American continent hundreds of years before Columbus.**

By using *and* to coordinate the two subjects, the combined sentence gives equal importance to the Vikings and to the Chinese monks.

The coordination signal *and* may be paired with the word *both* to give a little more emphasis to the coordinate elements.

> <u>***Both***</u> ***Chinese monks*** <u>***and***</u> ***Vikings*** **may have reached the American continent hundreds of years before Columbus.**

EXERCISE B

Using the example above as a model, combine each of the following pairs of sentences to produce a sentence that gives two subjects equal importance. Use *and* or *both/and* as the coordination signal.

1. Obedience to church authority characterized the Massachusetts Bay Colony.
   Attendance at religious services characterized the Massachusetts Bay Colony.

   _____

   _____

2. Roger Williams argued for individual religious freedom.
   Anne Hutchinson argued for individual religious freedom.

   _____

   _____

3. The civil authorities thought these opinions were dangerous.
   The religious authorities thought these opinions were dangerous.

   _____

   _____

4. The young minister left the Massachusetts Bay Colony.
   The outspoken woman left the Massachusetts Bay Colony.

   _____

   _____

5. Providence, Rhode Island originated as a result of this religious quarrel.
   Portsmouth, Rhode Island originated as a result of this religious quarrel.

   _____

   _____

In coordinating subjects with *and,* you have to watch out for one difficulty. Using *and* as a coordination signal between two subjects automatically creates a plural subject for the sentence. A plural subject must have a plural verb. Most of the time, this is not a problem, since most verbs look the same in their singular and plural forms. In a few cases, however, singular and plural verbs are different. The most notable example of this, as you may remember from Chapter 1, is in the present tense where the third person singular verb (used with *he, she,* or *it* subjects) has an *-s* ending. The verb *to be* also has different forms in the singular and plural.

Look at the sentences below:

> In the southern colonies, the average *settler lives* a hard life.
>
> In the southern colonies, the average settler's *family lives* a hard life.

Each of these sentences has a singular subject; each of them uses a singular verb. But look what happens when the subjects are coordinated:

> In the southern colonies, *the average settler <u>and</u> her family live* a hard life.

Here the coordinated subject—*the average settler and her family*—is plural; therefore, the verb must also become plural—*live.*

Here is another example of this pattern of coordination:

> *Hard work* often *leads* to early death among the settlers.
>
> *Disease* often *leads* to early death among the settlers.
>
> ↓
>
> *Hard work <u>and</u> disease* often *lead* to early death among the settlers.

Exercise C

Using the examples above as models, combine each of the following pairs of sentences to produce one sentence with two subjects coordinated by *and* or *both/and.* Be sure to use the appropriate verb form.

1. The Stamp Act provokes the American colonists.
   A tax on tea provokes the American colonists.

   _____

   _____

2. Radicals like Virginia's Patrick Henry oppose the British taxes.
   Moderates like Massachusetts's John Adams oppose the British taxes.

   _____

   _____

3. Remaining loyal to the English Crown sometimes divides families.
   Refusing to join the patriot cause sometimes divides families.

   _____

   _____

4. In 1775, Lexington sees the first battle of the Revolutionary War.
   In 1775, Concord sees the first battle of the Revolutionary War.

5. The Second Continental Congress has moved the colonists toward an open break with Britain.
   Thomas Paine's *Common Sense* has moved the colonists toward an open break with Britain.

6. After the Declaration of Independence, General Washington struggles against overwhelming military odds.
   After the Declaration of Independence, the Continental Army struggles against overwhelming military odds.

7. Germantown has been called the low point for the patriot forces.
   Valley Forge has been called the low point for the patriot forces.

8. Finally, Rochambeau joins forces with Washington.
   The armies of Baron von Steuben join forces with Washington.

9. Peace negotiations are begun after the British defeat at Yorktown.
   A preliminary treaty is begun after the British defeat at Yorktown.

_____

_____

10. The leaders of the Revolution face the responsibility of creating a new nation.
    Thousands of average citizens face the responsibility of creating a new nation.

_____

_____

■ *Coordinating Subjects with* or

Another common pattern for coordinating subjects uses *or* as the coordination signal. *Nor* works in the same way. When you use *or* (or *nor*), you are asking your reader to consider each subject separately. *Or* suggests a choice between two alternatives. *Nor* suggests two negative alternatives. In either case, you are giving the two alternatives equal weight. In coordinating, you may pair *either* with *or* (and *neither* with *nor*) as the examples below suggest.

> *Fear of strong executive power* motivated the drafters of the new state constitutions.
>
> *A desire for more legislative power* motivated the drafters of the new state constitutions.
>
> ↓
>
> <u>Either</u> *fear of strong executive power* <u>or</u> *a desire for more legislative power* motivated the drafters of the new state constitutions.
>
> *The state constitutions* were not adequate to govern the new nation.
>
> *The Articles of Confederation* were not adequate to govern the new nation.
>
> ↓
>
> <u>Neither</u> *the state constitutions* <u>nor</u> *the Articles of Confederation* were adequate to govern the new nation.

Notice that *nor* removes the need for using *not* in the second example. The negative needs to be stated only once.

EXERCISE D

Using the examples above as models, combine each of the following pairs of sentences to create a single sentence with a coordinate subject. Use *or* or *nor* as the coordination signal.

1. After the Revolution, administrative problems convinced many Americans of the need for a stronger central government.
   After the Revolution, foreign policy difficulties convinced many Americans of the need for a stronger central government.

   _____

   _____

2. Annapolis was the preferred site for the Constitutional Convention.
   Philadelphia was the preferred site for the Constitutional Convention.

   _____

   _____

3. John Adams did not attend the Constitutional Convention.
   Thomas Jefferson did not attend the Constitutional Convention.

   _____

   _____

4. Political idealism motivated most of the delegates.
   Economic self-interest motivated most of the delegates.

   _____

   _____

5. Small states could not be allowed to dominate the central government.
   Large states could not be allowed to dominate the central government.

   _____

   _____

As long as you use *or* or *nor* to coordinate two singular subjects or two plural subjects, you should have no problems with the verb form. What happens, though, when you coordinate a plural subject with a singular subject?

Look at the example below in which a singular and a plural subject are coordinated. Two different sentences may result from the coordination of the subjects.

James Madison's plan provides the basis for much of the new constitution.

William Patterson's proposals provide the basis for much of the new constitution.

↓

Either James Madison's *plan* or William Patterson's *proposals provide* the basis for much of the new constitution.

Either William Patterson's *proposals* or James Madison's *plan provides* the basis for much of the new constitution.

In the first sentence, the subject is singular—*plan.* In the second sentence, the subject is plural—*proposals.* Using *or* as the coordination signal means that you are asking your reader to consider each alternative separately. Using *or* does not automatically create a plural subject. In the case where you are coordinating a singular and a plural subject, then, how do you decide whether the verb should be singular or plural? As the examples show, you solve this problem by making the verb agree with the closer subject.

Thus, in the first combination, the verb is plural—*provide*—to agree with the plural subject—*proposals*—which is closer to it. In the second combination, the verb is singular—*provides*—to agree with the singular subject—*plan*—which is closer to it.

Most of the time, as you know, singular verbs and plural verbs look the same. It is only in the case of a present tense verb or the verb *to be* that you have to be careful about using the right verb form.

Here is another example of this pattern:

As a result of Roger Sherman's Great Compromise, a small state was not left powerless.

As a result of Roger Sherman's Great Compromise, large states were not left powerless.

↓

As a result of Roger Sherman's Great Compromise, *neither* a small *state nor* the large *states were* left powerless.

As a result of Roger Sherman's Great Compromise, *neither* the large *states nor* a small *state was* left powerless.

Exercise E
Using the examples above as models, combine each of the following pairs of sentences to create a single sentence with a coordinate subject. Use *or* or *nor* as the coordination signal. Be sure to make the verb in your new sentence agree with the closer of the two coordinated subjects.

1. Under the Constitution, the two houses of Congress check the power of the executive branch of government.
   Under the Constitution, the Supreme Court checks the power of the executive branch of government.

   _____

   _____

2. Freedom of speech was not guaranteed by the original version of the Constitution. Other personal freedoms were not guaranteed by the original version of the Constitution.

   _____

   _____

3. Later amendments to the Constitution assure these individual rights.
   Local legislation assures these individual rights.

   _____

   _____

4. James Madison himself has written most of the Federalist papers defending the new Constitution.
   Madison's supporters have written most of the Federalist papers defending the new Constitution.

   _____

   _____

5. With the Anti-Federalists on the verge of winning, the arguments in the Federalist essays finally persuade New York to ratify the Constitution.
   With the Anti-Federalists on the verge of winning, New York City's threat to secede from the state finally persuades New York to ratify the Constitution.

   _____

   _____

We, the people . . .

EXERCISE F
Combine each of the following pairs of sentences in two different ways. The first
time, use *and* to coordinate the subjects. The second time, use *or* or *nor* to coordinate the subjects. Be sure to maintain the verb tense and to select the appropriate
verb form for each combination. Be prepared to discuss the difference in meaning
between the two versions.

EXAMPLE:
    Spain has claimed Louisiana.
    France has claimed Louisiana.

    A. *Spain and France have claimed Louisiana.*

    B. *Either Spain or France has claimed Louisiana.*

1. Access to the Mississippi River was essential for the survival of the western
   settlers.
   Use of the port of New Orleans was essential for the survival of the western
   settlers.

   A. _____

   _____

   B. _____

   _____

2. By the time of Jefferson's presidency, thousands of farms and villages have
   been established in the western states.
   By the time of Jefferson's presidency, a chain of trading posts has been
   established in the western states.

   A. _____

   _____

   B. _____

   _____

3. Threatened with the loss of the port of New Orleans, President Jefferson was
   worried.
   Threatened with the loss of the port of New Orleans, the western settlers were
   worried.

    A. _____

    _____

    B. _____

    _____

4. Robert Livingston is sent to France to purchase New Orleans.
   James Monroe is sent to France to purchase New Orleans.

    A. _____

    _____

    B. _____

    _____

5. For $15 million, Napoleon Bonaparte agrees to turn over the entire Louisiana territory.
   For $15 million, the French government agrees to turn over the entire Louisiana territory.

    A. _____

    _____

    B. _____

    _____

6. Doubling the nation's size results from this purchase.
   Pushing back the frontier another 1,500 miles results from this purchase.

    A. _____

    _____

    B. _____

    _____

7. Ten future states were included in the Louisiana country.
    Some of the richest land in America was included in the Louisiana country.

    A. _____

    _____

    B. _____

    _____

8. The Senate never hears a word about the Louisiana Purchase until it is
    settled.
    The House of Representatives never hears a word about the Louisiana
    Purchase until it is settled.

    A. _____

    _____

    B. _____

    _____

9. Meriwether Lewis surveys the Louisiana Purchase.
    William Clark surveys the Louisiana Purchase.

    A. _____

    _____

    B. _____

    _____

10. Sacajawea, a Shoshone Indian, serves as their guide.
    Her French-Canadian husband serves as their guide.

    A. _____

    _____

    B. _____

    _____

● Coordinating Verbs

Besides coordinating subjects, coordination also allows you to involve the subject of a sentence in several actions, each of which gets equal emphasis. You can do this by joining two verbs in a sentence with a coordination signal. The sentences below illustrate the process of creating coordinate verbs:

The California gold rush *yielded* $555 million dollars in a single decade.

The California gold rush *set* a new record for mining.

↓

The California gold rush *yielded* $555 million dollars in a single decade *and* set a new record for mining.

Most prospectors *worked* feverishly.

Most prospectors *discovered* very little gold.

↓

Most prospectors *worked* feverishly *but discovered* very little gold.

Notice that each of the coordinate verbs may have its own object and its own modifiers.

If your sentence coordinates more than two verbs, you need to separate the coordinate verbs with commas, as the following example shows:

Large mining companies *owned* heavy equipment, *dug out* the deep veins of ore, *and made* most of the money.

EXERCISE G

Combine each of the following sets of sentences to create a sentence showing the same subject involved in two or more coordinate actions. The first few sets of sentences give you a suggested coordination signal. For the rest, you should supply an appropriate coordination signal.

1. Gold fever struck at Sutter's Mill.
   Gold fever swept through California like an epidemic.   (and)

_____

_____

2. Men left their plows in the field to go and dig for gold.
   Men locked up their businesses to go and dig for gold.   (or)

   _____

   _____

3. The Forty-Niners were encouraged by the promise of fabulous riches.
   The Forty-Niners were rewarded only occasionally by the wild thrill of
   discovery.   (but)

   _____

   _____

4. The Forty-Niners often lost their stakes.
   The Forty-Niners continued to hope for a big strike.   (yet)

   _____

   _____

5. The discovery of gold at Sutter's Mill brought more than 40,000 prospectors
   to California within two years.
   The discovery of gold at Sutter's Mill stimulated California's growth.   (and)

   _____

   _____

6. To reach California, gold seekers sailed around Cape Horn.
   To reach California, gold seekers traveled overland in wagon trains.

   _____

   _____

7. In 1848, San Francisco's population numbered about 800 people.
   San Francisco's population had grown to 225,000 by 1852.

   _____

   _____

8. Unfortunately, the city could not provide public services for its growing population.
   Unfortunately, the city could not maintain law and order for its growing population.

   _____

   _____

9. The California gold rush lasted about six years.
   The California gold rush made a few instant millionaires.
   The California gold rush produced a thousand broken dreams.

   _____

   _____

10. Only two years after the discovery of gold at Sutter's Mill, California became America's thirty-first state.
    California proudly called itself the "Golden State."

    _____

    _____

● Coordinating Objects and Complements

Sometimes an action may have several effects or an idea may be completed in several ways. Sometimes a subject may have more than one complement. Coordination lets you give equal emphasis to each of the ways in which an action or idea may be completed. The sentences below show coordinate objects or complements.

coordinate object   coordinate object
The railroad was called *"the iron horse" or "the splendid mechanical beast."*

coordinate complement
Building a transcontinental railroad was *a dream envisioned by*

coordinate complement
romantics and a proposition supported by investors.

If you are using a series of more than two objects or complements, be sure that you arrange the series in a logical order and use commas to separate the items in the series as the following examples show.

The railroads connected *towns, states, or regions.*

The race to finish the transcontinental railroad was *heroic, thrilling, but* also *comical.*

Exercise H

Using the examples above as models, combine each of the following sets of sentences to create one sentence that shows several completions of an action or several different aspects of a subject. Some sentences give you suggestions for appropriate coordination signals. For the rest, you should supply an appropriate coordination signal.

1. Early railroads showed little interest in what happened outside their region.
   Early railroads showed little concern for establishing a coordinated system.
   (or)

   _____

   _____

2. Building a transcontinental railway network was costly.
   Building a transcontinental railway network was essential for economic expansion.

   _____

   _____

3. The venture relied on private enterprise.
   The venture relied on government support.

   _____

   _____

4. Congress gave the railroads 6,400 acres of free land for each mile of track laid.
   Congress gave the railroads generous loans.   (not only/but also)

   _____

   _____

5. In return, the railroads transported the mail cheaply.
   In return, the railroads transported military supplies cheaply.

   _____

   _____

6. The winner of the transcontinental race would be the Central Pacific moving east from California.
   The winner of the transcontinental race would be the Union Pacific moving westward across the plains.   (either/or)

   _____

   _____

7. As the railroads raced across the country, their primary concern was not quality.
   As the railroads raced across the country, their primary concern was not safety. (neither/nor)
   As the railroads raced across the country, their primary concern was speed. (but)

   _____

   _____

8. The iron horse symbolized the age of energy.
   The iron horse symbolized an era of expansion.

   _____

   _____

9. By the end of the nineteenth century, America had more miles of railroad than Europe.
   By the end of the nineteenth century, America had more sophisticated trains than Europe.

   _____

   _____

10. The railroad dominated the imagination of a whole generation of Americans.
    The railroad dominated the politics of a whole generation of Americans.
    The railroad dominated the economy of a whole generation of Americans.

_____

_____

● Coordinating Modifiers

Sometimes, in order to communicate an idea clearly to your reader, you need more than one modifier. Coordinate modifiers can be arranged in several ways.

■ *Coordinate Adjectives: Before the Noun*

As you may remember from Chapter 3, most single-word adjectives appear right before the noun they describe, as in the following example:

> The *angry* Sam Houston would never forget the Alamo.

Another adjective could be added to the sentence by using a coordination signal:

> The *angry but determined* Sam Houston would never forget the Alamo.

A coordinate adjective could also be added by using a comma instead of a coordination signal to separate the two adjectives:

> The *angry, determined* Sam Houston would never forget the Alamo.

Not every pair of adjectives is necessarily coordinate. For example, even though the sentence below contains a series of adjectives, the adjectives are not coordinate.

> Before coming to Texas, Sam Houston had held *several important political offices* in Tennessee.

There are several ways that you can check to see if adjectives are really coordinate. First of all, you can insert a coordination signal between coordinate adjectives, as the first example above showed. You can't do that with the second example: "Several *and* important *and* political offices" doesn't make good sense. Second, coordinate adjectives can be rearranged without affecting the meaning. You can rearrange the adjectives shown in the first example—angry *but* determined/ determined *but* angry. In the second example, rearranging the order confuses the meaning: "political important several offices" doesn't mean much. These adjectives are not coordinate; they are not all equal modifiers for the word "offices."

Coordinate adjectives should be separated by coordination signals or by commas.

■ *Coordinate Adjectives: After the Noun*

Sometimes it is more effective to place coordinate adjectives after the noun they modify. Putting the adjectives out of their normal position gives them special emphasis. Coordinate adjectives placed after the noun should be set off with commas, as the following sentences show:

> Sam Houston was curious.
>
> Sam Houston was adventurous.
>
> Sam Houston ran away at the age of fourteen to live with the Cherokee for three years.
>
> Sam Houston, *curious <u>and</u> adventurous,* ran away at the age of fourteen to live with the Cherokee for three years.
>
> The Texans at the Alamo were courageous.
>
> The Texans at the Alamo were foolhardy.
>
> The Texans at the Alamo refused to surrender to the Mexican general Santa Anna.
>
> The Texans at the Alamo, *either courageous <u>or</u> foolhardy,* refused to surrender to the Mexican general Santa Anna.

■ *Coordinate Adverbs*

As you may remember from Chapter 3, adverbs are not strictly tied to one position in the sentence. Coordinate adverbs, therefore, can be placed in any of several positions in the sentence. The sentences shown below could be combined to produce several variations of a sentence containing coordinate adverbs.

The placement of the adverbs depends on the amount of emphasis you want to give the coordinate words and on your sense of the rhythm of the sentence. Notice that coordinate adverbs, like coordinate adjectives, may be separated by a comma or by a coordination signal.

> Culturally, the Anglo-American colonists in Texas often clashed with their Mexican rulers.
>
> Politically, the Anglo-American colonists in Texas often clashed with their Mexican rulers.
>
> *Culturally <u>and</u> politically,* the Anglo-American colonists in Texas often clashed with their Mexican rulers.
>
> The Anglo-American colonists in Texas often clashed with their Mexican rulers *culturally <u>and</u> politically.*

> The Anglo-American colonists in Texas often clashed, *culturally and politically,* with their Mexican rulers.
>
> *Culturally, politically,* the Anglo-American colonists in Texas often clashed with their Mexican rulers.

Modifiers should always be chosen carefully to point out some vivid or unusual detail. Coordinate modifiers should be chosen with even greater care. Don't just string together vague or colorless modifiers.

Exercise 1

Using the examples shown above as models, combine each of the following sets of sentences to create one sentence that uses coordinated modifiers. Remember to use punctuation in a series of two or more modifiers. Some sentences give you suggested coordination signals. For the rest, you should supply an appropriate coordination signal.

1. In the 1820s, Texans were not American citizens.
   Texans were Mexican citizens.   (but)

   _____

   _____

2. The Mexican government sometimes ruled inconsistently.
   The Mexican government sometimes ruled inefficiently.   (or)
   The Mexican government did not rule harshly.   (but)

   _____

   _____

3. Texans were frequently in conflict with the Mexican government.
   Texans were bitterly in conflict with the Mexican government.   (and)
   By 1835, Texans openly rebelled.

   _____

   _____

4. Because of the Mexican army's strength, the Texas rebellion seemed doomed.
   Because of the chaotic state of the Texas government, the Texas rebellion seemed doomed.

   _____

   _____

5. The soldiers at the Alamo were not strong in numbers.
The soldiers at the Alamo were not well equipped.   (neither/nor)
The soldiers at the Alamo were an easy target for General Santa Anna.

_____

_____

6. Davy Crockett was among the legendary heroes at the Alamo.
Davy Crockett was among the defeated heroes at the Alamo.   (but)

_____

_____

7. Six weeks later, shouting "Remember the Alamo," the Texans under Sam Houston crushed Santa Anna in a terrible battle.
Six weeks later, shouting "Remember the Alamo," the Texans under Sam Houston crushed Santa Anna in a bloody battle.

_____

_____

8. Like the British army in the American Revolution, the Mexican army seriously underestimated its opposition.
Like the British army in the American Revolution, the Mexican army fatally underestimated its opposition.

_____

_____

9. Since Mexico refused to acknowledge the independent Republic of Texas, the American annexation of Texas in 1845 quickly led to war.
Since Mexico refused to acknowledge the independent Republic of Texas, the American annexation of Texas in 1845 inevitably led to war.

_____

_____

10. Few people have had a more prominent role in the history of Texas than Sam Houston, its first president and governor.
    Few people have had a more colorful role in the history of Texas than Sam Houston, its first president and governor.

_____

_____

● **Coordinating Sentences**

Coordination signals can also be used to link together two complete sentences. Normally, as you remember from Chapter 2, a sentence begins with a capital letter and ends with a period so that your reader will be able to tell where one sentence ends and another begins. Sometimes, however, two sentences may be so closely related that you want your reader to consider them together, as part of the same idea. In that case, you can choose to coordinate the two sentences by replacing the period and the capital letter with a comma and a coordination signal, as the following examples show.

> In the 1860 election, the Republican Party was solidly opposed to the expansion of slavery, _but_ the Democrats were split on the question.
>
> The southern Democrats advocated federal protection of slavery in all territories, _and_ southern delegates walked out when the Democratic Party's convention refused to endorse this position.

Sometimes you might have a choice among several appropriate coordination signals that could join two sentences together. The signal word you chose would depend on what kind of relationship you wanted to set up between the coordinate ideas. For example, given the two sentences below, you might relate them in different ways.

> Southern states had threatened secession for many years.
> Abraham Lincoln's election set the drama in motion.

If you wanted to emphasize the contrast between threat and action, you might coordinate these sentences using *but* as the coordinate signal:

> Southern states had threatened secession for many years, _but_ Abraham Lincoln's election set the drama in motion.

If you wanted to emphasize a cause/effect relationship between the two sentences, you might coordinate them using *so:*

> **Southern states had threatened secession for many years, _so_ Abraham Lincoln's election set the drama in motion.**

All of the coordination signals put equal emphasis on each coordinate idea, but each signal word suggests a different kind of logical relationship between the ideas.

The box below shows the coordination signals arranged according to the kind of logical relationship each one suggests.

COORDINATION SIGNALS: LOGICAL RELATIONSHIPS			
Cause/Effect	**Contrast**	**Expansion**	**Alternative**
so	but	and	or
for	yet		nor

EXERCISE J

Use a comma and a coordination signal to join each of the following pairs of sentences. Write two different combinations for each pair, and be prepared to explain any differences in meaning between your two versions. The first five pairs give you suggested coordination signals. For the rest, you should choose appropriate coordination signals.

1. Lincoln did not support the Dred Scott decision.
   Lincoln did not support the outright abolition of slavery.   (but, yet)

   A. _____

   _____

   B. _____

   _____

2. The Supreme Court's decision in the Dred Scott case pleased southern Democrats.
   The Supreme Court's decision outraged abolitionists by saying Congress could not prohibit slavery in the territories.   (and, but)

   A. _____

   _____

   B. _____

   _____

3. The secessionists organized their cause more effectively.   (yet, so)
   Even after Lincoln's election, many southerners remained pro-Union.

   A. _____

   _____

   B. _____

   _____

4. These people hoped to avoid armed conflict.   (for, but)
   Some northerners recommended allowing the southern states to leave the
   Union.

   A. _____

   _____

   B. _____

   _____

5. Others, including Lincoln, thought secession was a bluff.
   They did not support a compromise with the southerners.   (so, and)

   A. _____

   _____

   B. _____

   _____

6. The South could not compete with northern industrial power.
   The South had to buy its guns from France and Britain.

   A. _____

   _____

   B. _____

   _____

7. The Union forces surrendered.
   The commander of the Confederate forces ordered his troops to attack Fort Sumter, South Carolina.

   A. _____

   _____

   B. _____

   _____

8. The Confederacy had difficulty raising the money to finance the war.
   The Confederacy relied on the bravery of its soldiers.

   A. _____

   _____

   B. _____

   _____

9. Lincoln was determined to save the Union.
   Lincoln stretched his presidential authority to the limit.

   A. _____

   _____

   B. _____

   _____

10. He did not hesitate to usurp the powers of Congress by ordering $2 million for military expenditures.
    Convinced of the rightness of his cause, Lincoln sometimes disregarded the civil liberties of citizens.

    A. _____

    _____

    B. _____

    _____

► USING EXPLAINING NOUNS

When you use coordination signals, you are giving equal emphasis to two different subjects, verbs, or other elements in a sentence. When you use an **explaining noun** to indicate coordination, you are showing two different versions of the same idea rather than joining two different ideas. The combination below illustrates this point.

> The abolitionists were opponents of slavery.
>
> The abolitionists pressured Abraham Lincoln to draft the Emancipation Proclamation.

↓

> noun   coordinate explaining noun
> The abolitionists, *opponents of slavery*, pressured Abraham Lincoln to draft the Emancipation Proclamation.

In the example above, the noun *opponents* (together with its modifier—*of slavery*) explains the noun *abolitionists*. The explaining noun pattern coordinates one noun with another. The explaining noun restates the first noun in some way. Instead of using a coordination signal, the explaining noun is set off by commas and always follows immediately after the noun it explains. Notice that an explaining noun may have its own modifiers.

Here are some additional examples of the explaining noun pattern:

> explaining noun
> The Emancipation Proclamation, *a document* granting technical freedom to more than three million slaves, switched world opinion from the underdog South to the liberating North.

> explaining noun
> Frederick Douglass, *a dynamic orator,* escaped from a Baltimore shipyard and lectured on slavery in Great Britain.

EXERCISE K

Underline the explaining nouns in each of the following sentences. Notice the position of each explaining noun and the punctuation used with this pattern of coordination.

1. Many progressive movements began in the nineteenth century, the great age of reform.
2. Women of the nineteenth century, the "angels of the house," were expected to look and act like fragile creatures.
3. Sarah and Angelina Grimké, daughters of one of Charleston's wealthiest and most conservative families, saw a connection between their own political powerlessness and the situation of the slaves.

4. A group of American women, delegates to an 1840 World Anti-Slavery Convention in London, were denied recognition because of their sex.
5. Lucretia Mott and Elizabeth Cady Stanton, would-be delegates, met with others in Seneca Falls at the Woman's Rights Convention.
6. Suffrage, the right to vote, was not gained by American or English women until after World War I.

7. In 1872, equal rights became the campaign theme of Victoria Woodhull, the first woman candidate for president of the United States.
8. Susan B. Anthony, the champion of women's rights, was active in the temperance and antislavery movements.
9. The temperance movement, a campaign to stop the drinking of alcoholic beverages, was supported by presidents Zachary Taylor and Abraham Lincoln.
10. The damaging effects of liquor were often shown in popular literature such as *The Bottle and the Pledge,* a novel about how excessive drinking ruined a happy home.

EXERCISE L

Using the examples above as models, combine each of the following pairs of sentences to create a sentence in which one noun is explained by a coordinate noun. Remember to put commas around the explaining noun.

1. Harriet Tubman was a former slave.
   She became a "conductor" on the Underground Railroad.

_____

_____

2. The Underground Railroad was a well-organized network of abolitionists.
   It funneled southern slaves to freedom in the North.

_____

_____

3. Harriet Tubman was a conductor for nineteen journeys into slave territory.
   She liberated at least three hundred people.

_____

_____

4. Harriet Tubman became a legend among fugitive slaves.
    She never lost a single "passenger."

    _____

    _____

5. In 1831, William Lloyd Garrison began publishing *The Liberator.*
    The Liberator was a newspaper dedicated to the abolition of slavery.

    _____

    _____

6. Garrison was a radical abolitionist leader.
    He opposed any form of gradual abolition.

    _____

    _____

7. Elizabeth Cady Stanton was the president of the National Women's Suffrage
    Association.
    She provoked a scandal by omitting the words "to obey" from her wedding
    vows.

    _____

    _____

8. Elizabeth Cady Stanton later drafted the *Declaration of Sentiments.*
    The *Declaration of Sentiments* was a document proclaiming that women had a
    right to all the privileges of American citizenship.

    _____

    _____

9. William Apes was the first major spokesman for the rights of Native
    Americans.
    William Apes pointedly criticized government efforts to move his people onto
    reservations.

    _____

    _____

10. "An Indian's Looking Glass for the White Man" was an essay published in 1833.
    In "An Indian's Looking Glass for the White Man," Apes angrily attacked the hypocrisy of white Americans.

    _____

    _____

EXERCISE M

Expand each of the following sentences by coordinating one of the parts—subject, verb, object, or modifier. You may use either a coordination signal or the explaining noun pattern where it is appropriate. Try to vary your techniques of coordination through the exercise.

EXAMPLE:

The president of the United States has a difficult job.

The president of the United States has a difficult but challenging job.

The president of the United States and the members of Congress have a

difficult job.

1. The presidency has become an office of great power.

   _____

   _____

2. Presidential actions can permanently change the lives of American citizens.

   _____

   _____

3. A president's philosophy can be stamped on the country by the judges he or she appoints to the federal courts.

   _____

   _____

4. The president's relationship with Congress can significantly enhance his or her ability to govern the nation.

_____

_____

5. Weeks of negotiation precede every presidential proposal.

_____

_____

6. An effective president knows the value of compromise.

_____

_____

7. Domestic issues may be a president's greatest challenge.

_____

_____

8. The president shapes America's policy toward friendly nations.

_____

_____

9. In recent years, the role of the president has grown considerably.

_____

_____

10. The presidency reflects the hopes of ordinary Americans.

_____

_____

▶ USING LINKING ADVERBS

You have already seen that using a comma and a coordination signal is one option for coordinating two sentences. Another option is using a semicolon or a semicolon and a **linking adverb** to coordinate two sentences. The examples below show these options.

> For many years, water routes were the only practical way to transport goods and passengers. Cities grew up along these water routes.

> For many years, water routes were the only practical way to transport goods and passengers, *so* cities grew up along these water routes.

> For many years, water routes were the only practical way to transport goods and passengers; cities grew up along these water routes.

> For many years, water routes were the only practical way to transport goods and passengers; *as a result,* cities grew up along these water routes.

A period at the end of a sentence indicates the end of an idea. A new sentence indicates the beginning of a new idea. When you coordinate sentences, you indicate that two ideas are somehow connected to each other. A semicolon indicates that two sentences are connected but doesn't spell out the nature of the connection. Coordination signals, as you saw in a previous section of this chapter, give your reader an indication of how two ideas are related. Similarly, linking adverbs also give your reader a clue about how two coordinate ideas are logically related.

The box below shows some of the most common linking adverbs arranged according to the logical patterns they suggest.

LINKING ADVERBS: LOGICAL RELATIONSHIPS				
Cause/Effect	**Comparison**	**Contrast**	**Expansion**	**Alternative**
accordingly	likewise	however	besides	instead
as a result	similarly	nevertheless	furthermore	otherwise
consequently		on the other hand	in addition	
therefore			moreover	
thus			then	

In this pattern of coordination, you use a semicolon to indicate the end of the first coordinate sentence. The semicolon tells your reader to expect a coordinate sentence to follow. The linking adverb is set off from the second coordinate sentence with a comma. Although the linking adverb usually appears at the beginning of the second coordinate sentence, it may appear elsewhere in the sentence. The examples below illustrate some possible arrangements of coordinate sentences using linking adverbs.

Early America was shaped by rural values; *however,* by 1900 America had moved to the city.

Early America was shaped by rural values; by 1900, *however,* America had moved to the city.

Early America was shaped by rural values; by 1900 America had moved, *however,* to the city.

EXERCISE N

Using the models shown above, supply appropriate punctuation for each of the following pairs of coordinate sentences. Remember to use a semicolon to indicate the end of the first coordinate sentence and to set off the linking adverb with commas.

1. By 1900 six American cities had populations of more than half a million people furthermore three cities had populations of more than a million people.
2. Children of American farmers migrated to the cities likewise children of European farmers left their native lands to swell the urban population of America.
3. By 1890, one-third of Bostonians and Chicagoans were of foreign birth New York meanwhile had two and a half times as many Irish as Dublin.
4. City dwellers endured many discomforts and inconveniences nevertheless outsiders continued to be attracted to the advantages of city life.
5. The glamour of the city was enhanced by telephones, trolley cars, and other wonders therefore farmers found their harsh lives even more intolerable.
6. Skyscrapers symbolized the dynamism and excitement of American cities the skyscrapers proved in addition to be functional and profitable.
7. Even an honest and efficient city government faced staggering difficulties few cities however had such a government.
8. Cities grew at the dictates of industrial enterprise otherwise there was no such thing as urban planning.
9. Cities supported incredible wealth and cultural resources on the other hand they also produced disease-ridden slums.
10. The city was a shock to America's rural consciousness Americans consequently were both fascinated and repelled by the cities' violent contrasts.

EXERCISE O

Use a semicolon to coordinate each pair of sentences below. Then use a linking adverb to bring out the specific logical relationship you want the reader to see between these two sentences. For the first few sentences, linking adverbs are suggested. For the rest, you should supply an appropriate linking adverb.

1. Louis Joliet and Jacques Marquette explored the mudflats of Lake Michigan in
   the 1670s.
   It was not until a hundred years later that Jean du Sable, a prosperous black
   fur trader, established the first permanent non-Indian settlement in what is
   now Chicago.   (however)

   A. _____

   _____

   B. _____

   _____

2. In 1830, Chicago was chosen as the terminal for the Illinois and Michigan Canal.
   The city began to boom.   (as a result)

   A. _____

   _____

   B. _____

   _____

3. By 1856, Chicago was the hub of ten railroad trunk lines.
   Chicago became the world's busiest rail center.   (consequently)

   A. _____

   _____

   B. _____

   _____

4. The railroad network helped make Chicago the center of trade for farm
   products.
   The Civil War made Chicago the meat-packing capital of the world.   (in
   addition)

   A. _____

   _____

   B. _____

   _____

5. The Great Chicago Fire of 1871 destroyed more than 18,000 buildings.
   A year later, some $40 million worth of new structures stood in place of the
   fire-charred ruins.   (nevertheless)

   A. _____

   _____

   B. _____

   _____

6. Many of America's most renowned architects, including William Jenney, Louis
   Sullivan, Dankmar Adler, and Frank Lloyd Wright, helped with the rebuilding
   of Chicago.
   The city became famous for a style of architecture known as the Chicago School.

   A. _____

   _____

   B. _____

   _____

7. The wretched living and working conditions of Chicago's factory and
   stockyard workers led to strikes and riots.
   These conditions also led to strong pressure for social reform.

   A. _____

   _____

   B. _____

   _____

8. Jane Addams's Hull House, opened in 1889, taught immigrants to speak
   English and set up day-care centers for working mothers.
   Hull House became a national model for social welfare programs.

   A. _____

   _____

   B. _____

   _____

9. Upton Sinclair's novel *The Jungle* graphically described the scandalous conditions in Chicago's meat-packing houses.
   After reading the novel, President Theodore Roosevelt established a federal meat-inspection law.

   A. _____

   _____

   B. _____

   _____

10. Chicago's Columbian Exposition of 1893, a fabulously successful world's fair, introduced the Ferris wheel and the exotic dancer Little Egypt to the world. The Exposition stimulated worldwide interest in city planning and the "City Beautiful" movement.

    A. _____

    _____

    B. _____

    _____

Exercise P

Add a coordinate sentence to each of the following sentences. Use coordination signals for half of the sentences and linking adverbs for the other half. Be sure to choose the coordination signal or linking adverb that most clearly expresses the relationship you want to show between the two ideas. Remember the punctuation that goes with each pattern.

1. Americans have put great value on individual freedom.

_____

_____

2. Women's roles have changed since the eighteenth century.

_____

_____

3. Life was not easy for America's early settlers.

_____

_____

4. The spirit of compromise has helped the country develop.

_____

_____

5. The expansion of the railroad changed America in many ways.

_____

_____

6. People from many backgrounds have shaped America's history.

_____

_____

7. Reformers were not afraid to criticize America's faults.

_____

_____

8. American history shows a continually evolving democracy.

_____

_____

9. America has encouraged strong leaders.

_____

_____

10. Cities can symbolize the best of American culture.

_____

_____

EDITING PRACTICE:

Read the following paragraphs carefully, checking them for problems in any of these areas.

1. Fragments
2. Run-on sentences
3. Subject–verb agreement
4. Correct verb form
5. Correct form of adjectives and adverbs
6. Correct placement of modifiers
7. Correct punctuation of coordinate word groups

Then, rewrite the paragraphs on separate sheets of paper.

1. From the most earliest days, Americans have put great stress on education. The Puritan settlers had a strong religious motivation for education they wanted their children to be able to read the Bible. Only six years after they had came to Massachusetts, the Puritans founded Harvard College. There were no mention of education in the U.S. Constitution, however America's founders stressed the importance of education in a democracy. At the time of the American Revolution, almost 90 percent of the men could read in New England. Compared with 50 percent of the men in England. Thus the average American man was equipped good to follow the events of his time. In the 1830s, Horace Mann championed free public education where children would learn reading writing and arithmetic. By 1900, almost all states had compulsory school-attendance laws. Women's educational opportunities expanded gradual throughout the 1800s. In 1837 Oberlin became the first coeducational college furthermore the first women's college Mount Holyoke open its doors in that same year. Before the Civil War, many states forbade teaching slaves to read and write so few African Americans received any education. In 1881, Booker T. Washington the son of a slave founded Tuskegee Institute helped construct its buildings and turned it into an internationally famous center for industrial education. Americans have always had faith in the power of education.

2. Because of their open-door policy, community colleges embodies the democratic ideal. Some two-year colleges existed as early as the nineteenth century but most people identify the early twentieth century as the real beginning of the junior college movement. Joliet Junior College the oldest public junior college in operation still was founded in 1901. By 1920, a total of eight thousand students enrolled in fifty-two junior colleges across twenty-three states. By 1950, there was about 600 two-year colleges in the United States. Curricular relevance accessibility and adaptability accounts for the remarkable growth of two-year institutions. Between 1921 and World War II, junior colleges emphasized vocational technical and career programs. Community colleges were more later development. After World War II, the limited mission of the junior college evolving toward a multipurpose community college. At a community college, students may begin their studies for a bachelor's degree receive training in specialized skills or improve basic skills. This broad range of services distinguish the community college from other forms of higher education. Today almost five million students attends America's community and junior colleges the community college represents the true democratization of education.

Writing Practice:

1. The exercises in this chapter of your text have focused on some of the important people and events in American history; however, history also has a personal dimension. Personal history can be lost if no one in a family ever writes down the family's story. Begin a family history by writing a paragraph of about 200 words giving some basic information about your parents and grandparents. Think of the future generations of your family—your own children and grandchildren—as the audience for this family history.

Planning:

A chart like the one shown below may help you to research the basic facts of your immediate family. If you can't fill in all the information yourself, ask your parents or other relatives to help you. Make the information as complete as possible, including the family names of your mother and grandmothers if you know them.

Name					
Date of Birth					
Place of Birth					
Date of Marriage					
Place of Marriage					
Occupation					
Date of Death					
Place of Death					

Drafting:

In writing out the facts about your immediate family, try to give equal emphasis to both sides of your family. Also look for similarities or differences in the family background that you can highlight in your presentation. Use coordination to help you present these points of similarity or difference. For example, you might include information such as:

Both my mother and my father were born in Maryland. My father was born there in 1935, but my mother was not born until 1938.

REVISING/EDITING:

When you have written a draft of your family history, go back and make sure that all your sentences are complete and correctly punctuated. You might want to have someone in your family read the draft to make sure that the family information is accurate.

2. Another important part of a family history, beyond just the facts of birth and death, is the traditions and customs that make your family unique. Add another piece to your family history by writing a paragraph of about 200 words on some tradition or custom in your family that is particularly important to you. For example, you might choose to write about the way your family celebrates birthdays or about some story that has been passed down in your family about a famous or infamous ancestor. Again, you should consider the future generations of your family as the audience for this piece.

PLANNING:

Make a list of three or four traditions in your family. Use the 5W's formula (the *who, what, where, why,* and *when*) to generate some details about each tradition.

DRAFTING:

Choose the tradition that interests you the most of the ones you have explored. Write out in sentences the details of what this tradition involves, who participates, where this tradition is celebrated, when it is celebrated, and why it is important in your family. Use the techniques of coordination to make sure that each aspect of the tradition gets similar emphasis.

REVISING/EDITING:

Ask a classmate to read your draft and tell you whether the details of the tradition or custom you have described are clear. Ask your reader to tell you any places where you need to give more detail or explanation. Read the draft yourself to make sure that all the sentences are complete and correctly punctuated.

◀ *Chapter 5* ▶

Subordination

• • • • • • • • • • • •

▶ USING ADVERB SUBORDINATION SIGNALS
▶ USING ADJECTIVE SUBORDINATION SIGNALS
  ● Choosing the Appropriate Adjective Sub-
    ordination Signal
  ● Distinguishing Between Interrupting and
    Narrowing Adjective Subordinate Word
    Groups
▶ USING VERBAL SUBORDINATION SIGNALS
  ● Arranging Word Groups with Verbals
▶ REVIEW OF METHODS OF SUBORDINATION

• • • • • • • • • • • • •

Subordination, like coordination, sets up a relationship between two ideas. Coordination, as you saw in Chapter 4, shows your reader that two ideas are equally important. For example, by using the coordination signal *but,* the following sentence gives equal emphasis to Mozart's death and to his undying reputation:

base sentence   base sentence
Mozart died in 1791 at age thirty-five, *but* his music remains immortal.

Subordination, on the other hand, shows that one idea is less important than another. The word *subordination* comes from two Latin words—*sub,* meaning below, and *ordinare,* meaning to arrange in order. Subordination, then, means to order one idea below another idea. Subordination moves a reader's attention away from one idea and toward another. The base sentence, the unsubordinated part of the sentence, contains the main idea. The subordinate word group contains the related—but less important—idea.

For instance, suppose that you wanted to include the information shown above in a paragraph about how Mozart's music remains popular with modern audiences. In that case, you might want to emphasize the second piece of information more than the first piece since it relates more closely to the point you want to make. Then you might use subordination to combine the two ideas this way:

> subordinate word group   base sentence
> *Although Mozart died in 1791 at age thirty-five,* his music remains immortal.

This sentence uses subordination to suggest that Mozart's death is less important than his continuing musical influence. Notice that the sentence contains the same information as the example shown earlier. The ideas have not changed. The relationship between the ideas has changed; the emphasis has changed.

In the sentence below, which idea is subordinated? Which is emphasized?

> **Mozart died in 1791 at age thirty-five although his music remains immortal.**

This sentence subordinates Mozart's musical immortality and emphasizes his early death. With this emphasis, it might fit well into a paragraph about the tragedies of Mozart's life.

When you subordinate an idea, you put it in some form that is less than a complete sentence. As you saw in Chapter 2, a base sentence expresses a complete idea by presenting a subject involved in some action set in a time frame and not introduced by a subordination signal. If any one of these requirements is lacking, you do not have a base sentence. You have, instead, a subordinate word group. Subordinate word groups usually define or describe part of the base sentence. Subordinate word groups function, in effect, as adjectives or adverbs.

As the box below indicates, there are three major ways that you can make a sentence into a subordinate word group: by using an adverb subordination signal, by using an adjective subordination signal, or by changing the verb in the sentence to a form that doesn't show time (a verbal).

CREATE A SUBORDINATE WORD GROUP BY:
1. Putting a subordination signal in front of the subject–verb unit. (adverb)
2. Replacing part of the base sentence with a subordination signal. (adjective)
3. Changing the verb to a non-time form. (verbal)

▶ USING ADVERB SUBORDINATION SIGNALS

Adverb subordination signals turn sentences into subordinate word groups that tell when, where, why, or how the main action occurs. Such word groups clarify the action in the base sentence. These word groups can be introduced by any of the adverb subordination signals shown in the box below.

<table>
<tr><th colspan="4">ADVERB SUBORDINATION SIGNALS</th></tr>
<tr><th>When</th><th>Where</th><th>Why</th><th>How</th></tr>
<tr><td>after</td><td>where</td><td>because</td><td>although</td></tr>
<tr><td>as soon as</td><td>wherever</td><td>if</td><td>as</td></tr>
<tr><td>before</td><td></td><td>in case</td><td>as if</td></tr>
<tr><td>once</td><td></td><td>in order that</td><td>as though</td></tr>
<tr><td>until</td><td></td><td>inasmuch as</td><td>even though</td></tr>
<tr><td>when</td><td></td><td>provided that</td><td>less than</td></tr>
<tr><td>whenever</td><td></td><td>since</td><td>more than</td></tr>
<tr><td>while</td><td></td><td>so that</td><td>so long as</td></tr>
<tr><td></td><td></td><td>unless</td><td>than</td></tr>
<tr><td></td><td></td><td>whereas</td><td>though</td></tr>
<tr><td colspan="4">(Some of these signals may fit in more than one category.)</td></tr>
</table>

EXERCISE A
Label the base sentence (BS) and the subordinate word group (SWG) in each of the following sentences.

1. Emily Dickinson was educated at Amherst Academy where she was trained in languages, literature, math, and science.

2. Her poetry, until after her death, was kept strictly private.

3. After Emily died, Lavinia Dickinson found almost two thousand poems among her sister's papers.

4. The poems, once they were discovered, presented a number of problems for their readers.

5. The poems were difficult to arrange since Emily did not put titles or dates on her work.

6. In addition, because Dickinson's rhythm, rhyme, and punctuation did not follow the usual rules, some people thought it needed to be "corrected."

7. Thus, her family tried to rewrite some of her work before it was published.

8. Although Emily Dickinson died in 1886, a complete edition of her poetry was not published until 1955.

9. During her lifetime, Emily Dickinson led a very private existence while her father and brother were well-known public figures.

10. When people hear the name Dickinson today, however, they think of quiet Emily, not of her father or brother.

This is my letter to the World
That never wrote to Me—
The simple News that
** Nature told—**
With tender Majesty

Her message is committed
To Hands I cannot see—
For love of Her—Sweet—
** countrymen**
Judge tenderly—of Me

Emily Dickinson (1830-1886)

If you look carefully at the sentences in Exercise A, you will see three basic ways to arrange sentences with subordinate word groups. In the first pattern, the sentence begins with a subordinate word group and ends with the base sentence. A comma at the end of the subordinate word group separates it from the base sentence:

introducing subordinate word group   base sentence
After he developed the first Native-American alphabet, **Sequoyah was revered by the Cherokee.**

In the second pattern, the subordinate word group comes in the middle of the base sentence. Commas are used before and after the interrupting subordinate word group to separate it from the base sentence:

base   interrupting subordinate word group   sentence
Sequoyah, *after he developed the first Native-American alphabet,* **was revered by the Cherokee.**

In the third pattern, the sentence begins with the base sentence and ends with the subordinate word group. Usually, you don't need to use any punctuation to separate the two parts. The subordination signal itself tells your reader that the base sentence is finished:

base sentence   following subordinate word group
Sequoyah was revered by the Cherokee *after he developed the first Native-American alphabet.*

EXERCISE B

Label the base sentence (BS) and the subordinate word group (SWG) in each of the following sentences. Using the patterns described above, insert any punctuation needed to separate the subordinate word group from the base sentence.

1. Because very little has survived of ancient Egyptian palaces most of our

   knowledge of Egyptian art comes from the royal tombs and their contents.

2. The survival of so many tombs is not surprising since they were built to last

   forever.

3. As a king prepared his tomb he saw it as a kind of insurance.

4. The king if he provided for his pleasures in advance could look forward to a

   happy afterlife.

5. When a king was buried his furniture,

   jewels, favorite foods, and sometimes even

   his servants and horses were buried with him to serve his spirit in the afterlife.

6. Although the outside of the pyramid was usually plain and dignified the inner

   walls of the tombs were covered with paintings of the king's activities.

7. The tomb after the king was buried was sealed as protection against enemies

   or thieves.

8. The pyramids appear today as if they are isolated structures in the middle of

   the desert.

9. When they were built they were actually part of a great complex of temples

   and other buildings.

10. This funeral complex was the scene of many religious celebrations even while

    the king was still alive.

EXERCISE C

Combine each of the following pairs of sentences so that one idea in each sentence is subordinated. Use the suggested adverb subordination signal if one is given. Otherwise, supply an appropriate adverb subordination signal. Be prepared to explain which idea you have emphasized and which you have subordinated. Be sure to include any punctuation needed to separate the subordinate idea from the base sentence.

EXAMPLE:

Chinese society has traditionally shown great respect for poetry.

Chinese society has no special class of people called poets.   (although)

Possible combinations:

introducing subordinate word group   base sentence
Although Chinese society has no special class of people called poets, **it has traditionally shown great respect for poetry.**

base sentence   following subordinate word group
Chinese society has traditionally shown great respect for poetry *although it has no special class of people called poets.*

base sentence   interrupting subordinate word group
Chinese society, *although it has traditionally shown great respect for poetry,* **has no special class of people called poets.**

1. Chinese poetry was written by common people as well as by educated scholars. Everyone considered poetry a good means of self-expression.   (since)

   _____

   _____

2. Poetic talent at one time became the chief means of selecting public officials. People who wrote poetry were considered wise and honorable.   (because)

   _____

   _____

3. Chinese poetry is deeply rooted in everyday life.
   The Chinese never forget poetry's goal of enriching ordinary experiences.
   (while)

   _____

   _____

4. Chinese poetry may appear simple on the surface.
   The reader concentrates on the hidden meaning.   (until)

   _____

   _____

5. A poem paints a picture with a single stroke.
   A poem captures a single moment of ecstasy.   (as)

   _____

   _____

6. Western poetry often uses metaphors.
   Chinese poetry rarely uses metaphors.

   _____

   _____

7. Chinese poetry avoids exaggeration and passion.
   Chinese poetry appeals through understatement and restraint.

   _____

   _____

8. Westerners usually read Chinese poetry in translation.
   Westerners do not hear the rhythmic tones of the poetry.

   _____

   _____

9. The poetry of Li Po, one of China's most famous writers, is often compared to an underground river.
   It has a powerful but hidden energy.

   _____

   _____

10. Li Po enjoyed imperial favor for a brief time.
    Li Po fell victim to court politics.

    _____

    _____

WRITTEN IN BEHALF OF MY WIFE

Since we parted, the grass before our gate
In the autumn lane has turned green in spring.
I sweep it away but it grows back.
Densely it covers your footprints.

Li Po (translated by Joseph J. Lee)

▶ USING ADJECTIVE SUBORDINATION SIGNALS

The adjective subordination signals—*who, whose, whom, which,* and *that*—can turn a sentence into a subordinate word group by replacing some part of the base sentence. For example, look at the two sentences below:

> **Lynn paints vivid landscapes.**
>
> **Lynn has just opened her first gallery show.**

To subordinate one of these ideas using an adjective subordination signal, you would follow these steps:

1. **Find the point of connection between the two sentences.** In this case, the connection is *Lynn.*
2. **Decide which idea you want to subordinate.** In this case, you'll subordinate the kind of paintings Lynn does—the first idea presented.

3. **Use the appropriate adjective subordination signal to replace the connecting word in the sentence you're going to subordinate.** In this case, you'll replace Lynn with *who*. The subordinate word group is then *who paints vivid landscapes.*
4. **Insert the subordinate word group into the base sentence right next to the word that the adjective subordination signal has replaced.** (Remember that adjectives are closely tied to the words they modify.)

Following these steps, you'll come up with the combination below. Because this subordinate word group is an interrupter, you need two commas to set it off from the base sentence.

> Lynn, *who paints vivid landscapes,* has just opened her first gallery show.

If you wanted to subordinate Lynn's gallery opening, you would follow the same steps and come up with this sentence:

> Lynn, *who has just opened her first gallery show,* paints vivid landscapes.

Here is another example of the use of adjective subordination signals.

> Pablo Picasso's *Girl Before a Mirror* violates the rules of perspective.
> *Girl Before a Mirror* shows several points of view at the same time.

In this example, the title of the painting, *Girl Before a Mirror,* is the connecting point between the two sentences; therefore, you can subordinate one of these ideas by replacing *Girl Before a Mirror* with an adjective subordination signal. If you decide to subordinate the first idea, the new sentence might look like this:

> Pablo Picasso's *Girl Before a Mirror, which violates the rules of perspective,* shows several points of view at the same time.

If you wanted to subordinate the second idea, your new sentence might look like this:

> Pablo Picasso's *Girl Before a Mirror, which shows several points of view at the same time,* violates the rules of perspective.

Exercise D
Underline the adjective subordinate word group in each of the following sentences and indicate with an arrow which word in the base sentence it modifies or describes.

1. Twentieth-century art, which reflects the cultural forces of its own time, often

   rebels against nineteenth-century artistic conventions.

2. Salvador Dali, whose paintings show things like melting watches, rejected the concept of realistic art.

3. Cubists like Mondrian used abstract shapes that eliminated all suggestions of real objects.

4. Lois Mailou Jones, whom the Cubists influenced, incorporated African tribal masks into her paintings.

5. Another experimental artist was Paul Klee who satirized modern culture with subtle pastel colors.

6. Kandinsky, on the other hand, whom the Soviet Communists forced to leave Russia, made his statements with bold contrasting colors.

7. Georgia O'Keeffe, whose paintings transformed flowers into abstract patterns, wanted to surprise people into looking at the ordinary.

8. Contemporary events provided many modern artists with subjects that have shocked their viewers.

9. Peter Blume, for whom fascism was a horror, painted *The Eternal City* as a powerful symbolic attack on Mussolini.

10. Pablo Picasso protested the brutality of war in *Guernica* which depicts a Spanish village destroyed by a bombing raid.

● Choosing the Appropriate Adjective Subordination Signal

To use adjective subordination signals effectively, you should recognize several points about them.

First, you should observe the positioning of adjective subordinate word groups within the base sentence. As you probably noticed in the exercise above, adjective subordinate word groups always appear right next to the word they modify or describe. For example, in sentence 10 above, the subordination signal *which* comes right next to the word *Guernica* because *which* stands for *Guernica* in the subordinate word group. A word like *who* or *which* doesn't mean anything to a reader unless the reader knows what the word stands for. To avoid any confusion, you should always put subordinate word groups beginning with these adjective signal words right next to the word that *who* or *which* has replaced.

Second, *who* and *whom* are usually used to refer to people. Sometimes, sentiment may make a writer use *who* when referring to a pet or some object she thinks of as having a personality (ships, the earth, the sea, and so on). Ordinarily, however, *that* and *which* are used to describe inanimate objects and animals.

Third, the signal words *who, whose,* and *whom* each have special functions. *Who* functions as a subject in a subordinate word group; *whom* functions as an object in a subordinate word group; and *whose* functions as a modifier in a subordinate word group.

For example, look at the following sentences:

D.W. Griffith began his film career reluctantly.

D.W. Griffith revolutionized the art of the motion picture.

To subordinate the first sentence, you would replace D.W. Griffith in that sentence with an adjective subordination signal. Since D.W. Griffith is the subject of the sentence, you would use *who* to replace it, as shown below:

who
(D.W. Griffith) began his film career reluctantly.

After you insert the subordinate word group into the base sentence, the new sentence would look like this:

D.W. Griffith, *who began his film career reluctantly,* revolutionized the art of the motion picture.

Here is an example where you would need to use *whom* as the subordination signal:

Biograph Studios hired Griffith to direct short features.

Griffith wanted to make epic films.

To subordinate the first idea, you would replace *Griffith* in the first sentence with an adjective subordination signal. Since *Griffith* is the object in that sentence, it would be replaced by *whom.*

whom
Biograph Studios hired (Griffith) to direct short features.

Before inserting this subordinate word group into the base sentence, you must move the subordination signal to the beginning of the subordinate word group. Thus the subordinate word group becomes

***whom* Biograph Studios hired to direct short features**

Now the subordinate word group can be inserted into the base sentence with the adjective signal next to the word it stands for:

> Griffith, *whom Biograph Studios hired to direct short features*, wanted to make epic films.

When the adjective subordination signal replaces an object of a preposition, as in the following example, notice that both the preposition and the object must be moved to the beginning of the subordinate word group.

> Silent films were a magical experience for their audience.
>
> The audience was the final creative contributor to the filmmaking process.

To subordinate the first idea, you would replace the word *audience* with the subordination signal. Since *audience* is the object of the preposition *for*, you would use the object signal, *whom:*

> whom
> Silent films were a magical experience for (their audience.)

Since the subordination signal needs to go at the beginning of the subordinate word group, and since prepositions can't be separated from their objects, you need to move both the preposition and its object to the beginning of the subordinate word group, like this:

> for *whom* silent films were a magical experience

Now the adjective subordinate word group can be inserted into the base sentence:

> The audience, *for whom silent films were a magical experience*, was the final creative contributor to the filmmaking process.

Finally, here is an example of *whose* as a subordination signal:

> California's sunny climate was ideal for movie making.
>
> California soon dominated the new industry.

To subordinate the first idea, you would replace *California's* in the first sentence with an adjective subordination signal. Since *California's* is a modifier, you would replace it with *whose* as shown below:

> whose
> (California's) sunny climate was ideal for movie making.

You can then insert the subordinate word group into the base sentence to create a sentence that subordinates California's climate and emphasizes its domination of the movie industry:

California, *whose sunny climate was ideal for movie making,* soon dominated the film industry.

The box below summarizes the forms of the adjective subordination signals.

ADJECTIVE SUBORDINATION SIGNALS		
Subject	**Object**	**Modifier**
who which that	whom which that	whose

Exercise E

In each sentence below, choose the appropriate adjective subordination signal and then insert the subordinate word group into the base sentence to create a new sentence. Be prepared to explain your choice of a subordination signal. Use appropriate punctuation to separate the subordinate word group from the base sentence.

1. Lillian Gish _____ often worked for Griffith.   (who/whom/whose)
   Lillian Gish was one of silent film's first big stars.

   _____

   _____

2. Griffith's _____ talent was enormous.   (who/whom/whose)
   Griffith produced the first blockbuster film, *Birth of a Nation.*

   _____

   _____

3. Griffith used Billy Bitzer _____ as his cameraman.
   (who/whom/whose)
   Billy Bitzer was a genius in his own right.

   _____

   _____

4. Billy Bitzer _____ was a genius in his own right.
   (who/whom/whose)
   Griffith used Billy Bitzer as his cameraman.

   _____

   _____

5. Griffith's _____ success with *Birth of a Nation* exhilarated him.
   (who/whom/whose)
   Griffith next attempted an even more ambitious film, *Intolerance*.

   _____

   _____

6. People in the audience _____ were confused by Griffith's cross-cutting of plots.   (who/whom/whose)
   People found the movie too difficult to follow.

   _____

   _____

7. Money was no object to Griffith _____.   (who/whom/whose)
   Griffith spent enough for forty ordinary films in making *Intolerance*.

   _____

   _____

8. The movie displayed Griffith's _____ talent well.
   (who/whom/whose)
   Griffith still lost money on *Intolerance*.

   _____

   _____

9. The silent film stars' _____ popularity was enormous.
   (who/whom/whose)
   The government used the silent film stars to sell Liberty Bonds during World War I.

   _____

   _____

10. Douglas Fairbanks, Mary Pickford, and Charlie Chaplin _____
    could draw a larger crowd than any politician.   (who/whom/whose)
    Douglas Fairbanks, Mary Pickford, and Charlie Chaplin raised thousands of
    dollars for the war effort.

    _____

    _____

EXERCISE F

Combine each of the following pairs of sentences using *who, whose, whom,* or *which*
as an adjective subordination signal. Be prepared to explain your choice of a subordination signal. Use appropriate punctuation to separate the subordinate word
group from the base sentence.

  1. Alvin Ailey founded the American Dance Theater in 1958.
     The American Dance Theater has probably been seen by more people than
     any other American dance company.

     _____

     _____

  2. Ailey's interest in dance was inspired by pioneer African-American concert
     dancer Katherine Dunham.
     Ailey saw Dunham when he was in junior high.

     _____

     _____

  3. Ailey's actual involvement with dance did not come until college.
     Ailey made his Broadway debut in 1954.

     _____

     _____

  4. Ailey trained with many of the best modern dancers.
     Martha Graham, Anna Sokolow, and Hanya Holm were among these
     dancers.

     _____

     _____

5. Ailey's American Dance Theater focuses on modern dance.
Modern dance can take a variety of forms including jazz, ballet, and ethnic idioms.

_____

_____

6. Ailey's company has provided a platform for African-American dancers and choreographers.
Ailey has choreographed many of the American Dance Theater's performances.

_____

_____

7. Ailey's jazz dance *For Bird—With Love* is a tribute to saxophonist Charlie Parker.
Charlie Parker led the "bop" movement in jazz.

_____

_____

8. *The River* is one of Ailey's best-known ballets.
The River was written for the American Ballet Theatre.

_____

_____

9. Ailey and his company have won many awards.
Ailey and his company have broken new ground in choreography.

_____

_____

10. Critics have recognized Alvin Ailey as a major creative artist of the twentieth century.
Alvin Ailey blends an African-American heritage with powerful modern choreography.

_____

_____

202

● Distinguishing Between Interrupting and Narrowing Adjective Subordinate Word Groups

As you have seen in the exercises above, adjective subordinate word groups frequently appear in the middle of a base sentence. They are set off with commas because they interrupt the flow of the base sentence. However, there is another type of adjective subordinate word group. This kind does not interrupt, even though it may come in the middle of the base sentence. Instead of providing extra information, it provides information necessary to the basic meaning of the sentence. It narrows or particularizes the meaning of some part of the base sentence.

Look, for instance, at the two sentences below:

> Tragedies, *which were performed as part of a religious festival,* originated in ancient Greece.

> Plays *that show the downfall of a hero* are called tragedies.

The first sentence follows the typical pattern of an adjective subordinate word group. It interrupts the base sentence to add some extra information. The extra information about the religious connection of the plays does not alter the statement that tragedies originated in Greece. The base sentence would convey the same meaning whether or not that subordinate word group was present. The interrupting subordinate word group is set off with commas and uses the signal word *which*.

The second sentence, however, does not operate the same way. If the subordinate word group were omitted from the sentence, the meaning of the sentence would change; in fact, the sentence would no longer be accurate without that subordinate word group. Not all plays are tragedies, only those that involve the downfall of a heroic character.

This second category of adjective subordinate word groups is called a narrowing word group. It narrows or defines which part of a larger group the sentence actually deals with. In this example, the narrowing word group identifies which segment of the literary works called plays this particular sentence discusses, i.e., plays that show the downfall of a heroic character. Narrowing subordinate word groups are not set off with commas and usually use the signal word *that*. In some cases, as the following example shows, the signal word may be omitted altogether:

> Only seven of the plays *(that) Sophocles wrote* have survived from the fifth century.

In this sentence as well, the subordinate word group is needed to identify which group of plays the sentence focuses on. Without the narrowing subordinate word group, the meaning of the sentence would change. Again, the base sentence would be inaccurate without the subordinate word group. More than seven plays have survived from fifth-century Greece. However, only seven of Sophocles' plays have survived.

A narrowing subordinate word group may also identify one specific person or item that might not otherwise be recognizable. The following sentence shows an example of this use of the narrowing subordinate word group:

> The man *who financed the drama festival* was a wealthy citizen chosen by the city.

Here the subordinate word group tells which particular man the sentence is discussing. This identification is essential to the meaning of the sentence, so it is not set off with commas.

To summarize, then, when the adjective subordinate word group narrows the focus of the sentence to a specific item or set of items within a larger category, it is not considered an interruption and it should not be set off from the base sentence with commas.

EXERCISE G

Underline the subordinate word group in each of the following sentences and identify it as interrupting (I) or narrowing (N). Insert commas where they are needed to set off an interrupting subordinate word group.

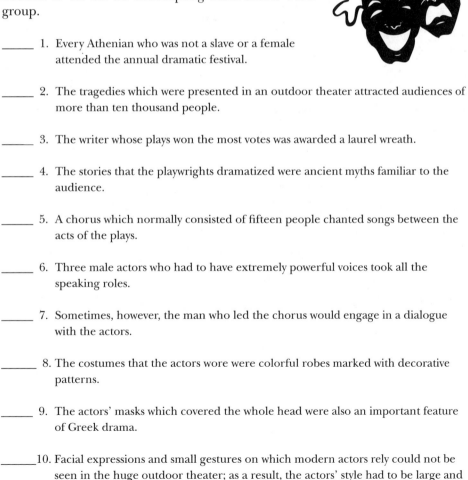

_____ 1. Every Athenian who was not a slave or a female attended the annual dramatic festival.

_____ 2. The tragedies which were presented in an outdoor theater attracted audiences of more than ten thousand people.

_____ 3. The writer whose plays won the most votes was awarded a laurel wreath.

_____ 4. The stories that the playwrights dramatized were ancient myths familiar to the audience.

_____ 5. A chorus which normally consisted of fifteen people chanted songs between the acts of the plays.

_____ 6. Three male actors who had to have extremely powerful voices took all the speaking roles.

_____ 7. Sometimes, however, the man who led the chorus would engage in a dialogue with the actors.

_____ 8. The costumes that the actors wore were colorful robes marked with decorative patterns.

_____ 9. The actors' masks which covered the whole head were also an important feature of Greek drama.

_____10. Facial expressions and small gestures on which modern actors rely could not be seen in the huge outdoor theater; as a result, the actors' style had to be large and distinct.

EXERCISE **H**

Combine the following sentences using adjective subordination signals. Punctuate each sentence appropriately depending on whether it contains an interrupting subordinate word group or a narrowing subordinate word group.

1. Rosa Bonheur was the child of two painters.
   Art was an almost inevitable career for Rosa Bonheur.

_____

_____

2. Bonheur's father trained her.
   Bonheur began painting and sculpting animals at an early age.

_____

_____

3. Nineteenth-century ideas of femininity held little power for Bonheur.
   Bonheur cropped her hair short and smoked cigarettes.

_____

_____

4. Bonheur also wore trousers.
   She needed a police permit for trousers.

_____

_____

5. Women wore trousers.
   Women were considered unusual.

_____

_____

6. Bonheur was concerned about anatomical accuracy in her art.
   Bonheur visited slaughterhouses and dissected animal parts.
   Bonheur obtained the animal parts from butcher shops.

_____

_____

7. Bonheur's most famous painting, *The Horse Fair,* shows Bonheur's familiarity with horses and their handlers.
   Bonheur had observed horses and their handlers for many years.

_____

_____

8. Queen Victoria admired *The Horse Fair* greatly.
   During its tour of England, Queen Victoria had *The Horse Fair* brought to Windsor Castle for a private showing.

_____

_____

9. Bonheur loved animals of all kinds.
   Bonheur's chateau was filled with exotic pets like lions and yaks.

_____

_____

10. In 1865, Rosa Bonheur became the first woman artist to receive the cross of the Legion of Honor, an award.
    Napoleon established the award to recognize special service to France.

_____

_____

USING VERBAL SUBORDINATION SIGNALS

The third method of subordinating an idea uses the three verb forms that don't show time. These forms are called **verbals.** Every verb has three verbal forms—that is, forms that don't indicate the time of an action. The box below shows these verbals.

VERBAL SUBORDINATION SIGNALS		
Verbal	**Examples**	
to + verb	to speak	to think
verb + *-ing*	speaking	thinking
past participle	spoken	thought

Any of these verbal forms may be used to make a subordinate word group.

Here are some examples of verbals used to subordinate an idea. Notice that verbal subordination signals follow the same principles of punctuation as the other methods of subordination. Subordinate word groups at the beginning of a sentence are set off by a comma. Subordinate word groups that interrupt the base sentence are set off with two commas. Subordinate word groups following the base sentence usually do not need punctuation.

> **Folk music calls people back to their roots.**
>
> **Folk music prepares people to worship, fight, work, or make love in ways normal to their community.**

To subordinate the first idea using a verbal, you would find the verb in the sentence—in this case *calls*—and change it to a verbal—*calling*. The subject of the sentence is dropped. Thus the subordinate word group would become: *calling people back to their roots*. The verbal subordinate word group would next be inserted into the base sentence:

> ***Calling people back to their roots,* folk music prepares people to worship, fight, work, or make love in ways normal to their community.**

Here is another example:

> **Each group of settlers in the New World reminded themselves of their homeland.**
>
> **They preserved the music of their native tradition.**

Here again, to subordinate the first idea, you would find the verb in the sentence—*reminded*—and change it to a verbal—*to remind*—and drop the subject. Thus the subordinate word group would be: *to remind themselves of their homeland*. You would then insert the subordinate word group into the base sentence:

> **Each group of settlers in the New World preserved the music of their native tradition *to remind themselves of their homeland.***

Here is a third example:

> **American folk music was created from various different strains.**
>
> **American folk music has no one "pure" source.**

To subordinate the first idea in this pair of sentences, you can use the past participle that is already in the sentence as part of the verb—*created*. You would drop the tense signal—*was*—and the subject to get the subordinate word group: *created from various different strains*. When you put the subordinate word group into the base sentence, you get this as one possible version of the sentence:

> **American folk music, *created from various different strains,* has no one "pure" source.**

Verbal subordinate word groups are sometimes adjectives and sometimes adverbs. Notice in the last example, for instance, that the subordinate word group—*created from various different strains*—functions as an adjective modifying the subject of the base sentence. In the second example, the subordinate word group—*to remind themselves of their homeland*—functions as an adverb explaining why the settlers preserved their music.

EXERCISE 1

Underline the verbal subordinate word group in each of the following sentences and show with an arrow what word in the base sentence it modifies as an adjective or an adverb.

1. Many American settlers wrote songs to express their individuality.

2. These songs, emphasizing nonconformity, often broke the rules of conventional music.

3. Frontier settlers, sometimes troubled by the awesome solitude around their little cabins, wrote "lonesome tunes," such as *I'm Just a Poor Wayfarin' Stranger.*

4. American folk music also incorporates a strong moral code to judge from lyrics like "I've told you once and I've told you twice, / There's sinners in Hell for shootin' dice."

5. Shrouded in gloom, nineteenth-century love ballads reflect people's suspicion of sexual pleasure: "There's not one boy in a hundred a poor girl can trust."

6. Narrative ballads, like *Barbara Allen* and *Fair Ellender,* often survive in several versions depending on the history and geography of a particular region.

7. Frontier poets usually started with a well-known traditional song and altered it to suit their new theme.

8. West African music, brought to America by slaves, added a different tradition to the American folk song.

9. To sing West African style, a leader raises a song and a chorus of blended

   voices answers.

10. Usually featuring a strong rhythmic beat, community songs of labor and worship

    and dance far outnumber narrative songs in the West African musical heritage.

EXERCISE J

Combine the following sentences by changing one sentence to a verbal subordinate word group. Be prepared to explain which idea gets the main emphasis
in your new sentence. The first few sets give a suggestion for an appropriate verbal.

1. Louis Comfort Tiffany worked from 1893 to 1933.   (-ing)
   Louis Comfort Tiffany brought the art of stained glass to new heights.

   _____

   _____

2. Tiffany is perhaps best known for his lamps.   (known)
   Tiffany also created vases, jewelry, small decorative items, and most
   importantly, magnificent windows.

   _____

   _____

3. Tiffany got the special colors he wanted.   (to ——)
   Tiffany made his own glass.

   _____

   _____

4. Many of Tiffany's designs were based on Tiffany's personal knowledge of
   flowers.   (based)
   Many of Tiffany's designs incorporate floral motifs such as wisteria, peonies,
   and Queen Anne's lace.

   _____

   _____

5. Tiffany portrayed leaves and flowers.
   Tiffany used a special mottled glass.

---

6. Tiffany also invented "drapery glass."
   Drapery glass is folded.
   Drapery glass creates a fabriclike appearance.

---

7. Tiffany achieved unique effects.
   Tiffany layered one piece of glass over another.

---

8. Tiffany developed a new technique for putting glass together.
   Tiffany created exquisite detail with small pieces of glass.

---

9. Tiffany experimented with many artistic media such as ceramics, metalwork, and enamel.
   Tiffany often incorporated several different kinds of art in his masterworks.

---

10. Tiffany's style is distinguished by its strong color and the richness of its materials.
    Tiffany's style is instantly recognizable.

● **Arranging Word Groups with Verbals**

Verbal subordinate word groups modify some part of the base sentence. Since these word groups do not have subjects, you must be particularly careful about placing them correctly in the base sentence. To avoid confusing your reader, you should place them as close as possible to the part of the base sentence they describe. If you don't do this, your reader may have difficulty seeing precisely what the verbal describes, as the following examples illustrate.

> *Varying in height from two feet to seventy feet,* the tribes of the Northwest produced elaborately decorated totem poles.

In this example, the verbal subordinate word group—*varying in height from two feet to seventy feet*—has been placed so that it seems to modify the subject of the base sentence—*the tribes of the Northwest.* This placement creates a very confusing sentence since humans aren't known to display such great variations in height. The writer almost certainly intended the verbal to describe the object of the base sentence—*totem poles.* This sentence can be corrected by moving the verbal so that it is next to the words it really describes:

> The tribes of the Northwest produced elaborately decorated totem poles *varying in height from two feet to seventy feet.*

Here is another example:

> *Attached to the front of the house,* the family proclaimed its clan affiliation and social status.

Here the verbal—*attached to the front of the house*—seems to modify the subject of the base sentence—*the family.* But it is not very likely that the family really attached itself to the front of the house. In fact, there seems to be nothing in the base sentence that might logically be attached to the front of the house. In this case, the sentence can't be corrected just by moving the verbal to a different location. The sentence needs to be rewritten. You must change either the subordinate word group or the base sentence so that the subordinate idea is clearly and logically connected to the base sentence. Here are two possibilities:

> *Attached to the front of the house,* the totem proclaimed a family's clan affiliation and social status.
>
> *Using a totem attached to the front of the house,* the family proclaimed its clan affiliation and social status.

Exercise K

In the following sentences, identify any verbals that are misplaced or unattached to the base sentence. Rewrite the sentences as necessary to ensure that every verbal has a logical connection to the base sentence.

1. Chosen from the birds, mammals, and fish in the area, each clan identified itself with a symbolic spirit guardian.

_____

_____

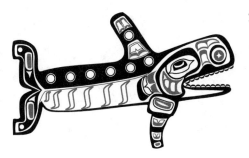

2. The totem sculptor, combined with human characteristics, created a rich network of symbolic relationships using animal figures.

_____

_____

3. To mystify the uninitiated, each animal was identified by certain typical characteristics—such as a hooked beak for the eagle—which the artist often blended in a complex pattern.

_____

_____

4. For example, representing a mythological creature, the eyes and brows of a figure might appear human while his nostrils and protruding tongue suggested a bear.

_____

_____

5. To interpret all the symbols in a totem design, only an experienced chieftain or medicine man had the required expertise.

_____

_____

6. Intermarriages among clans to enrich the totem pole called for the addition of new symbols.

_____

_____

7. Incorporating the same basic elements in each totem pole, variations were created by changes in scale and color and by three-dimensional relief carving.

_____

_____

8. Totem art emphasizes strong, bold contrasts characterized by its vigorous sense of form.

_____

_____

9. No two totem poles are alike requiring great imagination from the artists.

_____

_____

10. Carved on a smaller scale, the natives of the Northwest also made masks and stone sculptures with the same stylistic features as the totem poles.

_____

_____

▶ REVIEW OF METHODS OF SUBORDINATION

When you want to subordinate an idea, you can choose from among the methods presented in this chapter. For example, suppose you wanted to write about these two ideas:

Martha Graham celebrated life through her dance.
Martha Graham invented a whole new language of movement.

You could combine these two ideas with an adverb subordination signal:

When Martha Graham celebrated life through her dance, she invented a whole new language of movement.

You could also combine these ideas with an adjective subordination signal:

Martha Graham, *who celebrated life through her dance,* invented a whole new language of movement.

Or you could combine these ideas with a verbal subordinate word group:

Celebrating life through her dance, Martha Graham invented a whole new language of movement.

Each of these sentences is built on the same base—*Martha Graham invented a whole new language of movement*—but the subordinate idea can be expressed in a number of ways.

The box below summarizes the three basic methods of subordination.

METHODS OF SUBORDINATION

1. ATTACH AN ADVERB SUBORDINATION SIGNAL TO THE FRONT OF A SENTENCE:

Aztec artists made exquisite cloaks with feathers and gold.

↓

When Aztec artists made exquisite cloaks with feathers and gold,

↓

When Aztec artists made exquisite cloaks with feathers and gold, the cloaks were given to the city's greatest warriors.

2. REPLACE ONE WORD IN THE SENTENCE WITH *WHO, WHOSE, WHOM, WHICH,* OR *THAT*:

Aztec artists made exquisite cloaks with feathers and gold.

↓

who made exquisite cloaks with feathers and gold

↓

Aztec artists, who made exquisite cloaks with feathers and gold, taught their secrets only to their children.

3. REMOVE THE SUBJECT AND CHANGE THE VERB TO A VERBAL:

Aztec artists made exquisite cloaks with feathers and gold.

↓

making exquisite cloaks with feathers and gold

↓

Making exquisite cloaks with feathers and gold, Aztec artists achieved great heights of creativity.

EXERCISE L

Combine each of the following sets of sentences in two different ways. Each version should use a different method of subordination. Be prepared to identify the base sentence in each version and to explain the relationship between the base sentence and the subordinate word group.

<u>EXAMPLE:</u>
A Japanese garden is the focal point of the household.
The garden reflects the character of its owner.

A Japanese garden, which is the focal point of the household, reflects the character

of its owner.

Reflecting the character of its owner, a Japanese garden is the focal point of the house.

A Japanese garden reflects the character of its owner because it is the focal point

of the household.

1. A traditional Japanese landscape garden encourages relaxation and meditation.
   The garden is not intended for showy display.

   A. _____

   _____

   B. _____

   _____

2. The Japanese favor gardens with many different views.
   Japanese gardeners arrange paths, bridges, and hills very carefully.

   A. _____

   _____

   B. _____

   _____

3. Ideal Japanese gardens provide scenes for every season.
   The gardens feature different vegetation throughout the year.

   A. _____

   _____

   B. _____

   _____

4. Garden scenes often imitate famous natural landscapes or literary scenes.
   A knowledge of classical literature enhances one's appreciation of the
   garden.

   A. _____

   _____

   B. _____

   _____

5. A Japanese gardener plants a hill with wild cherries and maples.
   A Japanese gardener may suggest a famous mountain.

   A. _____

   _____

   B. _____

   _____

6. Japanese gardens give careful attention to the shape and placement of
   individual stones.
   Stones are considered the skeleton of the garden.

   A. _____

   _____

   B. _____

   _____

7. Stone lanterns constitute another important feature of Japanese gardens.
   The lanterns are seen as architectural ornaments rather than sources of light.

   A. _____

   _____

   B. _____

   _____

8. Trees, shrubs, and plants in a Japanese garden are considered embellishments
   for the stone ornaments.
   They serve as background for the striking shapes.

   A. _____

   _____

   B. _____

   _____

9. Japanese gardeners avoid rows of trees.
   They plant trees in an irregular pattern.
   The trees may then be viewed from several different angles.

   A. _____

   _____

   B. _____

   _____

10. Japanese gardeners value open spaces in their gardens.
    They do not crowd the garden with too many objects.

    A. _____

    _____

    B. _____

    _____

EXERCISE M

Expand the following sentences by adding a subordinate word group to each one. You should use each method of subordination at least three times in this exercise.

EXAMPLE:

Art has infinite meaning.

Art has infinite meaning because human beings are infinitely varied.

or

Art has infinite meaning which is what makes art endlessly interesting.

or

Art, which changes with the needs of each human community, has infinite meaning.

or

Reflecting the diversity of human beings themselves, art has infinite meaning.

or

To reflect the diversity of human beings themselves, art has infinite meaning.

1. Art is one of the oldest and most important means of human expression.

_____

_____

2. Art can take many forms.

_____

_____

3. Every human culture has developed distinctive musical, visual, and verbal forms of expression.

_____

_____

4. Art can express deeply personal feelings as well as the values of a whole society.

_____

_____

5. Art is often based on the observation of nature.

_____

_____

6. Art can change one's perception of the natural world.

_____

_____

7. Some artists are respected and successful.

_____

_____

8. Other artists lead difficult lives.

_____

_____

9. Art benefits people.

_____

_____

10. Creativity is a mysterious process.

_____

_____

EXERCISE N

Expand each of the following sentences by adding a coordinate sentence to it. Then change one of the coordinate ideas to a subordinate idea.

EXAMPLE:

Fairy tales usually involve magic.
Coordination:

Fairy tales usually involve magic, and they are filled with mysterious creatures.

Subordination:

Filled with mysterious creatures, fairy tales usually involve magic.

1. Fairy tales usually take place in or near an enchanted forest.

   Coordination: _____

   _____

   Subordination:_____

   _____

2. The same villains appear over and over in fairy tales.

   Coordination: _____

   _____

   Subordination: _____

   _____

3. The hero or heroine of a fairy tale is often the youngest of three brothers or sisters.

   Coordination: _____

   _____

   Subordination: _____

   _____

4. The hero of a fairy tale usually has a difficult task to perform.

   Coordination: _____

   _____

   Subordination: _____

   _____

5. The heroine of a fairy tale often gets help from animals.

    Coordination: _____

    _____

    Subordination: _____

    _____

6. Fairy tale creatures often use disguises.

    Coordination: _____

    _____

    Subordination: _____

    _____

7. The main character in a fairy tale may experience temporary defeat.

    Coordination: _____

    _____

    Subordination: _____

    _____

8. In fairy tales, the main character is always successful in the end.

    Coordination: _____

    _____

    Subordination: _____

    _____

9. In fairy tales, success means marriage, wealth, and wisdom.

    Coordination: _____

    _____

Subordination: _____

_____

10. Fairy tales try to fill readers with wonder.

Coordination: _____

_____

Subordination: _____

_____

EDITING PRACTICE:

Read the following paragraphs carefully, checking them for these kinds of problems:

1. Fragments
2. Subject–verb agreement
3. Correct form of adjectives and adverbs
4. Correct placement of modifiers
5. Correct punctuation of coordinate and subordinate word groups

Then, rewrite the paragraphs on a separate sheet of paper, making whatever changes are necessary to correct these sentence problems.

1. Walt Disney revolutionized animated cartoons. While early cartoons featured simple, two-dimensional figures Disney insisted on rounded, humanized figures. Pre-Disney cartoons were based on slapstick humor but Disney wanted humor, that developed out of personality. Creating a cartoon in which music and action were synchronized, the result was the legendary *Steamboat Willy*. This 1928 film in which the cargo of a riverboat are transformed into an orchestra marked the introduction of Disney's most famous character, Mickey Mouse. Previously shot in black and white, in 1932 Disney pioneered the use of full color for his animated features. "Who's Afraid of the Big Bad Wolf?" which was the hit tune from Disney's *The Three Little Pigs* swept the nation in 1933. Taking almost three years to produce *Snow White*, Disney's first full-length feature, was an overnight success. When it premiered just before Christmas, 1937. *Pinocchio* which many critics describes as Disney's masterpiece uses gorgeous background paintings, that contributes to the movie's brilliance. Special effects like live-action rain also make this a spectacular film. *Fantasia* an animated concert of orchestral pieces is another technical creation with animation ranging from hilarious hippos to delicate fairies. While many talented animators worked for him Disney himself was always the guiding spirit of his studio therefore the studio's success was Disney's success.

2. No great house in America more clearly reflect the vision of its creator than Monticello. Like the new American republic, the house seemed in a constant state of progress, as Thomas Jefferson put up tore down expanded and modified his house. Begun in 1768, Jefferson continually changed the building until his death in 1826. Jefferson was influenced by the design of other colonial buildings in Virginia such as Rosewell and Mount Airy. Jefferson also read extensive about architecture. By adapting classical architecture, Jefferson to symbolize the virtues of republicanism and rationality however his architecture broke away from traditional ideas. Although he borrowed from classical architecture Jefferson translated it into forms suitable for the climate materials and craftsmanship of Virginia. Not satisfied with commonplace rectangular rooms he created unusual interiors. No two of Monticello's internal spaces exactly identical. One innovation which became a kind of Jeffersonian signature was the use of octagons or eight-sided spaces. He designed the house to take advantage of all the spectacularly views. Large windows seems to dissolve the barrier between the inside and the outside of the house. Built into the hillside the kitchen and service areas of the house lie underneath the terraces as a result they do not block the views from the main rooms of the house. Emphasizing horizontal lines Jefferson created the illusion of a one-story house. The dome, which highlights the west porch, gave the building a monumental quality. As the house of the chief architect of the new republic Monticello continue to speak of the goals, that Jefferson held for himself and his country.

WRITING PRACTICE:

1. You have been given the opportunity to nominate your favorite creative or performing artist for a prestigious award in his or her field. You may choose a singer, a painter, an actor, a writer, or anyone engaged in creating or performing art. In a letter of about 150 words, you must explain to the award committee why your candidate should be considered for this award.

PLANNING:

Make a list of all the talents, skills, or special contributions of the artist you plan to nominate. Next to each item on your list, name a particular song, film, painting, story, or other example of his or her work that would demonstrate the quality you are trying to show. If another student in your class is planning to nominate the same artist, perhaps you could share your lists to help each other come up with ideas.

DRAFTING:

In writing your nomination, focus the committee's attention on one or two of the most important qualities of your candidate. Use coordination and subordination to keep the committee focused on those qualities.

EDITING:

When you have written a draft of your nomination, go back and make sure that all your sentences are complete and correctly punctuated. If your teacher allows it, you may want to have another student double-check your sentences.

2. In a psychology class, you have been discussing the phenomenon of creativity. What is it that makes people creative? The exercises in this chapter of your text have dealt with creative individuals and creative arts in general. Using this material as well as your own observations about creativity, write a paragraph of about 200 words explaining for your classmates what you think are the two or three most important characteristics of creative people.

<u>PLANNING:</u>

Using a web like the one shown below, generate a set of the characteristics of creativity. Your teacher may allow a group of you to work together in filling out this web. For each quality shown on your web, try to think of one or two examples of creative people who exhibit this quality. Use examples that your classmates will be likely to recognize.

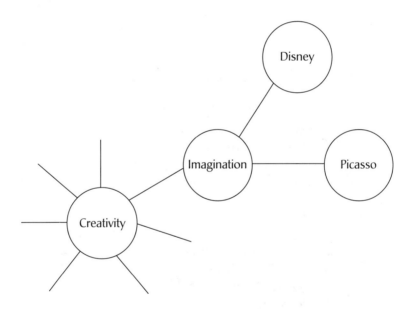

<u>DRAFTING:</u>

In writing your explanation, focus on one or two of the most important qualities of creativity, perhaps those where you have the best examples. Use coordination and subordination to keep your classmates' attention focused on those qualities.

<u>EDITING:</u>

When you have written a draft of your explanation, go back and make sure that all your sentences are complete and correctly punctuated. If your teacher allows it, you may want to have another student double-check your sentences.

◀ *Chapter 6* ▶

Sentences in the Context of Paragraphs

• • • • • • • • • • • • • •

▶ PRONOUNS
   ● Pronoun Forms
   ● Pronoun Function
   ● Pronoun Agreement
   ● Pronoun Reference
▶ CONSISTENCY
   ● Consistency in Verb Tense
   ● Consistency in Point of View
▶ SENTENCE VARIETY
   ● Methods of Variation
   ● Repetition

• • • • • • • • • • • • • •

In the first five chapters of this book, you have looked at various ways of putting ideas into a single sentence. However, since most writing situations require more than one sentence, you need to be aware of some of the special circumstances that arise when you write a series of sentences on the same subject. The use of pronouns, the need for consistency among sentences, and the use of variation in sentence patterns all come into play when you write sentences in the context of a paragraph.

▶ PRONOUNS

As soon as you write more than one sentence on the same subject, you will probably find a need for pronouns. For example, look at the following set of sentences:

> **Psychologists regard Sigmund Freud as the first explorer of the unconscious.**
> **Psychologists consider Freud's work one of the major revolutions in the**
> **psychologists' field.**

It is very likely that you would use pronouns in the second sentence instead of repeating the nouns.

> **Psychologists regard Sigmund Freud as the first explorer of the unconscious.**
> ***They* consider *his* work one of the major revolutions in *their* field.**

As the example shows, the pronoun *they* can substitute for the noun *psychologists*. The pronoun *his* can substitute for the possessive *Freud's*. The pronoun *their* can substitute for the possessive *psychologists'*. A **pronoun** is a word that can substitute for a noun.

In using pronouns, you need to keep four things in mind:

1. A pronoun must refer clearly and specifically to one noun. This noun is called the **antecedent** of the pronoun because it goes before (*ante*—before + *cedere*—to go). A pronoun has meaning only when the reader knows without doubt what noun the pronoun represents.
2. The pronoun has to agree with the noun it stands for. That is, a pronoun has to have the same number (singular or plural) and gender as the noun it replaces.
3. A pronoun must use the form that is appropriate for its function in the sentence—subject, object, or modifier.
4. Some pronouns refer back to other pronouns.

The adjective subordination signals that you used in Chapter 5—*who, whose, whom, which,* and *that*—function in much the same way as pronouns like *he, she,* or *it* and are often described as a kind of pronoun.

In addition to the personal pronouns and the adjective subordination signals, there is another category called **indefinite pronouns.** These words—as their name suggests—refer to nonspecific or uncertain antecedents. Most indefinite pronouns—words like *nobody, anything, everyone,* and *some*—are considered singular. The indefinite pronouns will be explained later in this chapter.

● Pronoun Forms

Depending on their function in the sentence and on the number and gender of their antecedent, pronouns may take different forms. As the next table shows, a pronoun that can function as the subject of a sentence may have a completely different form from a pronoun that can function as the object of a sentence.

PRONOUN FORMS						
Number / **Function**	**Singular**			**Plural**		
	1st Person	*2nd Person*	*3rd Person*	*1st Person*	*2nd Person*	*3rd Person*
Subject/ Subject Complement	I	you	he, she, it who, which	we	you	they who, which
Object/ Object of Preposition	me	you	him, her, it whom, which	us	you	them, whom, which,
Possessive Modifier	my	your	his, her, its whose	our	your	their, whose
Possessive Subject or Complement	mine	yours	his, hers, its	ours	yours	theirs
Indefinite Pronouns			*any each either *every neither *no none one *some *-body, -one, -thing			all few many most several

EXERCISE A

Using the chart above as a reference, underline each pronoun in the following sentences and the antecedent of each pronoun. In the chart that follows, indicate the function, person, and number of each pronoun.

<u>EXAMPLE:</u>
Sometimes students don't trust their intuitive thinking; they trust only their left brains.

Pronoun	Antecedent	Function	Person	Number
their	*students*	*possessive modifier*	*3rd*	*plural*
they	*students*	*subject*	*3rd*	*plural*
their	*they*	*possessive modifier*	*3rd*	*plural*

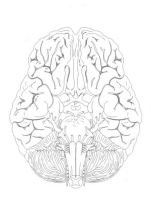

1. Although the two hemispheres of the brain look similar, they actually have physical differences.
2. A person's left brain is almost always larger than his right brain.
3. The right brain contains long fibers connecting it to many different areas of the brain.
4. The left brain contains shorter fibers, and its connections to other parts of the brain are more limited.
5. The two halves of the brain not only have physical differences, but they seem to specialize in different kinds of thinking.
6. The right brain makes connections between items; when you see a hamburger, fries, and a Coke, for example, your right brain recognizes them as "lunch."
7. The left brain, on the other hand, processes items one at a time; it breaks things down into parts and concentrates on their individual details.
8. For example, when an artist notices the individual brushstrokes in a painting, her left brain is at work.
9. The left brain focuses on factual information such as "I have just hit my head on the doorframe."
10. The right brain takes in facts and grasps their emotional significance: "Drat #%*!"
11. In left-brain thinking, we rely heavily on our organization of previously accumulated information; the left brain remembers rules and linear sequences.
12. Our right brains, on the other hand, allow us to transform the rules, to rely on intuition.
13. Scientists have long known of the connection between the left brain and language use; they noticed, for instance, that stroke victims with damage to the left brain have difficulty speaking and processing words.
14. The right brain deals with the world by using its graphic powers; it thinks in pictures more than words.
15. When someone sees the word "love," for instance, her left brain interprets it as a verbal sign meaning an intense affection for another person.
16. The right brain, meanwhile, may present her with a picture of two people hugging.

17. Right-brain thinking predominates in a young child as she experiences wonder, emotion, and curiosity about the world.
18. In older children, left-brain thinking becomes more dominant as they learn more about rules, rationality, and conventional patterns.
19. A good writer needs both the logical power of his left brain and the intuitive power of his right brain.
20. If you want to succeed, you should allow both sides of your brain to work for you.

Pronoun	Antecedent	Function	Person	Number
1.				
2.				
3.				
4.				
5.				
6.				
7.				
8.				
9.				
10.				
11.				
12.				
13.				
14.				
15.				
16.				
17.				
18.				

19. _____ _____ _____ _____ _____

20. _____ _____ _____ _____ _____

● Pronoun Function

The form of a pronoun varies according to its function. A pronoun may take a different form depending on whether it is used as a subject, object, or modifier.

In Chapter 1, when you conjugated verbs, you used the subject pronouns—*I, you, he, she, it, we, you, they*—to learn all the forms of a verb.

Object pronouns—*me, you, him, her, it, us, you, them*—function as the object of a verb or as the object of a preposition.

Possessive modifiers—*my, your, his, her, its, our, your, their*—show ownership of a particular item named in the sentence.

The pronouns in the last category, possessive subjects or complements, do double duty: they show possession and they function as a subject or complement in the sentence.

The examples below show each of the functions of pronouns.

When you replace a subject or a subject complement with a pronoun, you must use a subject pronoun.

> subject
> *Most people* daydream regularly.
> *They* daydream regularly.

> subject complement
> It is *young adults* who daydream the most.
> It is *they* who daydream the most.

When you replace an object or an object of a preposition, you must use an object pronoun.

> object
> Daydreams help *children* develop social skills.
> Daydreams help *them* develop social skills

> object/preposition
> For *children,* daydreams reduce impulsive behavior.
> For *them,* daydreams reduce impulsive behavior.

When you replace a possessive modifier, you must use a possessive pronoun.

> possessive modifier
> *Adults'* daydreams may provide a safety valve for aggressive thoughts.
> *Their* daydreams may provide a safety valve for aggressive thoughts.

When you replace both a possessive modifier and the noun it modifies, you may use a special form of the possessive pronoun.

> possessive subject
> *Children's daydreams* improve thinking ability.
> *Theirs* improve thinking ability.

EXERCISE B

In the following sentences, replace the underlined word or words with an appropriate pronoun. Determine how the underlined word functions in the sentence—as a subject, as an object, as a possessive—and rewrite the sentence using the appropriate pronoun.

EXAMPLE:
Walter Mitty spices up his routine life with exciting daydreams.

Function of the underlined word: *subject*   Pronoun: *he*

He spices up his routine life with exciting daydreams.

1. The story provides some real psychological insight.

    Function of the underlined word: _____ Pronoun: _____

    _____

    _____

2. In real life, people spend many hours daydreaming.

    Function of the underlined word: _____ Pronoun: _____

    _____

    _____

3. Such daydreaming may prepare people for future events.

    Function of the underlined word: _____ Pronoun: _____

    _____

    _____

4. Playful fantasies may increase <u>people's</u> creativity.

   Function of the underlined word: _____   Pronoun: _____

   _____

   _____

5. <u>Our daydreams</u> may not always be as dramatic as Walter Mitty's.

   Function of the underlined word: _____   Pronoun: _____

   _____

   _____

6. Our daydreams may not always be as dramatic as <u>Walter Mitty's</u>.

   Function of the underlined word: _____   Pronoun: _____

   _____

   _____

7. For <u>a woman</u>, daydreaming may be essential to mental health.

   Function of the underlined word: _____   Pronoun: _____

   _____

   _____

8. We should encourage <u>daydreaming</u>.

   Function of the underlined word: _____   Pronoun: _____

   _____

   _____

9. Daydreaming's benefits probably outweigh the drawbacks.

   Function of the underlined word: _____   Pronoun: _____

   _____

   _____

10. Psychologists will continue to study daydreaming.

    Function of the underlined word: _____   Pronoun: _____

    _____

    _____

Exercise C

Rewrite each sentence below using the verb in the exact form shown in parentheses. Be sure to choose appropriate pronoun forms in the revised sentences.

Example:

I am fascinated by the subject of sleep.

   (fascinates) *The subject of sleep fascinates me.*

   Pronoun: *me*_____   Pronoun Function: *object*_____

1. She and Professor Liu have studied thousands of volunteer subjects.

   (have been studied)_____

   Pronoun: _____   Pronoun Function: _____

2. The National Science Foundation has honored them and their colleagues.

   (have been honored) _____

   Pronoun: _____   Pronoun Function: _____

3. We were prepared by the researchers to study our sleep patterns.

   (prepared) _____

   Pronoun: _____   Pronoun Function: _____

4. The results of the experiment will be reported by you and me.

   (will report) _____

Pronoun: _____   Pronoun Function: _____

5. To measure brain activity, he has taped electrodes to our scalps.

   (have been taped) _____

   Pronoun: _____   Pronoun Function: _____

6. She and I were trained by Dr. Liu.

   (trained) _____

   Pronoun: _____   Pronoun Function: _____

7. Many observations have been recorded by the doctor and them.

   (have recorded) _____

   Pronoun: _____   Pronoun Function: _____

8. The reports show me and my sister dreaming about 20 percent of the time.

   (are shown) _____

   Pronoun: _____   Pronoun Function: _____

9. He and Steve were included in the next round of the study.

   (included) _____

   Pronoun: _____   Pronoun Function: _____

10. She and Pat wrote award-winning articles about the study.

    (were written) _____

    Pronoun: _____   Pronoun Function: _____

● Pronoun Agreement

Pronouns work effectively only when your reader can tell what noun the pronoun is supposed to stand for. One way that you alert your reader about the connection between a pronoun and its antecedent is by making a pronoun "agree" with its antecedent. If the antecedent is singular, then the pronoun that references it must be singular. If the antecedent is plural, then the pronoun that references it must be plural.

> When *Otto* experiences stress, *he* may be more subject to disease.
>
> When *people* experience stress, *they* may be more subject to disease.

If the antecedent is masculine, then the pronoun that references it must be masculine. If the antecedent is feminine, then the pronoun that references it must be feminine.

> When *Jennifer* experiences stress, *she* may be more subject to disease.

If the antecedent is in the first person, then the pronoun that references it must be in the first person. If the antecedent is in the second person, then the pronoun that references it must be in the second person. If the antecedent is in the third person, then the pronoun that references it must be in the third person.

> When *I* experience stress, *my* immune system is affected.
>
> When *you* experience stress, *your* immune system is affected.
>
> When *a manager* experiences stress, *his* (or *her*) immune system is affected.

EXERCISE D

In each sentence below, underline the pronoun that has the appropriate form for its function in the sentence and agrees with its antecedent. Be prepared to explain your choice.

EXAMPLE:

> A person's memory is (their, <u>her</u>, hers) storehouse of accumulated learning.
>
> Explanation: This slot in the sentence requires a possessive modifier; thus *hers* could not fit here. The possessive pronoun must be singular to agree with the antecedent, *person;* thus *her* is the correct choice.

1. Without memory, everyday tasks like dressing, cooking, or making a phone call would be a new experience every time. We would have to learn (they, them, it) all over again each day.
2. The first scientific studies of memory were conducted in the late nineteenth century by Herman Ebbinghaus. It was (he, him, his) who began to discover general principles of memory.
3. For information to be remembered, (they, it, its) must be encoded into the memory system.
4. Information can be encoded through images, through sounds, or through meaning. For example, if you and a friend tried to memorize a set of words, you and (she, her, they) might remember different characteristics of the words.
5. Scientists have suggested that humans have two types of memory. Short-term memory often stores items by sound; long-term memory usually stores (they, them, their) by meaning.
6. Short-term memory has a limited capacity. For most of us, seven items is the limit of our short-term memory span. When all the slots are filled, (you, we,

us) can only get new information into short-term memory by displacing some item that is already there.

7. When items are grouped in familiar patterns, (they, it, their) are easier to remember. This technique—called "chunking"—can expand short-term memory.

8. Long-term memory uses a complex system of categories to encode information. (Its, It's, It) organizational structure helps people remember general knowledge about words, symbols, concepts, and rules.

9. This background knowledge often affects the way someone remembers a specific event. A witness who associates hats with overcoats may report that a man wearing an overcoat was also wearing a hat even if (he, his, their) head were actually bare.

10. People remember by putting material into a context that makes sense to (he, him, them).

11. In other words, how and what someone remembers is often determined by (their, her, theirs) background, experience, and values.

12. In addition, research has shown that we often reconstruct memories. New information can distort (ours, our, their) memory of an experience.

13. For example, if one witness claims that the suspect had a mustache, other witnesses may suddenly "remember" (them, it, its) as well.

14. Retrieval—the process of getting information out of memory—may involve either recall or recognition of information. Between (they, them, it), these two methods are the most frequently used means of retrieving information.

15. "Forgetting" something may simply mean that you have not used the proper cues to retrieve the information or that some other information is interfering with (you, your, yours) ability to remember the desired item.

16. On the other hand, most of what we "forget" never got encoded in the first place. For example, most people cannot recall the exact details of a penny's appearance even after seeing thousands of them in (his, her, their) lifetime.

17. Memory is based on a web of associations. Retrieving a specific memory requires finding one of the strands that leads to (them, they, it).

18. Returning to a familiar location can trigger retrieval cues. For example, if someone returns to a former home, (they, he, her) may be flooded with memories associated with that place.

19. Emotional states may also trigger memories. We have a tendency to recall things that happened to (we, us, our) when we were in a similar mood. Happiness often triggers memories of other happy events. Depression often triggers memories of other depressing events.

20. Memory can be improved by maximizing retrieval cues. If a person forms many associations with an item—images, sounds, connections to previous knowledge—(you, she, they) will be more likely to remember the item.

EXERCISE E

Each of the numbered sentences contains one or more blank spaces that need pronouns. Underline the antecedent and then fill in a pronoun that will agree with the antecedent.

EXAMPLE:

If we could modify the behavioral sources of illness, *we*_____ could

alleviate much of *our*_____ physical suffering.

1. Many people are not aware of the link between _____ behavior and

   _____ health.

2. If a woman smokes, for example, _____ is much more likely to
   become seriously ill.

3. The National Academy of Science, in _____ most recent study,
   indicates that more than half the deaths from the ten leading causes of death in
   the United States can be traced to people's behavior.

4. Since concern about behavior's effect on health has
   grown, doctors have tried to deal with

   _____.

5. Traditional medicine assumes that illnesses have a
   single cause; in behavioral medicine, on the other

   hand, _____ are seen as a breakdown of
   interdependent systems.

6. If we can make ourselves sick by _____ behavior, behavioral

   medicine treats _____ by focusing on ways to prevent disease.

7. Stress management techniques such as biofeedback, for example, can help a

   person suffering from hypertension to lower _____ blood pressure
   and reduce the risk of stroke.

8. One doctor even studied the effect of laughter in preventing disease.

   _____ discovered that people who laugh readily are less disturbed
   by stress and less likely to suffer heart attacks.

9. Likewise, if pain is both a physical and a psychological experience, then

   _____ should be treated with both physical and psychological
   therapies.

10. For example, patients may need less pain medication and have shorter

    hospital stays if _____ are given a room with a pleasant view.

    While most pronoun agreement situations are fairly straightforward, some
types of nouns and pronouns may create particular problems with agreement.

Indefinite pronouns are one such category. As indicated in the chart on page 226, words like *another, anybody, anyone, each, either, everybody, everyone, neither, nobody, no one, one, somebody,* and *someone* are considered singular. Except in some informal situations, you need to use a singular pronoun when you refer to one of these words. For example:

> *Everyone* has *his* own unique personality.
>
> *Each* has *her* own unique personality.

On the other hand, words like *all, both, few, many, most, others,* and *several* are considered plural. You need to use a plural pronoun when you refer to one of these words. For example:

> *Few* have *their* own unique personalities.
>
> *All* have *their* own unique personalities.

When using these indefinite words or other nouns that do not have an obvious gender, like *student,* or *driver,* or *doctor,* writers have traditionally used the masculine pronouns *he, him,* or *his.* However, such language does not reflect the reality of both male and female students, drivers, doctors, and so forth. You can avoid this situation by using third-person plural pronouns or the phrase *he or she* when referring to nouns or pronouns that could be either masculine or feminine.

Here are some examples of these techniques for avoiding gender bias in pronouns:

> TRADITIONAL   When a child seeks affirmation, he should get it.
>
> REVISED   When a child seeks affirmation, he or she should get it.
>
> REVISED   When children seek affirmation, they should get it.

Certain nouns, called collective nouns, may also pose a problem when it comes to making pronouns agree with them. Words like *team, group, family,* and *committee* have a singular form, but they may require singular or plural pronouns depending on their meaning in a particular sentence. For example, when the collective acts as a single unit, you would use a singular pronoun:

> The *family* had *its* private celebration after the public ceremony.
>
> The *group* reluctantly decided to disband *itself.*

However, if the members of the collective act as separate individuals, then you would use a plural pronoun:

> The *team* have returned to *their* hometowns for the holidays.
>
> The *class* rose noisily from *their* seats.

EXERCISE F
Rewrite each sentence below changing the subject as indicated. Be sure that the pronouns in the new sentences agree with their antecedents.

EXAMPLE:

Most of the volunteers reported that they felt no change in their attitude.

Each *of the volunteers reported that she felt no change in her attitude.*

1. Both finished their treatment ahead of schedule.

   Everyone _____.

2. Leila and I examined our personality traits.

   I _____.

3. The scientists presented their findings in a 50-page report.

   The research team _____.

4. The group will receive their psychiatric treatments at Green Spring Hospital and at Pratt Institute.

   Everyone _____.

5. No one finds it easy to give up his or her ingrained habits.

   Few _____.

6. All have received their three weeks of vacation time.

   None _____.

7. Someone adjusts to his environment differently depending on his personality.

   Most _____.

8. Some believe that their personalities are inherited.

   Another _____.

9. Many insist their personalities result from their environment.

   Each _____.

10. Neither Raoul's nor mine changed despite our years of effort.

    Mine _____.

● Pronoun Reference

As you have seen in the previous exercises, a pronoun works effectively only when the reader knows what it stands for. Words like *he* or *they* have no particular meaning unless everyone understands to whom the words refer. When you use a pronoun, you need to be sure that it has a clear antecedent; otherwise, your readers will have difficulty in following your meaning.

Using a pronoun that has no antecedent can end up confusing your reader. For example, look at the sentences below:

> **Psychology is the study of human behavior. *They* need many years of training.**

In this example, the pronoun *they* in the second sentence does not refer back to any noun in the first sentence; it lacks an antecedent. The sentences below show how these statements can be rewritten to give the pronoun an antecedent.

> ***Psychologists* study human behavior. *They* need many years of training.**

Now the pronoun *they* refers back to the noun *psychologists* in the first sentence; it has an antecedent.

A pronoun may also cause a problem if it has more than one possible antecedent, as the following sentences show.

> **Psychologists can analyze human actions from many different perspectives. *They* are sometimes puzzling.**

The pronoun *they* in the second sentence doesn't communicate meaning effectively because it lacks a clear antecedent. The sentence doesn't really tell what is puzzling. *They* could refer to *psychologists* or to *human actions* or to *many different perspectives.*

Each of the revisions below clarifies the intended meaning:

> **Psychologists can analyze human actions from many different perspectives. Human actions are sometimes puzzling.**
>
> **Psychologists can analyze human actions, which are sometimes puzzling, from many different perspectives.**
>
> **Even though psychologists are sometimes puzzling, they can analyze human actions from many different perspectives.**
>
> **Psychologists can analyze human behavior from many different, and sometimes puzzling, perspectives.**

As the examples above show, a problem with pronoun reference can be corrected by replacing the pronoun with a noun, by rewriting the sentence so that the pronoun has only one possible antecedent, or by eliminating the need for a pronoun.

Here is another example of a sentence with a pronoun reference problem:

Dr. Wilson told her patient that she could help her.

Do you see the problem in this sentence? It is not clear whether the doctor or the patient can provide the help.

Here are some ways to clarify the meaning:

Dr. Wilson told her patient, "You can help me."

Dr. Wilson told her patient, "I can help you."

Dr. Wilson said that she could help her patient.

Dr. Wilson said that her patient could help her.

The patient was told that Dr. Wilson could help her.

The patient was told that she could help Dr. Wilson.

In general, you should use a pronoun only when you can make its antecedent clear.

EXERCISE G

Rewrite the following pairs of sentences to correct any problems with pronoun reference.

1. Psychology sometimes relates behavior to events in the brain and nervous system. It is probably the most complex structure in the universe.

   _____

   _____

2. Some emotional reactions such as anger or fear can be produced by electrical stimulation of certain areas of the brain. When applied to other areas of the brain, they can also induce vivid memories of past events.

   _____

   _____

3. In the early 1900s, American psychologist John B. Watson suggested that psychologists should study human behavior. Before that, it had focused on human mental experience rather than on actions like talking, laughing, or crying.

   _____

   _____

4. Watson argued that psychologists should study only what can be observed and measured; otherwise, he would lose his objectivity.

_____

_____

5. A behavioral psychologist may attempt to modify a patient's behavior by changing the pattern of rewards and punishments she associates with the behavior.

_____

_____

6. Cognitive psychology, on the other hand, focuses great attention on the mental processes by which an individual acquires knowledge, solves problems, and plans for the future. By understanding it, psychologists can predict a person's behavior.

_____

_____

7. A cognitive psychologist believes that a person's internal thought processes change his response to a situation. It is like a computer trying out various alternative responses.

_____

_____

8. Sigmund Freud developed the theory of psychoanalysis in the late nineteenth century. They used extensive case studies of individual patients to understand human behavior.

_____

_____

9. Psychoanalysis is perhaps the best-known approach to understanding human behavior. His theory suggests that behavior is influenced by unconscious thoughts, fears, and wishes.

_____

_____

10. Another school of psychology emphasizes the fulfillment of each individual's human potential. They try to work on their self-esteem and self-awareness.

_____

_____

EXERCISE H

After each of the following sentences, add two more sentences that use the pronouns you have been practicing. Be sure that the pronouns refer clearly to one noun and that they agree with the nouns to which they refer. Underline the pronouns you use.

EXAMPLE:

Studies offer somewhat different explanations of Fatemah.
They offer somewhat different explanations of Fatemah.
Studies offer somewhat different explanations of her.

1. *The Invisible Man* has become a classic in the study of psychology.

_____

_____

2. Juana thought Ethel was a jealous woman.

_____

_____

3. New Saturn cars are marketed as no other cars on the road are.

_____

_____

4. We sent telepathic messages to our sister in Sierra Leone.

_____

_____

5. Abdul took only a half hour to fill out the intake form.

_____

_____

6. The clinic aide cried when I could not untangle the knots.

_____

_____

7. Waving wildly to the people behind the observation glass, Regina hit her arm on the post.

_____

_____

8. Dr. Ula and I have been in charge of the psychiatric division for twenty years.

_____

_____

9. Your idea of mental health needs further study.

_____

_____

10. Clara and Otto had everyone laughing at the results of their research.

_____

_____

▶ CONSISTENCY

When you begin to write a series of sentences, you have to be careful that you stay consistent from one sentence to the next in verb tense and point of view.

● Consistency in Verb Tense

If you were telling a story about something that happened to you in the past, you would confuse your reader if you jumped around in time like this:

> I *have* never *forgotten* my first plane ride. I *was* four years old, and I *am* terrified of the noise of the engines. My mother *drags* me down the aisle and *strapped* me into my seat. Even the flight attendant's offer of a piece of gum *does* not calm me down. I *was* convinced that the monster *will eat* me.

Written this way, the story moves from the past to the present to the future without any logical reason. All these actions happened in the same time period, but the verb tenses don't make that clear. It would be correct to tell this story in the past tense since it happened in the past, but you could also tell it in the present tense as if you were reliving the events as you were describing them. You have to be sure, though, that you tell the story consistently in the present or the past tense. Both of the versions shown below use verb tenses consistently.

PRESENT TENSE   I *am* four years old, and I *am* terrified of the noise of the engines. My mother *drags* me down the aisle and *straps* me into my seat. Even the flight attendant's offer of a piece of gum *does* not *calm* me down. I *am* convinced that the monster *is going* to eat me.

PAST TENSE   I *was* four years old, and I *was* terrified of the noise of the engines. My mother *dragged* me down the aisle and *strapped* me into my seat. Even the flight attendant's offer of a piece of gum *did* not *calm* me down. I *was* convinced that the monster *was going* to eat me.

EXERCISE 1

Underline the verbs in each of the following sets of sentences. What time frame does each verb indicate: past, present, or future? Rewrite the sentences as necessary to make the time frame consistent in each set of sentences.

1. Since the 1920s, image-building has been used in cigarette advertising. At that time, women will start to smoke. Cigarette manufacturers want to encourage this trend and hoped to increase sales. The early advertisers are reluctant to show a woman smoking, so instead they picture a young woman asking a handsome young man, "Blow the smoke my way."

   _____

   _____

   _____

   _____

2. Buoyed by their success, manufacturers will try to reach weight-conscious women. Another 1920s ad suggests reaching for a cigarette instead of a sweet. The ads featured slim smokers and overweight nonsmokers. Such campaigns make smoking into a positive option for good health.

   _____

   _____

   _____

   _____

3. After World War II, cigarette companies employ psychologists. These experts researched ways to manipulate consumers' guilt, anxieties, and feelings of inadequacy. They also will design images connected with rewards and punishments.

_____

_____

_____

_____

4. Two famous advertisements play on snob appeal. They were promising purchasers the reward of enhanced sophistication. One is showing an aristocratic gentleman with a black eye patch. Another will show the smoker being rewarded with the company of a worldly-looking ex-officer in the British Navy.

_____

_____

_____

_____

5. Advertisements for other products threaten punishment if their product will be ignored. Soap ad customers usually are falling victim to this ploy. The person in the ad is sneered at by neighbors unless a particular detergent will be used.

_____

_____

_____

_____

EXERCISE J

For each numbered sentence, fill in the correct form of the verb. Show the pattern of time connections by a consistent use of verb tenses. If you use more than one verb tense, make sure there is a logical reason for doing so. You may use the verbs given in parentheses or use verbs of your own choice. Supply your own verbs in 8 through 10.

1. Our self-concepts (to represent) _____ our impressions of ourselves

   and our evaluation of our adequacy. They (to help) _____ us rate ourselves in terms of good–bad, intelligent–unintelligent, and strong–weak.

2. Carl Rogers (to state) _____ that we all (to have) _____ unique ways of looking at ourselves and the world. We (to judge)

   _____ ourselves according to different sets of values.

3. Rogers (to assume) _____ that we all (to develop) _____

   a need for self-esteem as we (to grow) _____. Self-esteem (to tend)

   _____ first to reflect the esteem in which others (to hold)

   _____ us.

4. Children in some families (to learn) _____ that it (to be)

   _____ bad to have ideas of their own. When they (to see)

   _____ their parents' disapproval, they (to see) _____

   themselves as rebels and (to label) _____ their feelings as selfish, wrong, or evil.

5. When we (to accept) _____ our feelings as our own, we (to

   experience) _____ psychological wholeness. There (to be)

   _____ a fit between our self-concepts and our behavior and
   emotions.

6. We should try to get in touch with our genuine feelings. Therapists (to help)

   _____ clients cope with the anxiety that (to go) _____
   with focusing on undesirable parts of the self.

7. We also (to have) _____ mental images of what we (to be)

   _____ capable of becoming. We (to need) _____ to
   reduce the difference between our self-concepts and our self-ideals.

8. The self-ideal _____ something like a carrot dangling from a stick strapped to a donkey's head. The donkey _____ to reach the carrot without recognizing that its own progress also _____ the carrot to advance.

9. We also _____ peak experiences. These experiences _____ brief moments of rapture that tell us that our actions _____ right for us.

10. What provides you with a peak experience may be meaningless to a friend or co-worker. An artist _____ a sketch that _____ his or her visual experience. A machinist _____ it in seeing a more efficient way to complete a task. We _____ a peak experience at the birth of our children or a major finding in our research.

● Consistency in Point of View

In writing a series of sentences, you must be consistent about the point of view you use. There are three points of view—the first person, the second person, and the third person.

With the first-person point of view, you focus the reader's attention on yourself, the writer or speaker, by using the first-person pronouns: *I, me, mine, my, we, us, ours, our.* The paragraph below is written from a *first-person point of view.*

My garden gives *me* many hours of enjoyment, even before *I* set foot in it. Early in the winter, *I* gather together *my* new seed catalogs and read about this year's developments in vegetables and flowers. Then *I* list the varieties *I* think *I'd* like to plant, usually two or three new ones each year plus a lot of *my* old favorites. *I* really enjoy planning *my* garden every winter.

With the second-person point of view, you focus attention on the audience—the person or persons being addressed—by using the pronouns *you, your,* and *yours.* The paragraph below is written from a *second-person point of view.*

You can begin to enjoy *your* garden even before *you* start to plant it. Gather up *your* seed catalogs early in the winter and read about the new vegetables and flowers developed in the last year. Then pick out a few that *you'd* like to plant along with *your* old favorites. *You* can then begin to anticipate *your* delicious rewards while snow is still on the ground.

With the third-person point of view, you focus attention on the subject you are discussing by using nouns that refer to the subject as well as the third-person pronouns: *he, she, it, him, her, his, hers, its, they, them, their, theirs*. Words like *anyone, someone, several,* and *each* are also third-person words. The paragraph below is written from a *third-person point of view.*

> An enthusiastic *gardener* enjoys *his* garden even before the planting season begins. *He or she* gathers up seed catalogs early in the winter to read about the latest developments in vegetables and flowers. Experienced *gardeners* usually try one or two new varieties each year along with *their* old favorites. For *them,* planning is as much fun as planting.

Which point of view you choose depends largely on the kind of relationship you want to have with your audience. The important thing is that you have to stick with a point of view once you have chosen it. Otherwise, your audience may become uncomfortable with your shifting perspective.

EXERCISE K

Identify the point of view in each sentence below. Then rewrite the sentence in the point of view indicated. Reword each sentence as necessary to change the point of view.

EXAMPLE:

If you exercise regularly, you are much less likely to suffer a heart attack.

second person (first person) *If I exercise regularly, I am much less likely to suffer a heart attack.*

1. If you start exercising as a child, it will be easier to stay active for the rest of your life. _____

   (third person) _____

   _____

2. Some people make vigorous physical activity an integral part of their everyday lives. _____

   (second person) _____

   _____

3. I played soccer when I was younger, but now cycling appeals to me more.

   _____

(third person) _____

_____

4. Instead of being a spectator, you should encourage yourself to participate in

    more physical activities. _____

    (first person) _____

_____

5. Most people think they should exercise more. _____

    (first person) _____

_____

EXERCISE L

On a separate sheet of paper, rewrite the following paragraphs so that each one maintains a consistent point of view.

1. Some people are dedicated to creation of their own stress. When studying physics, you may define stress as a force exerted on a body. Usually I think about that kind of stress in terms of types of physical stress. Psychological stresses also press, push or pull. You may feel crushed by the weight of a major decision. I may feel as though I am stretched to the point of snapping. Stress then is the demand made on people to adapt.

2. Pain and discomfort tax your ability to adjust. Athletes report that pain interferes with your ability to run even when the source of the pain does not directly weaken you. We can help ourselves by spacing painful tasks or chores as best we can.

3. Frustration is a source of stress. For adolescents, age is the barrier that requires you to delay drinking, working, driving. Therefore, we look at those years as a period of storm and stress. Older people sometimes set their goals too high. You may try too hard to earn other people's approval. You may try to be perfect at everything you do. Students sometimes judge themselves too harshly if their grades are not all As. A woman may fear moving up the corporate ladder and even turn down their promotion. We just have to learn to live with frustration.

4. Are you dedicated to the continuous creation of your own stress? If so, you are showing Type A behavior. Type A people are highly driven and deeply impatient. You feel rushed and under pressure. I am not only prompt but often early for appointments. We experience great frustration when stuck in a line. We would find it difficult to go to the tennis court just to bat balls around. We must be perfect and competent in everything we do.

▶ SENTENCE VARIETY

In the earlier chapters, you have seen that most sentences are built on a few patterns, all of which rely on the basic subject–verb unit:

subject–verb   S–V
Esperanza won.

subject–verb (passive)   S–V (passive)
The A.P.A. grant was awarded.

subject–verb–object complement   S–V–OC
Esperanza accepted the grant.

subject–linking verb–subject complement   S–LV–SC
Esperanza was excited.

When you begin to write a series of sentences, you need to think about varying the patterns occasionally. You can use variation to call attention to a particular point or just to make your writing more interesting to a reader.

For instance, look at the following series of related sentences:

Researchers questioned students.

These students did poorly in math.

They were convinced early in life that math was difficult.

Significant others told females that math was difficult for girls.

Students were told they should not expect to do well in math.

Many did not try to learn arithmetic well.

These negative statements had a profound effect.

Can you see how similar these sentences are? Every sentence is short; the longest is only twelve words. Every sentence begins with the subject, which is immediately followed by the verb. Although these sentences are perfectly correct and contain useful information, nothing in the series particularly stands out, and the sameness of the sentences could make the paragraph boring to read. What the paragraph could use is more variation in its sentence structure.

● Methods of Variation

■ *Variation 1: The Question*

A simple statement can be turned into a question in order to suggest uncertainty rather than certainty.

The nightmares stopped.

Have* the nightmares *stopped?

> The nightmares scared Niko.
>
> *Did* the nightmares scare Niko?
>
> Niko was scared by the nightmares.
>
> *Was* Niko scared by the nightmares?
>
> The nightmares were scary.
>
> *Were* the nightmares scary?

Notice that the question is formed by using a helping verb in front of the subject.

■ Variation 2: Reversing Word Order

You can call special attention to some part of a sentence by putting it out of its normal position. For instance,

> The patient was opposite the doctor.

could become

> Opposite the doctor was the patient.

In this second version, the descriptive word, *opposite* gets extra emphasis because it isn't where the reader would expect to find it.

Another example,

> An ugly beast was watching from the window.

could become

> Watching from the window was an ugly beast.

In this variation, the subject, *beast,* gets special emphasis. Again, the additional impact comes from the word's being out of its normal position.

■ Variation 3: Introducing or Interrupting the Base Sentence

You can call special attention to an adjective, adverb, or subordinate word group by using it to introduce or interrupt the base sentence. For instance,

> The analyst presented her case skillfully.

can become

> Skillfully, the analyst presented her case.

The second version calls more attention to *how* the analyst presented her case—*skillfully*—by opening the sentence with the adverb. The sentence

> The untrained analyst interpreted incorrectly.

can become

The analyst, untrained, interpreted incorrectly.

In the second version, the reader is forced to pause over the adjective *untrained,* and so it gets more emphasis. Notice that any construction that introduces or interrupts the base sentence is set off with commas.

Here is one way these techniques could be applied to the sentences on p. 250 so that the sentence patterns are more interesting.

> S   V   OC   interruption   V
> **Researchers questioned students *who did poorly in math* and found**
>
> **that these students had been convinced early in life that math was difficult.**
>
> Introduction
> ***When many females were told by significant others that math was difficult for***
>
> S   V
> ***girls,*** **they believed that they should not expect to do well in math.** *After*
>
> introduction   S   V
> *hearing these negative remarks,* **many did not try to learn arithmetic well, so**
>
> S   interruption   V   OC
> **these statements *made to young students* have a profound effect on their**
>
> **performance in math.**

Here the sentence patterns are varied by introductory and interrupting word groups. Because some sentences have been combined, there is also a greater variety in the lengths of the sentences.

Besides making your writing generally more interesting, variation can also be used to call attention to one point. When there are several sentences in a row that use the same pattern, one different sentence will stand out for the reader. For example, a short sentence following several long sentences will get more emphasis in a reader's mind.

Look at the way this paragraph uses sentence patterns:

> **The average West Point cadet has scored better on the S.A.T. than the average American college freshman.(17 words) More significantly, most cadets have been "A" students in high school, with one out of ten having been class valedictorian or salutatorian.(22 words) In one recent year, over 200 of the plebes had been Eagle Scouts.(13 words) Cadets are, in short, overachievers.(5 words)**

The last sentence in this paragraph should get the reader's full attention because its pattern is significantly different from the sentences that came before it.

● Repetition

It is also possible to use pattern repetition to emphasize a point, if the point is that two ideas are quite similar or quite different. For instance, look at the way repetition is used here:

> My two uncles are completely different in temperament. *While Bob is* thoughtful and slow to show emotion, *Randy tends* to speak his feelings before he has thought about them. *While Bob is* home-loving and has never been farther than fifty miles from home, *Randy* is a wanderer who has visited forty states and six foreign countries. Most telling of all, *while Bob has* few friends and keeps mainly to himself, *Randy is* always accompanied by half a dozen of the friends he has acquired in his travels. How can twin brothers be so different?

(Notice how variation is used in the last sentence. A question stands out from all the direct statements.)

The important thing to remember in using any variation of the basic sentence pattern is:

NEVER WRITE A SENTENCE THAT WILL CONFUSE YOUR READER.

EXERCISE M

Write one variation for each basic sentence below. Try to use all the patterns of variation in this exercise: the question, reversing word order, and introducing or interrupting the base sentence. You may need to add onto the base sentence.

EXAMPLE:

A newborn child benefits from a stimulating environment.

Does a newborn child benefit from a stimulating environment?

1. An eight-week-old baby frequently exercises the skill of focusing.

2. Tracing family histories suggests that artistic ability is inborn.

3. Babies develop their own timetable for walking or crawling.

4. How the parents act toward a child determines how the child develops.

5. Children need to gain a sense of security.

6. Two-year-olds often prefer toys to one another.

---

7. Four-year-olds play almost always in groups.

---

8. Parents use a system of giving rewards for acceptable behavior.

---

9. Can most people reach their potential?

---

10. Research has shown the existence of different kinds of intelligences.

EXERCISE N
Rewrite the following paragraphs on a separate sheet of paper so the sentences show more variety in length and structure.

1. A dreamer awakens. He has had a dream. He gets information from his dream. He cannot be honest with himself. He is more honest while dreaming. He views himself cautiously. He tests his own ability. Information is in the dream imagery.

2. Dream appreciation can be accessible to everyone. Parents and teachers can use dreams. Children's dreams offer an honest connection. Counselors in halfway houses can use dream work. Senior citizens can open up new aspects in dream work.

REVIEW	
Basic Sentence Patterns	
S–V	Freud frowned.
S–V–OC	The patient was observing him.
S–V (passive)	He was observed by the patient.
S–LV–SC	Freud's anger was deep.
Variations	
Question	Was Freud's anger deep?
Reversal	Observing him was the patient.
Introduction	Deeply angry, Freud frowned.
Interruption	Freud, deeply angry, frowned.

Exercise O

Using a separate sheet of paper, combine each of the following sets of sentences to produce an effective paragraph. You may use any form of modification, coordination, or subordination in putting together your paragraphs. You may follow the suggested groupings of ideas, or you may set up groups of your own. Either way, be sure that your finished paragraph uses verb tenses and pronouns consistently. Also try to use appropriate repetition and variation of sentence patterns.

Men and Their Feelings

1. Men still do not share.
   The sharing is of feelings.
2. Men have companions.
   Men have buddies.
   Men have pals.
   They do not have someone to tell how they feel.
3. Women say they do not know the men.
   The men are people they live with.
   They talk of long silences.
   They talk of keeping feelings hidden.
4. Men are like this with other men.
   Men suffer setbacks.
   Men have problems in their families.
   They pretend otherwise.
5. Children think men have real friends.
   Children believe women do not have real friends.
6. Men feel uncomfortable.
   The feeling occurs when feelings are discussed.
7. Men and women have problems in common.
   Sharing feelings will help.

Creativity

1. Creativity is in every human being.
   All people have a need for self-expression.
   The urge is universal.
2. Everyone has tried to translate thoughts and feelings.
   The thoughts and feelings are innermost.
   The translation is into a visible outward form.
3. A small child may write in chalk on the street.
   A singer might perform.
   A cook might make an exceptional pudding.
4. A first-rate story could be fresh.
   A first-rate story could be valuable.
5. Every act could be a creative achievement.
   The act shows talent.
   The act shows inventiveness.
   The act shows originality.

6. To be human is to yield to the urge.
   The urge is of self-expression.

Hypnosis

1. Hypnosis is derived from the Greek word for sleep.
   Hypnosis has useful applications.
   Hypnosis is not sleep.
   It is a trance state.
2. Hypnosis is used as an anesthetic.
   The anesthetic is for dentistry.
   The anesthetic is for childbirth.
   The anesthetic is for surgery.
3. Surgeons have used hypnosis.
   A man had his leg amputated.
   The amputation was without discomfort.
4. Psychologists use hypnosis.
   Their use is to help teach.
   Clients are taught to relax.
   Clients are helped to imagine vivid imagery.
5. Police use hypnosis.
   Their use is to prompt memories.
   The memories are of witnesses.
6. Some people have high hypnotic suggestibility.
   These people enjoy daydreaming.
   These people have vivid imaginations.
7. Many people are unsure about hypnosis.
   The concept of hypnosis cannot be explained.
   The explanation is not adequate.

EDITING PRACTICE:
Review the following paragraphs for any errors in using the sentence patterns you have learned. Be sure that all sentences are complete and correctly punctuated. Make sure there are no inconsistencies in point of view or verb tense that might distract a reader. See that pronouns are used correctly. On a separate sheet of paper, rewrite each paragraph to correct any sentence problems you find.

1. Many people relax by meditating. You actually alter the relationship between yourself and your environment. Planning, worry, and problem-solving will be suspended. Meditators have reported that you merge with the object of meditation or a repeated phrase. They transcend the focus and became one with the universe. Psychology has no way to measure oneness with the universe, but psychologists will measure bodily changes. You can induce bodily changes by meditation. The blood pressure of people with hypertension decreased. Meditators will produce more frequent alpha waves. These brain waves are associated with relaxation. They also will show lower heart and respiration rates. Just taking time out might be helpful for all of us.

2. Psychologists once believed that one's memory was fixed. You had a good or poor memory, and you were stuck with it. Now they will know that there are ways to improve our memories. The first one is called the method of loci. You select a series of related images to attach to your shopping list, for example. The person actually combines several items into one chunk of information. Another method of improving your memory is the method of mediation. People link two items with a third that ties them together. If these methods do not work, try mnemonics. This method helps you chunk pieces of information into a format. The format itself, like a jingle, helps the person remember the items. There are several other methods, but I have forgotten them.

WRITING PRACTICE:

1. You are about to leave Earth for a newly established moon colony. Because of limited space, you are allowed to take only one personal item with you to your new home. Write a statement of 200 words or less for the NASA archives explaining what item you have decided to take and why the item will be good for your mental health. Before composing the statement, you may want to explore your choices in a private journal entry. After you have composed a draft of your statement, check your writing (or have a classmate check it) to see that your sentences are sufficiently varied and that they are complete, consistent, and correctly punctuated.

2. It is now thirty years after you joined the moon colony. The colony has prospered and so has your family. You now have several lovely grandchildren who, unfortunately, know very little about your home planet, Earth, and its customs. Because you don't want knowledge of the old traditions to die out completely, you have decided to write a book for your grandchildren and great-grandchildren about your memories of Earth. Prepare a short article for your book about some traditional celebration that you were familiar with on Earth—for instance, Thanksgiving or the Fourth of July.

Before writing, try to recreate the celebration in your mind. Make notes about the sights, sounds, smells, and tastes associated with this celebration. See if you can focus your article to create one dominant impression of the scene.

After you have composed a draft of your article, check your writing (or have a classmate check it) to see if your sentences are sufficiently varied and if they are complete, consistent, and correctly punctuated.

◆ Part II ◆

Basic Paragraph Patterns

A sentence, clear and well-constructed, can be a very useful tool for communicating ideas. Through the use of modification (adjectives and adverbs), coordination, and subordination, all of which are presented in Part One of this book, you can express some fairly complicated ideas and also show a precise relationship between one idea and another within the same sentence.

However, sentences do have limits. If you try to squeeze too much information into one sentence, you can easily confuse or distract your readers. If you try to relate too many ideas within a single sentence, your readers may not be able to figure out which idea you really want them to pay the most attention to. So the paragraph—a series of sentences carefully developing one idea—can be even more useful than a single sentence for sharing your idea with someone else.

Part Two of this book presents a basic model for paragraphing and then shows you some strategies for arranging the ideas that go into paragraphs. You will also have a chance to practice shaping paragraphs from series of sentences.

◀ *Chapter 7* ▶

Basic Paragraph Structure

• • • • • • • • • • • • •

▶ BASIC PATTERN
▶ LEVELS OF GENERALITY
▶ TOPIC SENTENCE
▶ SUPPORT
▶ CONCLUSION
▶ FROM PARAGRAPH TO ESSAY

• • • • • • • • • • • • •

In some ways, paragraph structure is an extension of sentence structure. In a sentence, one subject–verb unit serves as the focus, and all the other ideas are arranged around it. In a paragraph, one sentence gives the focus, and all the other sentences are arranged to explain, expand, and generally clarify that idea.

▶ BASIC PATTERN

Although there are many possible forms for a paragraph, in this book you will concentrate on one basic pattern for paragraph construction: a *topic sentence,* which focuses the main idea; *support,* an arrangement of subordinate ideas; and a *conclusion,* which coordinates with the topic sentence by restating the focus.

PARAGRAPH STRUCTURE		
TOPIC SENTENCE	← SUPPORT ← SUPPORT ← SUPPORT	CONCLUSION

Here is a typical paragraph that uses the pattern of a topic sentence, followed by supporting detail, followed by a concluding sentence.

(main idea)	According to our study, the legends of Hina portray women as stubborn.
(supporting details)	For instance, when the moon is full, Hina can be seen in the dark markings continuing to beat her tapa cloth. She will not stop. Moreover, her accidentally breaking a branch of the tree which then fell through space and became the first banyan tree is the result of her endless beating of tapa cloth even through eternity. Originally, villagers killed Hina because of her stubborn refusal to stop beating the tapa cloth she wanted to use to make the god Ta'aroa a cloak. Ta'aroa was bothered by Hina's noise, but she had refused to stop.
(restatement of main idea)	She died but in the many versions of the Hina legend, Hina is still busy with her tapa board and mallet.

In this paragraph, which is being used to summarize a longer report, the focus idea is stated in the topic sentence. Then three reasons, which are supports to the topic sentence, are given to show why the focus idea is valid. Finally, the conclusion, referring back to the topic sentence, restates the main point in slightly different words.

▶ LEVELS OF GENERALITY

To construct this kind of paragraph, you need to understand how ideas relate to one another on a scale of generality. To borrow some mathematical terms, you can think of "books," for example, as a set that includes many members. However, "books" itself is but one member of a larger set of "reading material," which includes even more members than the set "books." "Reading material," therefore, is more general than "books" because it includes more members. Likewise, "novels" is one member of the set "books." Although you may have a set called "novels," that set will not have as many members as the set called "books." "Novels," therefore, is more specific than "books" because it has fewer members in its set. The following chart illustrates one example of such a scale of generality.

Levels of Generality

3	4	5	6	7 etc.
	More General ⟷ More Specific			
	Newspapers	→ Novels	Nigerian	→ Hemingway's
	Magazines	Biographies	Russian	Faulkner's
Reading Material	→ Books	Encyclopedias	→ American	Twain's
	Signs	Legends	Spanish	Wharton's
	Cereal boxes	etc.	Japanese	etc.
	etc.		etc.	

In writing a paragraph, you are moving back and forth on a scale of generality. Your topic sentence makes a relatively general statement. Your support moves across the scale one or two levels. And then your conclusion moves back to the level of your topic sentence. Another way you might visualize your paragraph is something like this:

Levels of Generality

More General ←   11   12   13   14   → More Specific

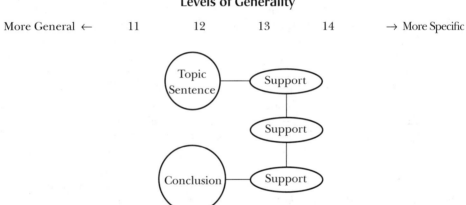

When you have mastered this form of paragraphing, you may wish to develop other paragraph structures, as many professional writers do. In the meantime, however, this basic three-part paragraph can be used for many different kinds of writing, from letters to term papers to professional reports.

EXERCISE A

Supply an appropriate term for each blank in the following scales of generality.

1. Living things → _____ → dogs → Great Danes → my dog Metro →

   _____ → Metro's cute pointy ears

2. _____ → grains → wheat → _____ → a slice of whole wheat
   bread

3. Means of transportation → _____ → Fords → _____ → the

   mechanical systems of my car → _____

4. Government → _____ → legislative branch → Senate → Senator

   Goodtime → _____ → _____

5. _____ → Christian → _____ → Presbyterian →

   _____ → Rev. Brimstone → Rev. Brimstone's knowledge

Exercise B

Identify the topic sentence, support sentences, and conclusion in each of these student paragraphs. Be prepared to explain how these parts relate to each other on a scale of generality.

1. Although eyeglasses were invented in the thirteenth century, the problem of how to keep them on comfortably wasn't solved until nearly 350 years later. The first spectacles, two lenses in metal or leather frames attached in an inverted V-shape, balanced on the bridge of the nose. These spectacles pinched the nose, and wearers had to hold their heads at an odd angle to keep the contraption from falling off. By the fifteenth century, the Italians had rigged a wire hat with the glasses dangling down over the forehead. The Spanish later experimented with silk ribbons that tied behind the wearer's ears. The Chinese attached small weights to strings that ran behind the ears. Around 1730, a London optician named Edward Scarlett perfected the use of rigid sidepieces. Finally, eyeglass wearers could enhance their vision in comfort.

2. My first day of college left me thoroughly confused. I drove around the campus for what seemed like hours before locating a parking space. Then I had to dig out my campus map to figure out where I was and where I had to go for my first class. Heading in what looked like the right direction, I soon reached the main highway without catching a glimpse of anything that looked like the Farrell Building. When I asked a group of students for directions, I got three conflicting sets of instructions on how to find the place. I finally stumbled into the right building through sheer luck, only to find a sign on the classroom door announcing that the class had been moved to some building that wasn't even shown on my campus map. Thoroughly bewildered, I decided to return to the parking lot and start over. I haven't felt so confused since I was lost in a shopping mall at the age of five.

▶ TOPIC SENTENCE

The topic sentence in a paragraph has two main purposes: to identify the subject of the paragraph and to show the focus you are going to use in discussing that subject. Look at the topic sentence in the sample paragraph at the beginning of this chapter. What is the subject of the paragraph, according to the topic sentence? *The legends of Hina.* That subject could be written about from a number of different angles: other women in legends from Tahiti, Hina's relationships to men in the legends, Hina compared with women in other legends about the moon. But, in a paragraph, you really can't do justice to more than one of these. You have to choose one aspect to focus on. What focus does this sentence give for the subject? *Portray women as stubborn.* In other words, the topic sentence tells the reader right away what to expect from this paragraph. It will present the ways in which Hina is stubborn.

SUBJECT + FOCUS = TOPIC SENTENCE

EXERCISE C
Circle the subject and underline the focus of each of the following topic sentences.

1. Myths tell how others have made the passage through life.

2. The earliest evidence of anything like myths is connected with graves.

3. Guilt, especially about killing an animal, is wiped out by the myth.

4. The Blackfoot tribe tell of the buffalo fall in a myth about a young girl.

5. The aborigines in Australia tear the young boys from their mothers to tell them the mythology of the tribe.

6. Myths can sanctify a local landscape more than a ritual can.

7. Because woman gives birth and nourishment, in the early tradition she is the first planter.

8. An Algonquin story about the origin of maize tells of a boy having a vision.

9. A similar story, coming up throughout Polynesia, is about a girl who loves to bathe in a certain pool.

10. More than any other goal, getting back into the Garden is the aim of the myth.

As you were doing the exercise above, you may have observed some characteristics of topic sentences. The following box shows some important qualities of a useful topic sentence.

TOPIC SENTENCES

1. A TOPIC SENTENCE MUST BE A COMPLETE SENTENCE, NOT A FRAGMENT.
2. A TOPIC SENTENCE IS USUALLY A DIRECT STATEMENT, NOT A QUESTION.
3. THE SUBJECT OF THE TOPIC SENTENCE IS USUALLY THE SUBJECT IDEA OF THE PARAGRAPH.
4. THE VERB AND COMPLEMENT OF THE TOPIC SENTENCE USUALLY SHOW THE FOCUS OF THE PARAGRAPH.
5. THE FOCUS PART OF THE TOPIC SENTENCE USUALLY PRESENTS A JUDGMENT OR ATTITUDE ABOUT THE SUBJECT.
6. A SUBORDINATE WORD GROUP IS SOMETIMES USED IN THE TOPIC SENTENCE TO DEFINE THE FOCUS STILL FURTHER.

EXERCISE D

Keeping in mind the characteristics shown above, combine each of the following sets of sentences into one effective topic sentence. Identify the subject and focus of each topic sentence.

Compare your topic sentences with those of your classmates and discuss any differences in wording or arrangement. Does one version of the sentence seem better to you than another? Can you explain why?

EXAMPLE:

    Myths give accounts.
    The giving is often.
    The accounts are about a creation.
    The creation has the Sacred.
    The Sacred breaks through.

Myths often give accounts about a creation that has the Sacred break through.

or

Accounts about the Sacred breaking through in a creation are often given by myths.

1. Myths are stories.
   The stories are true.
   Myths are sacred.
   Myths are exemplary.
   Myths are significant.

---

2. Models are offered.
   The models are for activities.
   The activities are human.
   The activities are significant.
   The offering is by myths.

---

3. The beginning is told.
   The beginning is of death.
   The explanation is told.
   The explanation is of mortality.
   The explanation is by myths.
   The telling is by myths.

---

4. Myths have told.
   The myths were about origins.
   The telling was of how the world changed.
   The telling was of how time was a circle.
   This has happened for thousands of years.

---

5. Myths explain.
   The explaining is that sicknesses appear.
   Myths also tell.
   The telling is of the ways.
   The ways are how sicknesses can be remedied.

---

6. Myths are rendered.
   The myths are about the trickster.
   The rendering is with humor.
   They try to describe.
   The description is of extraordinary experiences.
   They use images.
   The images are of human yearnings.

   _____

   _____

7. The ceremony is in Fiji.
   The ceremony is called.
   The ceremony belongs to the king.
   The ceremony is of his enthronement.
   It is called creation.
   The creation is of the world.

   _____

   _____

8. The coronation was regarded.
   The coronation was of a pharaoh.
   The pharaoh was new.
   The pharaoh was in Egypt.
   The regarding was as the creation.
   The creation was of an epoch.
   The epoch was new.

   _____

   _____

9. The inauguration is taking place.
   The taking place is at New Year's.
   The inauguration begins.
   The beginning is of Creation.
   The Creation is over again.

   _____

   _____

10. The aborigines are in Australia.
    The aborigines repaint.

The repainting is of the rock paintings.
The rock paintings are in Kimberley.
They repaint to reactivate.
The reactivation is of their force.
The force is creative.
The force is mythical.

● Limiting the Subject and Focus

Each of the topic sentences below contains some sort of a subject and a focus but one of each pair presents these two basic parts more clearly than the other. Which one in each pair gives the reader a clearer idea of what to expect in the paragraph that will follow?

1. I like myths.
    My favorite Navajo myth is about the creation of the first man and first woman.

2. The Aleut myth is nice.
    The Aleut myth called "The Fight for a Wife" portrays a young man throwing his rival into a pit of shaman worms.

3. Native American myths are interesting.
    I like Native American myths that have hair-raising trials of endurance to test a commitment.

4. Legends about war are interesting.
    In the ancient legends, men rode into war with protective medicine bundles, miracle-working pebbles, or medicine shields—all intended to make the wearer arrow-proof.

5. The Blackfoot idea of death is better than the Caddo legend.
    The Blackfoot Old Man sees death as a component of life when he fashions the first men and women whereas Coyote in the Caddo legend encounters death as a whirlwind.

In each case, you should have noticed that the second topic sentence gives the reader a more precise statement of the subject and the focus than the first topic sentence. Words like *nice, interesting,* and *better* don't work very well to focus an idea because they suggest so many different meanings that a reader isn't really sure what to focus on. Similarly, a broad subject like *Native American myths* or *legends about war* doesn't help your reader understand which particular aspect of that topic you want to tell about.

The terms of a topic sentence have to be placed very carefully on the scale of generality. Your subject and focus have to be general enough that they can include details from a more specific level, but not so general that they can't be dealt with adequately in a paragraph. A single paragraph usually starts near the more specific end of the scale rather than near the more general end.

Exercise E

Rewrite the word groups below so that each one is a topic sentence with a clearly limited subject and a well-defined focus.

1. Hurricanes are better than tornadoes.

   _____

2. A time when Icarus made a funny mistake.

   _____

3. He is a mean man.

   _____

4. Exchanging an article of clothing.

   _____

5. That myth is a nice story.

   _____

6. Why should you work in the old manuscript department?

   _____

7. Heroines are great.

   _____

8. Heroes are interesting.

   _____

9. An African myth is different from mine.

   _____

10. That quest sounds good.

    _____

11. I don't like myths about the trickster.

    _____

12. The heroine's castle was pretty neat.

_____

13. That monster was terrible.

_____

14. The worst way to read a myth.

_____

15. Can you appreciate stories with unhappy endings?

_____

▶ SUPPORT

The second important part of a paragraph is the support. You write a paragraph so that someone else can understand and perhaps accept your idea. Therefore, you have to do more than just present a general statement of your idea. You have to move to a more specific level of reasons, explanations, or examples that will clarify the idea for your reader.

For example, the paragraph on Hina shown earlier in the chapter doesn't just keep making coordinate statements:

> **Hina legends portray women as stubborn.**
>
> **Hina legends show women as being obstinate.**
>
> **Hina legends portray a negative image of women.**

Instead, it moves from a general statement that legends of Hina portray women as stubborn to specific, subordinate details of her image when the moon is full, her creation of the banyan tree, and her stubbornness causing her death.

Just as subordinate parts of a sentence help to clarify and define the base sentence, so does the support part of a paragraph help to clarify and explain the topic.

Read the topic sentence below. Then look at the student paragraphs that follow. Which paragraph more effectively supports the topic sentence?

Roberto Montoya deserves to receive this year's Citizen of the Year Award.

A. For one thing, Bob is an all-around nice guy. There is really no better choice for this award. Bob is always willing to help. He is a special person. Besides his good personal qualities, Bob has worked hard for our community too. He has served

B. Since being elected to the City Council three years ago, Bob has worked tirelessly for our community's interests. He established a tax credit system for the elderly and made sure we got an appropriate share of the library and the town well through his many public activities. Bob has worked for the community's interests at the state level too. The town of Bradley can be proud of an outstanding man like Roberto Montoya.

recreation funds. Bob has been the leader in our fight to have the Interstate rerouted around our community. Besides his public work, Bob has also served us in a private capacity. He devotes many hours to coaching soccer and teaching camping skills to the scout troops.

Because of his many years of public and private service to our community, Roberto Montoya should be named Citizen of the Year.

What differences do you see in the kind of support provided in the two paragraphs above?

Paragraph A provides almost no specific detail to back up the nomination of Montoya. Most of the sentences stay on the same level. Paragraph B, on the other hand, moves to a more specific level to mention five of Montoya's particular contributions to the community, such as his legislation and his coaching activities.

Paragraph B, then, shows two important qualities of support: there should be enough support, without padding, to make your point convincingly (the more difficult the point, the more support is needed), and it should be as specific and as factual as possible. A few vague generalizations will not make your ideas clear to an audience.

Topic sentences tend to present attitudes or opinions about which people may disagree. Support, on the other hand, tends to be more substantial. The details used for support may be observable by your senses, such as what a person looks like or sounds like. Or you may use the events of your own life and those of your family and friends to support some idea. Or you may use the written experiences of others for support. (Historical fact and the attitudes of experts in various fields, for instance, are frequently presented in books and magazines, which are good sources of support.)

Exercise F

Decide which sentences in the following list would be appropriate statements of factual support and which are statements of opinion. Where would you place these statements on a scale of generality? Be prepared to explain your choices.

1. Hodja, the hero of Turkish tales, probably lived during the thirteenth century.
2. Hodja is viewed by the Turkish people as a culture hero.
3. Many of the early Hodja stories were coarse and off-color.
4. Hoca is another term for Hodja.
5. Tamerlane had already invaded and was approaching Aksehir.
6. The people believed that the hoca, a trickster, could do something to help protect them.
7. The hoca had the people build a huge camelskin tent outside the city walls.
8. The hoca took off all his clothes except for a bright-orange turban.
9. He climbed on top of fifteen overstuffed mattresses.
10. The hoca told an advance guard of Tamerlane, "I am the God of Earth."

11. Seeing the audacity of the man standing naked, the guard slithered back to Tamerlane's army.
12. The hoca was later asked to do a miracle or have his head chopped off.
13. The hoca seemed unafraid of the cruel sultan.
14. He claimed he could not violate his agreement with the God of the Sky.
15. The hoca won with a crude summary statement.

EXERCISE G

For each topic sentence shown below, check off the three best supporting details from the list under it. Be prepared to explain your choices.

1. In Chinese mythology, creation was the act of reducing chaos to order.

_____ Shu and Hu used to meet halfway in the territory of Hun-tun.

_____ To thank Hun-tun, Shu and Hu decided to give Hun-tun one opening a day for seven days.

_____ Hun-tun could then see, hear, eat, and breathe.

_____ Hun-tun's name means Chaos.

_____ Hun-tun died at the same moment the world came into being.

2. From the various parts of Phan-ku's body came different natural elements.

_____ All the mountains came from his head.

_____ The sun and moon came from his eyes.

_____ The rivers and seas came from his flesh.

_____ The plants came from his hair.

_____ Another version says his sweat was the rain and the fleas on his body became the human race.

3. The origins of climatic change, the cycle of seasons, and day and night rest upon a dragon.

_____ A monster Kung Kung damaged a mountain and tore a hole in the sky.

_____ The flaming dragon had a human face and a dragon's body.

_____ The dragon's exhaling is winter; its inhaling is summer.

_____ When the dragon stops breathing there is neither rain nor wind; when it resumes breathing the wind blows.

_____   When its eyes are open it is day; when they are closed it is night.

4. The goddess Nu-kua created human beings.

_____   Nu-kua tried to repair the damage done by Kung Kung.

_____   Nu-kua set about modeling people out of yellow earth.

_____   The process was tedious, so to speed up, she dipped a rope into the mud and trailed it about so that drops fell off.

_____   From the modeled specimens came the rich and the noble.

_____   Those who dripped from the muddy rope were the humble and the poor.

_____   How did the crippled come to Earth?

5. A Chinese myth explains why oxen exist on Earth.

_____   The Emperor of Heaven sent the Ox star to tell people that if they worked hard, then they would always be able to eat every third day.

_____   The Jade Emperor was afraid the humans would eat the ox's flesh.

_____   Mistakenly, the Ox told them they should eat three times a day.

_____   Since he had made a mistake, the Ox was sent back to help with the plowing.

_____   With just human hands and feet, they would not be able to prepare sufficient food.

EXERCISE H

Each topic sentence below makes a general statement about a subject. Supply three more specific details that could support each topic sentence.

EXAMPLE:

Several of my friends have started to look like their pets.
A. Catherine → cat Juliet
B. Juan → dog Tobias
C. Kobe → dog Fiji

1. Our downtown area has several interesting historic buildings.

A. _____

B. _____

C. _____

2. Doing team sports is not always good for teenagers.

    A. _____

    B. _____

    C. _____

3. Today's movies are presenting a more positive (*or* negative) image of the family than those of a few years ago.

    A. _____

    B. _____

    C. _____

4. Three distinct types of instructors teach at our college.

    A. _____

    B. _____

    C. _____

5. My uncle is (*or* is not) a very organized person.

    A. _____

    B. _____

    C. _____

6. The success of my favorite team (name) depended on the work of several key players.

    A. _____

    B. _____

    C. _____

7. My wardrobe reflects my personality.

    A. _____

    B. _____

    C. _____

8. To be effective with teenagers, youth workers need three basic qualities.

    A. _____

    B. _____

    C. _____

9. Owning a home is too expensive for most young couples.

    A. _____

    B. _____

    C. _____

10. A successful wedding reception is easy if you plan ahead.

    A. _____

    B. _____

    C. _____

▶ CONCLUSION

The final part of paragraph structure is the concluding sentence. This sentence should bring the discussion of the main idea to a close by returning to the general level of the subject and the focus of the paragraph. For example, in the paragraph on Hina presented earlier, the topic sentence states: "The legends of Hina portray women as stubborn." The conclusion coordinates by restating that idea in slightly different language: ". . . she is still busy with her tapa board and mallet."

The conclusion also brings the discussion to a close by means of the phrase "in the many versions of the Hina legend," which asks the reader to recall the arguments that have been made.

Notice the relationship between the topic sentence and the conclusion of the Montoya paragraph earlier in this chapter:

TOPIC SENTENCE   **Roberto Montoya deserves to receive this year's Citizen of the Year Award.**

CONCLUSION   **Because of his many years of public and private service to our community, Roberto Montoyo should be named Citizen of the Year.**

The conclusion repeats the key words of the topic sentence and uses the phrase "because of his many years of public and private service to our community" to sum up the points made in the paragraph. The conclusion moves back to the same level of generality as the topic sentence.

EXERCISE I

From the list below, select a concluding sentence that would fit with each topic sentence given. Write your choice for a conclusion underneath each topic sentence. Be prepared to explain the relationship between each topic sentence and conclusion.

Concluding Sentences

Antigone disobeys the king's order and buries her brother.

The entire Greek army sailed to Troy to rescue Helen.

Medusa's murderer was able to aim his sword by looking at her reflection in a shield.

Antigone is condemned to death for her decision.

Giving the answer to the riddle, Oedipus finally put the beast to rest.

Women sometimes complain that they look like Medusa when they have become victims of an inept hairstylist.

Perhaps running around as swine was the crew's worst spell.

Circe, a powerful sorceress, turned the crew into swine.

Many travelers to Thebes were killed because they could not figure out the riddle.

Helen's face was "the face that launched a thousand ships."

1. Medusa had the power to turn people who looked at her to stone.

   Conclusion: _____

_____

2. Paris abducted the most beautiful woman in the world, Helen of Troy.

   Conclusion: _____

   _____

3. Antigone is torn between human laws and the laws of the gods.

   Conclusion: _____

   _____

4. Odysseus's crew fell prey to several women.

   Conclusion: _____

   _____

5. In the story of *Oedipus,* the sphinx with the head of a woman and the body of a
   lion threatened people with her famous riddle.

   Conclusion: _____

   _____

EXERCISE J
Study the following paragraphs, particularly the topic sentences, and then try to
write for each one a concluding sentence that coordinates with the topic sentence.

   1. Even if you are a nonmechanic you can do some things to keep your car
running efficiently. For one thing, you can check the oil level. First, pull the dip-
stick out of the engine and wipe it off with a rag. Then put it back in the engine
again. This time, when it is pulled out, see where the oil level is on the stick. If it
is low, add however many quarts of oil it will take to make it full. Another thing you
can check is the water level in the radiator. First, make sure the radiator is not hot
when you take the cap off. As long as the water level is within one inch of the top
of the radiator, it is fine. Finally, you can make sure the tires are properly inflated.
Most gas stations have an air pump. Set the air pump for the number of pounds of
pressure shown on your tires. When the bell on the pump stops ringing, your tires
are fully inflated.

_____

_____

_____

2. Our inspection team found incredibly unsanitary conditions at Fred's Restaurant. The counters and floors were littered with scraps of meat and vegetables, some of which were starting to rot. The garbage cans were uncovered and overflowing. Insects and rodent droppings were discovered in several boxes of flour and crackers. Milk and butter were left standing at room temperature because the refrigeration system was broken. The kitchen staff did not observe the hand-washing rule.

_____

_____

_____

3. As I looked out over the huge audience, I was overwhelmed with nervousness. First, my throat became clogged, and no amount of coughing could clear it. Then my hands began to shake. When I tried to steady myself against the podium, I just succeeded in scattering the pages of my speech across the stage. I thought my legs would collapse as I tried to collect the pages. Once I finally began to speak, my voice was so soft it could hardly be heard over the loud BA-BOOMP of my heart.

_____

_____

_____

4. Fernandina Beach in October can still be a great vacation spot. You don't have to worry about not finding a room. All the major motels stay open year round. And most of them offer big discounts for late fall visitors, sometimes as much as 50 percent. You can also find good prices on resort clothes in the fall. Your savings on next summer's wardrobe could finance another vacation next fall. During the fall, too, the cool weather is perfect for exhilarating walks along the ocean. And, perhaps best of all, you won't have to share all these benefits with a crowd of other vacationers.

_____

_____

_____

5. If your child doesn't seem to respond to your questions, perhaps you need to raise the level of the conversation. First-level conversations begin with a question that asks for a factual reply: "Do you have any homework, dear?" There's no real opportunity for give-and-take here. The second level of conversation asks for opinions: "Did you like that movie?" This kind of question can lead to a more interesting discussion since more thought is required to reply. However, the third level, abstraction, can lead to the most rewarding conversations because it requires the use of imagination. "What do you think it would be like to be a pilot?" This level offers a chance for stimulating discussion both for your child and for you.

_____

_____

_____

EXERCISE K

Using a separate sheet of paper, combine each set of sentences below to produce a paragraph with a well-defined topic sentence, specific support, and a conclusion that echoes the topic sentence. In each paragraph you will be asked to supply one part.

Overcoming

Topic Sentence: You supply this.
Support:
    Mpaca attached himself.
    The attachment was to Nturo's back.
    Nturo wanted to commit suicide.
    Nturo hid.
    Her hiding was in a snail shell.
    Nturo made beer.
    The beer was drunk by Mpaca.
    He was drunk.
    He fell asleep.
    Nturo slashed.
    The slashing was of Mpaca's throat.
Conclusion: Do not consider suicide.

The Theft of Fire

Topic Sentence:
    Maui is the hero.
    The hero is great.
    The hero is Polynesian.
    The hero is responsible.
    The responsibility is for snaring.
    The snaring is of the sun.
Support:
    Maui sat.
    The sitting was by a tree.
    The tree was a wiliwili.

He tied the legs.

The legs were of the sun.

The tying was to the tree trunk.

The sun compromised.

Maui compromised.

The sun will go.

The going will be fast.

The going will be for six months.

The going will be slow.

The going will be for six months.

Human beings benefited.

Conclusion: You supply this.

My Favorite Storytellers

Topic Sentence:

Storytellers are relatives.

The storytellers are my favorites.

They are relatives of mine.

There are three storytellers.

Support: You supply three examples to support the topic sentence.

Conclusion:

Reunions are my favorite time.

The reunions are of the family.

The time is of the year.

These happen with all the storytellers present.

EXERCISE L

Using a separate sheet of paper, combine the group of sentences below to produce a paragraph that follows the topic sentence–support–conclusion format. When you have finished, you will have the first of a pair of paragraphs. Using this one as a guide, write the second paragraph on your own.

A shepherd pretended.

The pretension was about wolves.

The wolves were attacking.

The attack was of his sheep.

The villagers rushed.

The rushing was to his aid.

The shepherd laughed.

The laughing was at the villagers.

Then this happened one day.

The wolves came.

The coming was actual.

▶ FROM PARAGRAPH TO ESSAY

Longer pieces of writing are built on the same basic principles as single paragraphs. In many ways, an essay is just a larger version of a paragraph. Just as you related individual sentences in a paragraph, moving from general to specific to general, so you relate paragraphs to one another in an essay.

In an essay, you still need to provide your reader with a general statement of your subject and the focus you are taking on this subject (a *thesis*). You also need to move to a more specific level and provide examples, reasons, and details to explain your point about this subject. At the end of an essay, you need to restate the general point you made in your writing.

Here is a student essay of several paragraphs that follows the pattern of introducing the subject with a thesis, supporting it, and then summarizing the main idea.

thesis (focuses main idea)	For two months, I could think only about getting a divorce. However, being divorced has caused me financial, emotional, and parenting problems that I did not have to face when I was married.
support (presents subordinate details)	Since the divorce, my financial situation has certainly changed. Before, I could depend on my husband's salary to pay the rent, buy groceries, and clothe the three of us. The extra money that I made as a part-time bookkeeper could be used for extras like a vacation or new dining room chairs. However, since Ben and I separated, my full-time salary is barely enough to rent a small apartment, buy groceries and gasoline, and pay for babysitting for my son, Mark.
	The financial strain has not made my emotional adjustment to divorce any easier, either. The divorce raised all kinds of frightening questions for me about my value as a person. Instead of Ben telling me that I'm lovable, I have to convince myself that I am. The loneliness is hard, too. There's no one but my four-year-old to confide my problems to. I often feel depressed because I don't think I can handle all the responsibilities I have now.
	Of course, my chief responsibility is raising Mark, and the divorce has made parenting more difficult. Ben was able to be firm with Mark, while I find discipline very hard to maintain. Since I'm working all day, I find I have less energy at night to

play with Mark. In fact, sometimes I'm just plain irritable with him. I never realized before how much easier it is to be able to share the responsibility for child raising. A single parent doesn't get much time off from parenting.

conclusion (coordinates with thesis)   All in all, the first few months after my divorce have caused great changes in my financial situation, in my emotional situation, and in my relationship to my son. But, as each day passes, I'm more and more sure that I'll make a good life for Mark and me.

Notice how the thesis of this essay tells the reader that it will deal with three main problems: financial problems, emotional problems, and parenting problems. The essay then devotes one paragraph to each kind of problem.

Each individual paragraph within the essay has its own topic sentence, which focuses on one aspect of the larger subject raised in the introduction. These individual paragraphs supply specific details about a financial, emotional, or parenting problem the writer faced. However, each paragraph does not have its own conclusion. Instead, the writer uses some linking phrases to move a reader from one paragraph to another and uses one paragraph at the end of the essay to sum up the points she has made.

The outline below shows one way of visualizing the structure of this essay.

Problems of Divorce

Thesis: General statement about kinds of problems faced
   I. First kind of problem (more specific than thesis)
      A. Supporting detail about problem I (more specific than topic sentence I)
      B. Supporting detail about problem I (about as specific as detail A)
   II. Second kind of problem (about as specific as problem I)
      A. Supporting detail about problem II (more specific than topic sentence II)
      B. Supporting detail about problem II (about as specific as detail A)
   III. Third kind of problem (about as specific as problem I)
      A. Supporting detail about problem III (more specific than topic sentence III)
      B. Supporting detail about problem III (about as specific as detail A)
Conclusion: General statement about problems of divorce (about as general as thesis)

The following diagram is another way you can visualize the relationship between the parts of an essay.

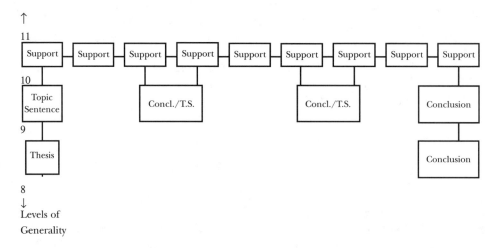

In general, any comment made in this book about paragraphing can be applied equally to longer pieces of writing.

EXERCISE M

Study the multiparagraph essay shown below and find its major parts. Be prepared to explain how the parts of this essay fit together using the general pattern described above.

African Myths of Eshu

Even though Africa is home to an enormous diversity of cultures and its peoples speak more than 1,000 languages, the same trickster, commonly called Eshu, is found in different guises in many myths. In some stories, Eshu breaks up lifelong friendships, and in others he tricks the High God.

Perhaps the best-known story portrays Eshu walking on the path that divides the farms of two men who have been lifelong friends. He puts his pipe at the back of his head and hooks his club over one shoulder so that it hangs down his back. He is wearing a hat that is black on one side and white on the other. After Eshu has passed by, the two friends quarrel about the direction the stranger has taken and the color of his hat. While each accuses the other of lying, Eshu comes and tells the king that neither is a liar but that both are fools.

In another story, Eshu tells the High God that thieves are planning to raid his yam garden. During the night, Eshu steals the High God's sandals, wears the sandals, and steals all the yams. When Eshu reports the theft of the yams, he explains that it will be easy to identify the thief from the clearly defined footprints. All the people are called but nobody's feet fit such big prints. Eshu suggests that perhaps the High God himself took the yams in his sleep. The divinity denies it, but his foot matches the prints exactly. He accuses Eshu of tricking him and as punishment makes Eshu come to the sky every night to report what has happened below.

So even though Eshu is said to be responsible for quarrels between human beings, he is also portrayed as the cunning mediator between heaven and earth.

EXERCISE N

Each set of topic sentences shown below represents the supporting paragraphs of an essay. Compose a thesis that might introduce each essay and a conclusion that might close each essay.

EXAMPLE:
A. On the one hand, Maui was a bold sea-rover.
B. But Maui was also a gifted fisherman.

Possible Thesis: *Maui had an unusual combination of navigational skills and*

fisherman instinct.

Possible Conclusion: *Through this genius for navigation and his fishing skills, Maui*

became one of the greatest heroes of the New Zealand Maori.

1. *Thesis:* _____

_____

   A. In the first stage of remodeling, we will make major structural changes in the building.
   B. During the next three weeks, we will take care of the utility services necessary to support the new structure.
   C. Finally, we will make the cosmetic changes to the interior of the building.

Conclusion: _____

_____

2. *Thesis:* _____

_____

   A. Reducing the speed limit would be one way to make Route 17 safer.
   B. We should also consider adding several traffic signals.
   C. As a last alternative, we could ban trucks from the road altogether.

Conclusion: _____

_____

3. *Thesis:* _____

_____

    A. Many homebuyers choose Arlington because of its great location.
    B. Others are interested in the excellent design and construction of the homes.
    C. Still others move here because the houses are so affordable.

    Conclusion: _____

_____

EXERCISE O

For each thesis–conclusion pair shown below, write appropriate topic sentences as indicated for the supporting paragraphs of the essay.

1. *Thesis:* In just two months, Barbara's new diet changed her from a sullen, withdrawn child to a cheerful, outgoing one.

    A. _____

       _____

    B. _____

       _____

    Conclusion: The elimination of certain foods from Barbara's diet worked an almost miraculous change in her personality.

2. *Thesis:* Because of Ms. Beaman's outstanding performance in the classroom, in her department, and in the college as a whole, I would enthusiastically recommend her promotion to associate professor.

    A. _____

       _____

    B. _____

       _____

    C. _____

       _____

Conclusion: Florida Community College is fortunate to have such an effective teacher who works so well with her colleagues in the Communications Department and serves the whole college with such generosity.

3. *Thesis:* What kind of computer you should buy depends on what you want to do with it, how much technical knowledge you have, and how much money you want to spend.

A. _____

_____

B. _____

_____

C. _____

_____

Conclusion: If you shop for a computer with your needs, your level of expertise, and your budget clearly in mind, you should find your way more easily through the confusing computer market.

WRITING PRACTICE:

1. You have a work-study job at the public relations office of your college. The college is hosting a group of Chinese high school students for a week, and your concerned boss has asked you for some recommendations about what activities should be planned for the visitors. Write a memo to your boss laying out your top choice of an activity for the visitors. Be aware of your audience and purpose. Explain why you think this activity should have a high priority in the visitors' schedule by referring to the stories they will tell about their visit to your college.

Before you draft your memo, list about ten possible activities you think the students might enjoy. Then choose your top priority from the list.

After you have drafted the memo, look over your paragraphing, or trade papers with another student in the class and comment on each other's work. Is the main point clearly stated and adequately supported? Did you close with a strong restatement of your recommendation? Check your sentences to make sure they are complete and correctly punctuated. When you have made any necessary revisions or editing changes in your memo, complete a final draft.

2. Because of your excellent suggestion for the visiting students, the head of the public relations office has asked you to plan a two- or three-hour tour of your area (it may include the campus and/or surrounding city or region) for the guests of some deans who will be attending a conference at the college. Write a one-page description of the tour you have planned. This flyer will be mailed to all conference participants. For your work in setting up the tour, you will receive a commission for each person who signs up, so make your tour sound as interesting as possible. Keep in mind that you are offering the participants the experiences they will use for word-of-mouth promotion of your area.

While you are planning your tour, you might want to confer with relatives or friends familiar with your area to get suggestions about sights to visit. You might also consult the college library or the public library or call your local chamber of commerce or tourist bureau for suggestions.

In planning your tour, it might be helpful to have a theme—for instance, famous historical events, unusual natural features of the region, ethnic cultures in your area.

When you have composed a draft of your flyer, review your paragraphing, or trade papers with another student and review each other's work. Have you stated the main idea clearly? Have you given enough supporting details to make the nature of the tour clear? Also check your sentences to see that they are complete and correctly punctuated. When you have made any necessary revisions or editing corrections, make a final copy of your tour description.

◀ *Chapter 8* ▶

Basic Paragraph Strategies

• • • • • • • • • • • • •

- ▶ STRATEGY: TELLING A STORY
- ▶ STRATEGY: DESCRIBING
- ▶ STRATEGY: LISTING EXAMPLES, REASONS,
    OR STEPS
- ▶ STRATEGY: BREAKING DOWN INTO CATEGORIES
- ▶ STRATEGY: COMPARING OR CONTRASTING

• • • • • • • • • • • • •

Chapter 7 showed you a general structure for paragraphs (and, by extension, for longer pieces of writing): a topic sentence, followed by supporting detail, followed by a conclusion. Within that general format, however, you can arrange information in dozens of different ways. In this chapter, you will see five of the most common strategies for arranging information within the basic topic sentence–support–conclusion framework. The discussion of each strategy gives you some guidelines for using that strategy effectively. (These general guidelines are covered in greater detail in separate chapters elsewhere in this book.)

FIVE BASIC PARAGRAPH STRATEGIES

TELLING A STORY
DESCRIBING
LISTING EXAMPLES, REASONS, OR STEPS
BREAKING DOWN INTO PARTS OR CATEGORIES
COMPARING OR CONTRASTING

EXERCISE A

The paragraphs below illustrate the use of these five strategies. The new management of Computer Lanes Stores has hired five people to shop in its various branches and report on the conditions, service, and merchandise they find. These paragraphs are taken from the shoppers' reports. Can you identify the strategy each writer has used? Be prepared to show the parts of each paragraph's structure.

1. *From Carl's report:* The PC Department at the Westside Mall's Computer Lanes projects an image of quiet elegance. Soft, diffused lighting gives the whole area an atmosphere of understated luxury. The rich, dark burgundy of the upholstery and carpeting and the gleaming mahogany of the furniture also reinforce the air of polished sophistication. Accent pieces such as rock crystals and photographs of Saturn further suggest the good taste and refinement customers should associate with Computer Lanes. In sum, the decorating scheme of the PC Department seems to complement perfectly the high quality of the technology sold there.

Carl's strategy: _____

2. *From Jaime's report:* When compared with Computer Lanes, Computer Warehouse at Harbour View offers less satisfactory customer services. In the first place, while the customer service area at Computer Lanes is conveniently located on the first floor and marked with prominent signs, Computer Warehouse has hidden its customer service center in a corner of the basement with very few signs to guide shoppers in finding it. And even if customers do locate the service area, they won't find as many services offered at Computer Warehouse as at Computer Lanes. Computer Lanes, for example, provides a hardware upgrade service and a children's software demonstration area, neither of which is available at Computer Warehouse. Although Computer Warehouse provides boxes for customer purchases, it does not have a gift-wrap counter as Computer Lanes does. In the Har-

bour View shopping area, customers looking for convenient service would do better at Computer Lanes than at Computer Warehouse.

Jaime's strategy: _____

3. *From Rita's report:* Trying to buy a color laser printer at the downtown Computer Lanes store was an exercise in frustration from start to finish. When I arrived in the Printer Department at about 6 p.m. on Friday, the 10th, there seemed to be no salespeople on the floor. I wandered through the rows of printers for about twenty minutes before I found the printers that had been advertised in that week's sale booklet. It then took me 10 more minutes to spot an open cash register on the other side of the floor in the CD Department. When it was finally my turn, the clerk rang up my purchase at the regular price instead of the sale price. I politely pointed out his mistake, but he insisted quite rudely that this was not the printer that was on sale. Finally, I pulled out my copy of the advertisement, and he grudgingly redid the sale. Meanwhile, I had discovered that the tray was missing from my printer. When I asked if I could exchange that printer for another one, the clerk insisted that I had to go down to the customer service area to get an exchange ticket. If Computer Lanes wants to prevent the kind of frustration I experienced, it needs to take a close look at its staffing patterns and staff training procedure.

Rita's strategy: _____

4. *From Hannah's report:* The salespeople I observed at Computer Lanes's Memorial Plaza store ranged from aggressive to indifferent in their attitudes. The aggressive clerks began to bear down on me if I so much as looked in the direction of their sales area. One woman in the CD Department even took me by the arm and almost pulled me over to her games. These pushy salespeople made me so uneasy I wanted nothing except to escape from their clutches. Fortunately, a very large percentage of the sales staff was genuinely helpful and friendly. They allowed me to look around at my own pace but immediately offered assistance when I asked for it. I also came across a few clerks who seemed to be afraid of me. These timid souls would scurry out of sight if I looked as if I might ask a question. The last, and I am happy to report, the smallest group of sales clerks was the indifferent ones. They would keep me waiting while they finished up conversations with their buddies in the next department or be too busy fixing their makeup to find the item I needed. I have attached a list of the salespeople I observed at the store, putting each into one of the categories described above. I think Computer Lanes would do well to find more of the friendly types and dismiss or retrain the aggressive, the timid, and the indifferent clerks.

Hannah's strategy: _____

5. *From Wilma's report:* All things considered, then, I found shopping at Computer Lanes in Cedar Grove a pleasant experience. The selling areas seemed logically arranged, and the general look of the store was fresh and appealing, conducive to relaxed shopping. In the majority of departments, there was an adequate selection of items in several price ranges. In addition, the salespeople, on the whole, seemed knowledgeable and polite in dealing with me, as did the managers and office personnel. With the few exceptions I have noted in my report, Computer Lanes in Cedar Grove seems like an excellent place to shop.

Wilma's strategy: _____

▶ STRATEGY: TELLING A STORY

● Guidelines:

■ *Focus*

Focus on a limited series of events. Don't try to tell about your whole vacation, for instance, in one paragraph.

■ *Topic Sentence*

Be sure that your topic sentence explains the significance of the story.

EXAMPLES:

> Last summer's marine biology trip on the Bay turned into a *nightmare.*
> Jerry's behavior at the research facility just shows *what a gentle person he is.*
> *I've never been so embarrassed* as I was the day I took my licensing exam.

■ *Organization*

Arrange events in a logical time order, making sure that no important part of the story is left out.

■ *Coherence*

Use joining words like *after, next, while, then,* and *before* to emphasize time relationships between events.

■ *Word Choice*

Use sentences with strong verbs to emphasize action in telling a story.

EXAMPLES:

> WEAK VERBS   There *was* a certain tension in the air before the liftoff.
> Millie *put* the package on the lab bench.

> STRONG VERBS   Tension *crackled* in the air before the liftoff.
>
> Millie *slammed* the package down on the lab bench.

■ Sentence Structure

Try to put an action in each base sentence.

EXAMPLES:

> ACTION NOT EMPHASIZED   *It was late summer* in 1996 when we set out for our archaeological dig.
>
> *The sun shone cruelly overhead* as the drivers clocked mile after mile.
>
> ACTION EMPHASIZED   In late summer 1996, *we set out for our archaeological dig.*
>
> *The drivers clocked mile after mile* as the sun shone cruelly overhead.

■ Conclusion

Use a concluding sentence to reemphasize the significance of the story.

EXAMPLES:

> At last, *the nightmare* was over.
>
> *Jerry's compassion* that night touched everyone in the group.
>
> With my family, I've never quite been able to live down *my "run-in" with the state licensing board.*

EXERCISE B

Using the guidelines suggested above, evaluate each of the following paragraphs. Which one uses the storytelling strategy more effectively? Where could each paragraph be improved?

1. Ibn Yunus, author of *The Large Astronomical Tables of al-Hakim,* predicted his own death in A.D. 1003. Seven days before the predicted event, he cleared up his personal business and then locked himself in his house. Next, Ibn Yunus washed the ink off his manuscripts and recited the Qu'ran until he died. He died on the day he had predicted.

2. In 1898, Marie Curie continued to search for an unknown chemical element. Just as she had done for eight years, she headed out her back door to the slag heap in her yard. She carefully stuck her spoon into the mound for another sample. She then returned to the warmth of her living room and with mathematical precision spread the spoonful so she could pick out the particles that contained the missing element. She sought carefully for the exact color variation. After years of such patient sampling, she had finally collected a few grams of radium. From this small sample, Marie Curie became the first person in the world to distinguish and name alpha particles, beta particles, and gamma radiation.

EXERCISE C
Keeping in mind the guidelines suggested above, combine the following groups of sentences to produce a paragraph that makes its point by telling a story. Use a separate sheet of paper.

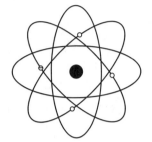

1. Wilhelm Roentgen had a complaint.
    His complaint turned.
    The turning was a discovery.
    The discovery was important.
2. Roentgen complained to the janitor.
    He complained about the laboratory.
    The laboratory was dirty.
3. The janitor feared a ghost.
    Something had glowed.
    The glowing was at night.
4. Barium salt glowed.
    The barium salt was in the back of the lab.
5. The next day, the glowing increased.
    The increase was caused by static electricity.
    The increase was caused accidentally.
6. Mrs. Roentgen came for lunch.
    Roentgen put her hand.
    Her hand was put in front of the glow.
    On the wall were shown all the bones of her hand.
    One bone had a ring.
7. The person was zapped.
    The person was the first.
    She was a woman.
    The zap was by an X-ray.

WRITING PRACTICE:
Most of us have had or seen others have a slip-on-the-banana-peel experience. These life experiences are what make cartoonists wealthy. We all can relate to the skier crashing into the only tree on the slope. Psychiatrists tell us it is healthy to laugh *at* ourselves and *with* others. Laughter is good medicine. Write a funny story of such an event to enter in your writing class's humor contest. Remember the importance of audience appeal and the guidelines for telling a story.

▶ STRATEGY: DESCRIBING

● Guidelines:

■ *Focus*

Focus on the physical characteristics of one person, place, or thing.

■ *Topic Sentence*

Be sure that your topic sentence presents one central impression you want to give your reader.

EXAMPLES:

> My lab partner's area is always *a mess.*
>
> Shirley looked *exhausted* after her first day in the lab.
>
> The outer office is the *most cheerful* room in our facility.

■ *Support*

Reinforce that central impression by using details that will appeal to the senses. Show your reader what the subject looks like, sounds like, smells like, tastes like, and/or feels like.

■ *Organization*

Arrange the descriptive details in a logical order, such as top to bottom, left to right, or far away to close up.

■ *Coherence*

Use transitions like *beside, under, against, where,* and *on* to emphasize the spatial relationships between details.

■ *Word Choice*

Use vivid adjectives to get your reader really involved in your description. Show your reader the exact color, size, shape, position, etc., of each detail.

■ *Sentence Structure*

Put these descriptive details into your base sentences.

EXAMPLES:

> DESCRIPTION NOT EMPHASIZED   Her bench top, *which is covered with books, chemicals, and half-eaten food,* stands near the door.

You walk in *as the acidic smell of sulfur dioxide overwhelms you.*

DESCRIPTION EMPHASIZED   *Open books, unsealed chemicals, and half-eaten food littered her desk,* which stood near the door.

The acidic smell of sulfur dioxide overwhelms you as you walk in.

■ Conclusion

Restate the central impression in the conclusion.

EXAMPLES:

Amelio's bench top is a *man-made disaster area.*

Altogether, Shirley's fatigue *completely obscured her normally healthy appearance.*

With its bright colors and open layout, *the outer office lifts everyone's spirits.*

EXERCISE D
Using the guidelines suggested above, evaluate each of the following paragraphs. Which one uses the description strategy more effectively? Where could each paragraph be improved?

1. Chang Heng's primitive earthquake instrument looked like a six-foot bronze wine jar. Around the jar's surface were eight dragon heads, each holding a ball. On the floor around the jar were placed eight bronze toads with open mouths. The heavy pendulum inside did not respond to light disturbances. In the event of the rumbling of an earthquake, however, one of the dragon's mouths would open and drop its ball into the mouth of the appropriate toad. The dragon that spewed the ball indicated from which direction the tremor had come. Even though Heng's earthquake instrument looked like a wine jug, his apparatus measured more powerful rumblings than even the best bottle of Chardonnay.

2. In Chinese, the abacus is called "a calculating plate." It has a frame that is a rectangle. It is made with wires that have seven balls. The abacus was first described in A.D. 1593. In earlier texts, they called a similar instrument "ball arithmetic." Some writers claim that a form of the abacus goes as far back as the second century A.D. People in many different cultures have used types of pebbles for counting.

EXERCISE E
Keeping in mind the suggestions above, combine the following groups of sentences to produce a paragraph that describes. Use a separate sheet of paper.

1. Stephen Hawking has a body.
   The body has not stopped him.
   He is well known.
   The knowledge is of him as a living Einstein.

2. Hawking has suffered adversities.
   The adversities were physical.
   The adversities were extraordinary.
3. In his early twenties, he was afflicted.
   The affliction is known as Lou Gehrig's disease.
4. Since then, he has been confined.
   The confinement has been to a wheelchair.
5. Now he is unable to move.
   The exception is his eyes.
   The exception is three fingers.
   The fingers are on his left hand.
6. In 1985, he lost the use.
   The use was of his voice.
   He relies on a synthesizer.
   The synthesizer computerizes his voice.
7. His body is ugly.
   His body is crippled.
   His mental abilities are honed.
   His mental abilities are incredible.

WRITING PRACTICE:
Look in the mirror for several minutes. Exaggerate your features, perhaps by making a distorted face. Hold the pose and discover an overall impression of the mood and what your face expresses. Next, notice the hair, its color, length, texture. Look into your own eyes and describe their alertness, their colors. Notice a particular mark on your face. Exaggerate the mark and describe its color and texture. Continue by describing your mouth and facial hairs. For your concluding sentence, answer this question: what story does your face tell?

▶ STRATEGY: LISTING EXAMPLES, REASONS, OR STEPS

● Guidelines:

■ *Focus*

Focus on a process or event that you are familiar with so that you will know the examples, causes, or steps involved.

■ *Topic Sentence*

State the subject as clearly as possible in the topic sentence and try to indicate the examples, causes, or steps you will be discussing.

<u>EXAMPLES:</u>

> The Drama Club's production of *The Time Machine* failed *because of poor casting and poor directing.*

You can make a deadly poison *in five simple steps.*

Throughout American history, *women scientists have had to struggle for educational opportunities* that men took for granted.

■ *Support*

Be sure that all necessary steps or significant causes have been mentioned. If you are giving examples, use enough to show your reader that there is a pattern present rather than just one isolated incident. Generally, three to five examples should be enough for one paragraph.

■ *Organization*

Arrange the examples, reasons, or steps in a logical order; either a time order or an order of importance works well with this kind of paragraph. If reasons or steps have been laid out in the topic sentence, they should be developed in the paragraph in the same order in which they appear in the topic sentence. In the first topic sentence above, for instance, the two reasons for the play's failure are listed in chronological order. (Casting takes place before directing.) Therefore, in the paragraph, casting should be discussed before directing.

■ *Coherence*

Use transitions like *next, then, even more important, another example, a hundred years later,* and *most significant of all* to show the logical connections between your examples, causes, or steps.

■ *Word Choice*

Use specific, concrete statements rather than general or abstract ones.

EXAMPLES:

GENERAL   Cars today are more efficient.

Tighten the bolts.

The *Ohio* is a big submarine.

SPECIFIC   A 1997 Nissan averages 33 miles per gallon.

Use an 8-centimeter torque wrench with a rubber handle to tighten the bolts.

The nuclear submarine *Ohio* is 560 feet long and has an 18,700-ton displacement.

■ *Sentence Structure*

Put important examples, causes, or steps into your base sentence.

EXAMPLES:

UNIMPORTANT IDEAS EMPHASIZED *The first computers,* which had vacuum-tube memories and occupied an entire room, *were developed in the 1940s.*

Next, *a medicated pad,* which should be wiped over the entire face, *can be very effective.*

IMPORTANT IDEA EMPHASIZED *The first computers,* developed in the 1940s, *had vacuum-tube memories and occupied an entire room.*

Next, *a medicated pad,* which can be very effective, *should be wiped over the entire face.*

■ Conclusion

Make the conclusion a restatement or summary of your main point.

EXAMPLES:

Although the sets were elegant, *poor acting and poor direction ruined this play.*

With little more than an hour's work, *you can now kill your worst enemy and escape detection.*

So, little-known women scientists like these have *forced open the doors of American educational institutions.*

EXERCISE F

Using the guidelines suggested above, evaluate each of the following paragraphs. Which one uses the listing strategy more effectively? Where could each paragraph be improved?

1. Space law governs the use and control of outer space by different nations on Earth. The first treaty that governs space activities is *Treaty on Principles Governing the Activities of States in the Exploration and Use of Outer Space.* This treaty was proposed in 1967 and is also called the "Outer Space Treaty." The next year, scientists had additional concerns and wrote *Agreement on the Rescue of Astronauts, the Return of Astronauts and the Return of Objects Launched Into Outer Space.* As space shots increased, the focus centered on the objects launched. As a result, space law later included *Convention on International Liability for Damage Caused by Space Objects* (1972) and *Convention on Registration of Objects Launched into Outer Space* (1975). Few human undertakings have stimulated so great a degree of legal scrutiny on an international level as has the development of modern space law.

2. The servo robot represents several categories of robots. This type of robot has mechanisms to enable it to change direction in midair without having to trip a mechanical switch. Therefore, five to seven directions of motion are possible.

Another type, the computerized robot, is a servo robot run by a computer. This kind of robot is programmed by instructions fed in electronically. These "smart" robots may even have the ability to improve upon their basic work instructions.

Exercise G

Keeping in mind the techniques discussed above, combine the following sentences to produce a paragraph that lists reasons and examples. Use a separate sheet of paper.

1. Mars has an atmosphere.
   The atmosphere is hostile.
   The hostility is to life.
   The life is human.
2. Here is the first reason.
   There is little air pressure.
   The reason is the atmosphere is so thin.
   It resembles air on Earth.
   The air is at an altitude.
   The altitude is 32 kilometers.
3. This air makes an animal's blood boil.
   It makes a person's blood boil.
4. Mars has thin atmosphere.
   Mars has low pressure.
   The liquid water escapes.
   It escapes instantly.
5. Mars also does not have.
   It does not have enough ozone.
   The ozone is in the Martian atmosphere.
   The atmosphere will not shield radiation.
6. At night, the temperature falls.
   The fall is below zero.
   The fall is as low as minus 150 degrees Fahrenheit.
7. The Martian atmosphere contains nitrogen.
   The Martian atmosphere contains carbon dioxide.
   The Martian atmosphere contains oxygen.
   The Martian atmosphere contains water vapor.
   The Martian atmosphere cannot support life.
   The life is human.

Writing Practice:

Remember a time when you had to ask someone for a date or a favor. For whatever reason (and you may explain this to your reader), you feared disapproval or rejection. Explain your steps of preparation and then the actual asking. Toward the end of your explanation of the process, you may consider using dialogue to make the event realistic. In your concluding sentence, share with your reader the relief you felt just getting through asking the question.

▶ STRATEGY: BREAKING DOWN INTO CATEGORIES

● Guidelines

■ *Focus*

Focus on a group of people or objects that you are very familiar with so that you will know the various types within the group. Find some principle that you can use to classify the members of the group you are writing about. Teachers, for example, might be classified according to how strictly they grade. Restaurants might be classified according to price or according to kind of food served. Be sure this classification principle reveals some *significant* similarities or differences among members of the group. (Most people would not be interested in a division of teachers according to height, for instance.)

■ *Topic Sentence*

If possible, name the major categories (usually three to five) in your topic sentence.

EXAMPLES:

> **Three kinds of students roam the astronomy lecture hall of LaGuardia Community College:** *the scholar, the jock,* **and** *the loner.*
>
> *Nervousness, calm,* **and** *enjoyment* **are the three stages in learning to calculate.**
>
> **Laboratory research requires** *varying degrees of athletic skill.*

■ *Support*

Explain each category and/or give examples of items that would fit in each.

■ *Organization*

Present the categories in a logical order: from smallest group to largest, from most expensive to least expensive, from first stage to last stage.

■ *Coherence*

Use transitions like *slightly more expensive, the highest degree of skill, most boring of all,* and *last* to emphasize your principle of classification.

■ *Conclusion*

Use a conclusion that will sum up the whole classification system, not just the last point.

<u>Examples:</u>

> Though the actual students change from year to year, *the same types seem to appear again and again.*
>
> It is a rare student who does not pass through *each of these stages* in the course of his or her development.
>
> The particular research subject demands levels of athletic skills from none to super-jock.

Exercise H

Using the guidelines suggested above, evaluate each of the following paragraphs. Which one uses the categorizing strategy more effectively? Where could each paragraph be improved?

1. The ancient Chinese seem to have had a special partiality for insects. First of all, they bred crickets for sport, keeping them in cages and releasing them for fighting. They also kept bees, though the honey obtained was used mainly for medical purposes. However, the most unusual Chinese use of insects was to protect crops from other pests. In the third century A.D., a writer described how citrus farmers would hang bags of ants on their trees as a protection against spiders, mites, and other pests. Modern scientists were delighted to identify the actual species of ant, so they can use natural methods to protect plants. Do the novelty chocolate-covered ants in the mall get our attention because of a similar fascination with critters?

2. Many people believe that Galileo Galilei advanced the frontiers of science more than any person before him. He is the first person known to have used a telescope for observing the stars. He did this in 1610. He also was the first person to study sunspots with a telescope. His discovery of Jupiter's moons showed that the Earth was not the only center of motion. In short, Galileo was one of the greatest originators of all time.

Exercise I

Using the suggestions above, combine the following groups of sentences to produce a paragraph that could introduce the study of exobiology. Use a separate sheet of paper.

1. The field is exobiology.
   The field is multidisciplinary.
   The field is new.
   It covers several aspects.
   The aspects are of outer space environments.
2. The first approach is to study.
   The study is of samples.
   The samples are material.
   The samples are from alien worlds.

3. The Viking Landers have given.
   They have given information.
   The information is chemical.
   The information is about the soil.
   The soil is Martian.
4. The second direction involves experiments.
   The experiments are in laboratories.
   The laboratories are terrestrial.
   The experiments try to simulate.
   The simulation is of conditions.
   The conditions are extraterrestrial.
5. One approach is the most exciting.
   The approach has a goal.
   The goal is to communicate.
   The communication is with other life forms.
   The life forms are intelligent.
   The life forms are within our galaxy.
6. Life is probably not unique.
   The life is on Earth.
   Life may be widespread.
   It may be throughout the galaxy.
7. Exobiology is a career choice.
   The career choice is good.
   The career choice could be exciting.
   The career choice could be fascinating.

WRITING PRACTICE:

For a moment, become a reporter for your college newspaper. You are assigned, along with a photographer, to do a feature article on incoming freshmen. You interview some of them and then you get the idea to categorize this year's specimens into three categories. Share with your readers a description of the types, using stick figure drawings to represent the photos.

or

From your experience as a consumer or an employee, describe three categories of disgruntled shoppers. Give names to typical individuals. Describe their facial expressions and other body language along with their attitudes and tones of voice.

▶ STRATEGY: COMPARING OR CONTRASTING

● Guidelines

■ *Focus*

Focus on two subjects between which you see some clear differences or similarities that will interest your readers.

■ *Topic Sentence*

Name both subjects in the topic sentence and define the similarity or difference as clearly as you can.

EXAMPLES:

> The *computer differs* from the *human brain* in its *speed of operation, number of components,* and *degree of free will.*
>
> *College science* is *more academically demanding* than *high school science.*
>
> *My two physics professors* share the *same easygoing temperament.*

■ *Support*

List several examples of the similarity or difference you are emphasizing. Make sure that your two subjects are developed in equal ways, with just about the same space given and the same ideas developed for each subject. You can't, for example, compare two stories by writing two sentences about the plot of one story and ten sentences about the characters in the other.

■ *Organization*

Arrange the points of comparison or contrast in the block pattern or the alternating pattern.

EXAMPLE:

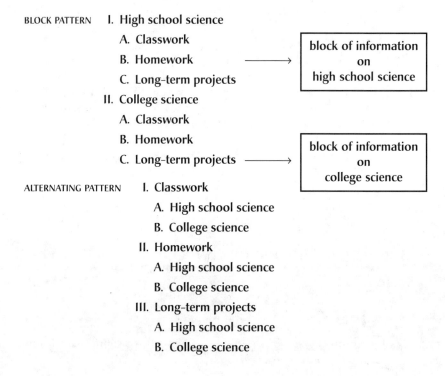

Also consider the order in which you present the major points. High school science, for instance, would logically be discussed before college science; classwork might (since it is less demanding) logically come before long-term projects.

■ *Coherence*

Use transitions like *similarly, likewise,* and *compared with* to suggest similarity between ideas. Use transitions like *on the other hand* and *however* to suggest contrast between ideas.

■ *Word Choice*

Use concrete, specific language rather than vague or abstract words to point out similarities or differences.

EXAMPLE:

> VAGUE LANGUAGE Microbiology is interesting, like anatomy and physiology.
> Summer is more pleasant than winter.
>
> SPECIFIC LANGUAGE Like anatomy and physiology, the study of microbiology offers answers to questions I have had about human diseases.
>
> With its drowsy, mint-julep evenings, summer in Atlanta is far more attractive to me than the cold, harried evenings up North when school is in session.

■ *Sentence Structure*

Put the similarities or differences you are trying to emphasize into the base sentence.

EXAMPLE:

> SIMILARITY EMPHASIZED Although I am more interested in geology than in meteorology, *my zeal for learning new material in each course is remarkably equal.*
>
> DIFFERENCE EMPHASIZED Although my zeal for learning new material in each science course is remarkably equal, *I am more interested in geology than in meteorology.*

■ *Conclusion*

Restate the two subjects and the main points of similarity or difference in the conclusion.

EXAMPLES:

> In *speed, complexity,* and *autonomy,* the *computer* is still not the equal of the *human brain.*
>
> Anyone who says that *college science* is just another four years of *high school science* hasn't looked carefully at the *academic demands* of college.

I could never hope to find two more *evenly matched*, *unflappable* personalities than those of my two physics professors.

Exercise J

Using the guidelines suggested above, evaluate each of the following paragraphs. Which one uses the compare/contrast strategy more effectively? Where could each paragraph be improved?

1. The ancient Greeks and Indians struggled with the concept of why an object continues in motion. Aristotle tried to explain his idea of natural and violent motion. He thought the pressure of the air forced the motion of the body once it had been given its initial push. The Indian view, however, suggested that when an object first experiences the force that sets it moving, the very application of this force imparts a quality. This quality or "vega" causes the object to continue to move in the same way. Even though Aristotle's idea caused the West to be stuck for many centuries, what the Indian physicists suggested became the forerunner of what was developed mathematically much later in the West.

2. Educators disagree about the use of graphing calculators in the classroom. The argument on one side is that the act of calculation involves practice and training. If you do not get it, you can never expect to develop the necessary skills. The opposition questions whether it really matters if these skills are not developed. Calculators are cheap, universal and quick, so why bother to fumble around with sums in your head? One side insists that you have to be able to manipulate and understand the basic skills of math, and the other side argues that such formal discipline might stifle natural mathematical powers.

Exercise K

Keeping in mind the guidelines suggested above, combine the following groups of sentences to produce a paragraph that contrasts bonds of carbon atoms. Use a separate sheet of paper.

1. The carbon atom forms bonds.
   It can form a single bond.
   It can form a double bond.
   It can form a triple bond.
2. Bond strengths can be compared.
   Bond strengths can be measured.
3. To break a bond between a single C–C requires 347 KJ.
   To break a bond between a double C=C requires 614 KJ.
   To break a bond between a triple C≡C requires 839 KJ.
4. Bond lengths can be compared.
   Bond lengths can be measured.
5. The single bond is 1.54 Å.
   The double bond is 1.34 Å.
   The triple bond is 1.20 Å.

6. We can draw a conclusion.
   The conclusion is about the C-C bonds.
   Stronger bonds have shorter lengths.

WRITING PRACTICE:

Your boss asks you for input about two employees with whom you have worked for two years. She needs your write-up first thing in the morning. She wants you to compare them in three categories: being a team player, generating solutions and not problems, and putting clients first. Your job is secure, but she must dismiss one of the employees in question because of downsizing in the company. Your response paragraph will be held in the strictest confidence.

EXERCISE L

Using a separate sheet of paper, combine each of the following groups of sentences to produce a complete paragraph. In some cases, you may have to add a topic sentence, a conclusion, or transition words. In other paragraphs, you may have to rearrange the sentences to get the most effective order. In writing these paragraphs, use whatever techniques are appropriate to the strategy being used.

Emergency Room Report

1. The patient was admitted.
   The admitting was at 7:10 a.m.
   It was in the emergency room.
   The patient was complaining of severe pain in his ankle.
2. The region was swollen.
   The region was below the left distal fibula.
   The region was discolored.
   The discoloration covered an area.
   The area had a diameter of 7 centimeters.
   The area was circular.
3. The right side showed swelling.
   There was no discoloration.
4. The patient made a statement.
   He had pain when he moved the foot.
   The movement was from side to side.
   The pain was sharp.
5. The swollen area was tender.
   The tenderness was to the touch.
   The patient complained about it.
6. No signs appeared.
   The signs were of injury.
   The appearance was on the leg above the ankle.
   The appearance was on the foot.

7. X-rays were needed.
   The need was to determine the extent.
   The extent was of the injury.
   Bones might be broken.

Preparing for a Hurricane

1. There is a way to prepare for a hurricane.
   The way is methodical.
   The way is efficient.
   It can be learned in a few minutes.
2. Listen to local radio.
   Listen to television stations.
   Listen every three hours.
   Listen for weather updates.
   This should take top priority.
3. Organize supplies.
   The supplies are for emergencies.
4. The most important supply is water.
   The water must be stored.
   The storage should be in the bathtub.
   The storage should be in bottles.
   The storage should be in containers.
   The storage should be sterilized.
5. Clear your yard.
   Objects can become missiles.
   Bicycles can become missiles.
   Trash cans can become missiles.
   Lawn furniture can become missiles.
   Anchor objects that cannot be moved inside.
6. Tape windows.
   Taping will not prevent breaking.
   Taping will reduce flying glass.
   Open indoor trap to attic.
   Close all windows.
   Board up windows.
   Board up doors.
7. Be sure your automobile is ready.
   Check gas.
   Check oil.
   Check water.

Studying Petroglyphs

1. Most archaeologists avoid making.
   The avoidance is of interpretations.
   The interpretations are of petroglyphs.
2. They focus their efforts.
   Their efforts are on recording of sites.

  The recording is descriptive.
  Their efforts are toward analysis of designs.
  The analysis is stylistic.
3. It was four thousand years ago.
  Rock art appeared.
  The style was dramatic.
  The style was visionary.
  The art appeared among the bands.
  The bands were nomadic.
  The bands were of the Southwest.
4. The purpose was to convey information.
  The purpose was of the petroglyphs.
  Petroglyphs are forms pecked into rock.
5. Archaeologists study artifacts.
  The artifact is in its own place.
  The place is the context.
  The context is important.
6. Damage comes.
  The damage is to the petroglyphs.
  The damage is from an admirer.
  The admirer touches the glyph.
  The admirer has hand oils.
  Hand oils quicken deterioration.
7. The locations of sites need to remain obscure.
  The sites are numerous.
  The sites are of little-known rock art.

Excitement for Scientists

1. Physicists experiment in laboratories.
  They try to understand.
  Their understanding is of the natural world.
2. Frederic Joliet was at work in a lab.
  Irene Joliet was at work in a lab.
  The lab was at a university in Paris.
  This happened in January 1934.
3. They were exposing a piece.
  The piece was aluminum.
  The aluminum was ordinary.
  The exposing was to a stream.
  The stream was of tiny charged bits.
  The bits were of matter.
  The bits were called alpha particles.
4. The aluminum became radioactive.
  The aluminum was ordinary.
5. The news was exciting.
  The excitement was for scientists.
  The news traveled.

The travel was rapid.
6. Enrico Fermi altered.
   The alteration was of their experiment.
   He produced radioactivity.
   The radioactivity was artificial.
   He did this by using neutrons.
7. These breakthroughs could be done.
   The breakthroughs were exciting.
   The breakthroughs were scientific.
   They could be done only through experiments.
   The experiments were in labs.
   The experiments were methodical.

EXERCISE M

In each of the following exercises, you are given a group of sentences to combine into an effective paragraph. When you have finished combining, you will have the first of a pair of paragraphs. Using it as a guide, write the second paragraph. Use a separate sheet of paper.

1. There are reasons for exercising.
   The reasons are two.
   One reason is appearance.
   The other reason is health.
   Most people look better when fit.
   Exercise keeps weight down.
   Exercise burns up calories.
   The calories are excess.
   Exercise increases circulation.
   Increased circulation improves complexion.
   Exercise develops coordination.
   Coordination gives precision and grace to movement.
   Exercise tones muscles.
   The tone improves posture.
   Exercise has other effects.
   These effects go beyond cosmetics.
   Exercise also affects health.
2. The elderly enjoy reading books.
   The elderly enjoy using CD-ROMs.
   Books and CD-ROMs are different.
   Books are portable.
   Books usually are read from front to back.
   Books are structured.
   Readers use hypertext in CD-ROMs to branch to different topics.
   CD-ROMs require a computer.
   CD-ROMs show the characters in motion.
   CD-ROMs help the reader interact with the characters.
   Books cannot have the reader physically interact with the characters.

◆   **Part III**   ◆

The Writing Process

In Parts One and Two of this book, you looked at the relationships between ideas within sentences and between the parts of paragraphs and longer pieces of writing, and you started to get a feel for what a finished paragraph or essay looks like. It is important for you as a writer to have an idea of the overall structure you're aiming for in a piece of writing. But this kind of knowledge, all by itself, isn't necessarily enough to help you compose a well-written paragraph.

An architect, for instance, needs to have a basic knowledge of the structure of a building, needs to know the essential parts, needs to understand how these parts relate to one another. When she begins to design an actual building, however, the architect goes through a long process of considering all the factors in the design situation— what will the building be used for? where will the building be located? how much does the client want to spend on this building? and so forth. In other words, the architect adapts her basic knowledge to a particular situation.

Once she has gotten a feel for the situation, the architect begins trying out building designs, sketching a general shape, noting some particular features that might work well in this building, maybe reviewing other buildings that have been designed for a similar purpose or built in a similar location, consulting with the client about various options. In the course of her work, she may go through a dozen different versions of the building, adding or subtracting details as she gets a clearer sense of what will suit this situation. Only after a long process of exploring, drafting, and redrafting, does she come up with a design that satisfies her.

As a writer, you need to go through a similar process. Although you know the general shapes of sentences and paragraphs, you have to adapt them to a particular situation if you want to write well. A paragraph that has a topic sentence, support, and a conclusion is not necessarily a good paragraph any more than a building with a roof, walls, and a floor is necessarily a good building.

Writers usually go through several different kinds of activities in the process of composing. At various points in the process, writers explore, focus, organize, draft, revise, and edit, but not always in that order. A writer may move back and forth among these activities, skipping some, repeating others. In fact, the writing process tends to be somewhat messier than it looks when it is neatly laid out in a textbook. However, you will find that knowing the process may help you get through a period or assignment that otherwise makes you feel as though you are wandering aimlessly in a desert. Therefore, shown below is one somewhat neatened-up way of visualizing the writing process.

THE WRITING PROCESS								
Exploring	▮	▮	▮			▮		
Focusing	▮		▮					
Organizing	▮	▮		▮				
Drafting				▮	▮		▮	
Revising					▮	▮	▮	▮
Editing					▮		▮	▮

As you read the text's discussion of these various stages, you need to keep in mind that, although a book can deal with only one activity at a time, these activities may, in fact, overlap when you are actually writing.

◀ *Chapter 9* ▶

Exploring

• • • • • • • • • • •

- ▶ EXPLORE THE SUBJECT
- ▶ STUDY THE AUDIENCE
- ▶ ESTABLISH A PURPOSE
- ▶ SELECT A VOICE

• • • • • • • • • • •

In the exploring part of the writing process, you are trying to see just what you have to work with in a particular writing situation. You want to consider as many options as you can for dealing with this situation, so when you are exploring, you want to stimulate the creative side of your brain and generate as many ideas as you can without being too concerned about how good each idea is. As that brilliant thinker Linus Pauling once noted, "The best way to have a good idea is to have a lot of ideas."

To explore a writing situation, you need to focus on the general areas of subject, audience, purpose, and writer's voice, as the box below shows. You don't have to explore them in any particular order; in fact, it's quite likely that thinking about any one of these factors will generate ideas about all of them. So don't worry if your exploration seems to jump around almost at random.

EXPLORING THE WRITING SITUATION

1. WHAT IS SIGNIFICANT ABOUT THE SUBJECT?
2. WHO AM I WRITING FOR?
3. WHAT IS MY PURPOSE IN WRITING?
4. WHAT IMAGE OF MYSELF DO I WANT TO PROJECT TO MY AUDIENCE?

Although you may do some exploration of subject, audience, purpose, and voice early in your composing, you will be refining your ideas about them throughout the writing process. So stay alert for those sparks of inspiration that may flash as your ideas begin to rub against each other.

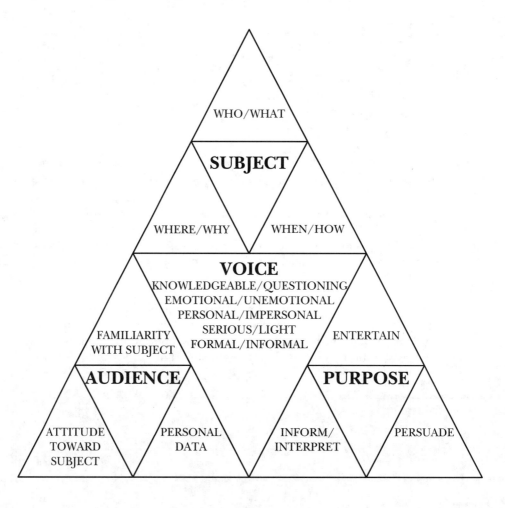

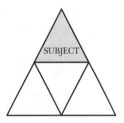

▶ EXPLORE THE SUBJECT

All writing is *about* something. Sometimes you may have a completely free choice of your subject; more often, the subject is determined to a greater or lesser degree by someone else. Although you might want to write about your pet beagle, what your boss has asked for is an analysis of the county's proposed changes in utility rates. Although you may be dying to explain the intricacies of the new style of rock music, what the community association needs is a good fund-raising proposal.

Whatever the subject you are dealing with, you have three basic sources of information about it: your own memory, your immediate observations of the world around you, and the memories and observations of other people that you may discover through personal interviews, e-mail, books, films, or tapes.

Many writers combine several of these sources by keeping a journal or a computer file where they record their own memories, observations, and responses and also those of others that they have come across in their reading or conversations. Such a journal, electronic or written, may suggest a subject that you would like to write about or may provide details about a subject that someone else has asked you to write about.

Since your journal is basically for your own use, you don't need to be particularly concerned about recording only completely formulated ideas or about such mechanical considerations as spelling and punctuation. In fact, writers refer to entries in their journals as "zero drafts." (They're not even polished enough to be first drafts.) One of the nice things about a journal is that it gives you a place to try out ideas on yourself before you try them out on someone else. Your writer's journal will be a good place to use some of the other exploration techniques suggested later in this chapter.

In using these techniques, remember that their main purpose is to prime the pumps of your thinking apparatus, to get your brain working on a subject. If one method doesn't help you come up with ideas, try another one. And be sure to allow yourself enough time to explore your subject. Ideas may seem to come very slowly at first. But gradually, as you activate your creative processes, ideas come faster. The techniques are based on brain and creativity research; trust the methodologies even though some may seem awkward for you at first.

● Brainstorming

One way to begin exploring a subject is to brainstorm it with a friend or a group of people working on the same project. In a brainstorming session, the group pools its collection of memories, observations, and research on a certain subject. Everyone contributes ideas about the subject, and the whole group keeps working to expand the pool of ideas. Many times, one person's idea, even if it sounds strange at first, can jar another person's mind to come up with a new approach to the subject. So, in brainstorming, don't stop the flow of ideas to criticize; keep the flow moving. Each participant can then take whatever ideas seem useful and develop them. If you are brainstorming alone, you will find your brainstorming richer if you plan three separate sessions to add to your original list. Try not to judge items until after your third session. Being critical beforehand dries up the flow of ideas.

● Freewriting

Freewriting is another kind of private brainstorming. You just take your journal and write whatever comes into your head on the subject. Don't stop to analyze your thoughts; just keep your pen moving on the paper. If you get stuck, just repeat, write the opposite, or rhyme the last word you just wrote. You don't have to worry about organizing your thoughts or putting them into correct language. You just write until you've filled up a whole page or until you have written for ten minutes. Later you can select, refine, and organize your thoughts. For now, generate as many ideas as possible. When you have filled a page, you might stimulate your thinking by rereading what you have written and putting a circle around what you think is your best idea.

Page 315 shows an example of some freewriting done by a student who needs to evaluate a day-care facility in her neighborhood.

● Webbing

Another technique that many writers find useful is webbing. Webbing is related to brainstorming and freewriting, but it is a little more visual. To use this technique, write your subject in the middle of a blank page. Then draw a line leading out from your subject and write down the first thing you associate with your subject. Draw a line leading away from that idea and write down whatever you associate with that idea. Keep going with that line until you run out of associations. Then go back to your subject in the center of the page and start a new set of associations. Page 315 shows a web done by the student who is evaluating the day-care facility.

● Self-interviewing

Some writers prefer to explore their subjects in a little more structured way. For example, you can explore a subject by interviewing yourself. Make up ten questions about your subject and then write out your answers to your questions. Page 316 shows some self-interview questions for the student evaluating the day-care center.

● Alphabet Cuing

You can also use a system of cues to force yourself to think about a subject from several different angles. You can even use the alphabet as a cue. You just write down one idea about your subject for each letter of the alphabet. Page 316 shows a sample of this technique.

● **Freewriting**

Tiny Tots School
small classes, Julio attended three years ago — rather strict
discipline — emphasis on learning — Mrs. Gregory — still
stern face — high school girls in charge in play yard —
learn responsibility — pick up toys — clean areas after eat-
ing — Suzuki piano lessons — Julio always sick — even
working parents involved in fund raising — charged for day
don't attend — children's birthdays all same → cup cakes
— smaller school better? new learning areas like Montessori
— summer once a week at pool — plumbing problems —
Amanda will still be teacher next year — children from other
neighborhoods — cost up $15/week — lots of music activities — children happy
— time out — no spanking.

● **Webbing**

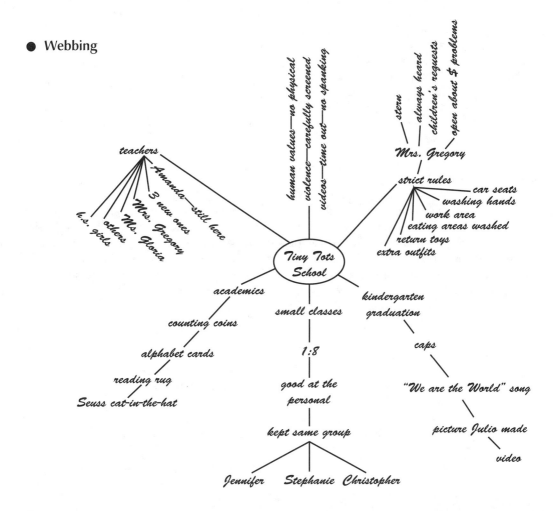

● **Self-Interviewing**

1. *What did Julio enjoy most when he went to Tiny Tots?*
2. *What did Julio like least about Tiny Tots?*
3. *What picture comes to mind when I think of Tiny Tots?*
4. *What event do I remember best from Tiny Tots?*
5. *What do we want from Tiny Tots for Maria?*
6. *Which person at Tiny Tots had most influence previously?*
7. *How is Julio different because of Tiny Tots?*
8. *Does Maria have different needs from Julio?*
9. *Why had we sent Julio to Tiny Tots?*
10. *What would I like to change about Tiny Tots?*

● **Alphabet Cuing**

a — Amanda
b — bus outings
c — community image
d — discipline
e — educational goals
f — Friday birthday celebrations
g — going home ritual
h — high school girls
i — instructions for trips
j — junk food no-no.

● **Five W's Cuing**

You can also cue yourself with the five W's—*who, what, where, when, why*—as many journalists and other professional writers do. Using a cue word like *who,* you begin to write down all the *who*'s you associate with your subject or any questions related to your subject that begin with *who.* When you run out of *who* associations or questions, move on to the next cue. Of course, you can always fill in more ideas if they occur to you while you're working on another cue.

Tiny Tots

who
— Mrs. Gregory   *— who started the school?*
— Amanda   *— who went there?*
— high school girls   *all income levels*
— new teachers   *different neighborhoods*
— familiar but nameless   *ethnic mix*
what
— private   *— lots of singing and acting out*

— *strict discipline*
— *emphasize numbers and alphabet*
   skills
— *fun — parties, shows, field trips*
— *Suzuki piano lessons*
— *Montessori learning areas*   — *plumbing problems*
<u>*where*</u>
— *three blocks from home*
— *old building*
— *somewhat isolated*
— *fenced-in yard*
<u>*why*</u>
— *provide solid background*   *why not?*
— *licensed facility*   — *cost*
— *convenient*   — *Maria might need different*
— *Julio — good experience*   *experience*

● **Five Senses Cuing**

You may also find the five senses useful as cues for exploring. To use them, try to recreate in your mind some scene that you associate with your subject. Then review each sense in turn, making notes about what you see, hear, and so on, in that scene.

Tiny Tots

<u>*See*</u>
   — *cubicles with names*
   — *groups of children on mats*
   — *teachers listening*
   — *children wandering outside circles*
   — *bright charts on walls*
   — *window → playyard with equipment*
   — *familiar faces*
<u>*Hear*</u>
   — *children's voices, two crying*
   — *thuds of objects dropped*
   — *singing*
   — *requests*
   — *teacher playing guitar*
   — *counting in Spanish*
   — *clicking of Mrs. Gregory's necklace*
<u>*Touch*</u>   <u>*Smell*</u>
   — *soapy water*   — *clorox*
   — *sponge*   — *soup*

— *hard folding chairs for parents*   — *crayons*
— *sticky handrail*   — *Mrs. Gregory's perfume*
                                                        — *urine??*

Taste
    — *tomato soup*
    — *peanut butter*

● Observing and Researching

Any of these methods of exploring a subject can help you find out what is in your memory about that subject. Just as important, these techniques can help you discover what kinds of additional information you may need to find by observation or research.

For example, the student who has been exploring the subject of Tiny Tots Day Care might need to check with parents of children attending now, H.H.S. for negative reports or warnings, and teachers who are new to the school. She might also decide to spend some time at the school observing what is happening to see how it compares with what she remembers when her son attended. The exploring techniques of the five senses or the five W's could help her organize her observations.

After she has done some reading and observing, she can try some further explorations to see what new ideas may have been stimulated by her new information.

EXERCISE A

Keep a writer's journal for at least two weeks. You should make at least four entries per week, some based on something you have observed, the others based on something you have read. Stay attuned to newspaper articles and assignments you read for other courses. Watch for occasions in which happiness or tension is expressed. Then use the exploring techniques described in this chapter or any other format you choose for your journal entries. The journal entries should be about subjects that you might choose later to develop into finished pieces of writing.

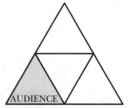

▶ STUDY THE AUDIENCE

After doing some exploration of your subject, you will probably find yourself with lots of ideas, maybe even more ideas than you can use in one writing project. To help you select from among these ideas, you need to explore your audience. What you write has to be shaped to some degree by who will be reading it. Sometimes, you have no choice about your audience. You may know from the beginning, for instance, that the report you are preparing will be read by your supervisor or your professor. Other times, you are free to choose the most suitable audience for what you want to say.

In any case, to write well, you must consider who will be reading what you write. Is it a person you know well, like your brother? Or is it a group of people you don't know personally—the members of the city council, for example? Is your audience already interested in the subject you are writing about—a group of fellow skin-divers, perhaps? Or do you have to convince your audience of the importance of your idea—for instance, are they potential contributors to your group's fund-raising project?

For each kind of audience—personal or public, knowledgeable or uninformed—you have to write in a somewhat different way. You would choose different arguments, use different words, take a different attitude, depending on your audience.

For example, if you were writing something about inflation for the local food co-op newsletter, you would want to choose examples that your audience could immediately recognize, like food prices. If you were writing about inflation for your economics class, though, you would have to choose other kinds of examples, since members of this audience might not do the family grocery shopping.

Also, your language would be different for each group. For the food co-op members, you would try to use fairly nontechnical terms so that you could be easily understood by everyone. Your economics class, on the other hand, should be more familiar with the professional language of economists, and so you could use words like *commodities market, the Fed,* and *prime rate* and expect to be understood.

You can explore your audience using the techniques described earlier. The audience simply becomes another subject you want to explore. For instance, this writer is working on a letter to city council members about the need for an investigation of toxic wastes in the local landfill areas. Here is his private brainstorming on the audience.

Who are Council members?
  Clarke — chair,
  Nolan — my district, Barrett,
  Freeson (?) Ventre — woman,
  one other?
How many have children?
Clarke said in newspaper he would
  introduce the bill
Don't know how others feel
All council members Democrats
Public hearing — two weeks
All members know about proposal
Professional backgrounds
  Barrett — tax lawyer
  Clarke — insurance
  others — don't know

Met Nolan once at high school graduation
He gave talk on necessity for future health care needs
— relate this to need for investigation
Only existing landfill is in Clarke's district

This exploration has revealed several things that the writer needs to consider. First, there are some significant gaps in his knowledge of his audience. He is not sure of all the names. He doesn't know how many council members have children. He doesn't know the professional backgrounds of the council members. But he needs this information to compose an effective letter. Therefore, he is probably going to have to go down to the public library or call City Hall to get some more information about his audience.

Studying the audience has also shown that it may not be possible to write just one letter that will appeal to the interests of all six council members. So he may decide to write just one letter, addressed to the chairperson and appealing to him, and to send copies to the other members. More time-consuming, but more effective, would be six different letters, each using what the writer knows about that recipient to gain his or her support.

For instance, since Nolan is from the writer's own district and he has heard him speak, he might make his appeal to him a little more personal than one to those members whom he does not know at all. Since Clarke is the sponsor of the bill, the writer knows he is already very interested in the subject. His letter to Clarke could be a simple statement of support and encouragement, or it might include suggestions for improving the bill. Barrett, a tax lawyer, might be appealed to on the basis of economic benefits to the city. If Ms. Ventre is a mother, the writer might appeal to a sense of fellowship with her concerns for the health not only of herself but of future generations. And so on for each council member.

Knowledge of the audience can affect the content of writing.

You can vary the brainstorming technique by giving yourself a set number of things (say ten) that you will list about your audience.

1. religion?
2. business-oriented people mostly
3. worried about city's finances
4. interested enough to listen
5. all older
6. gender
7. health issue should be important to them
8. busy people
9. parents
10. ecology concerns

Once you have made a list like this, you need to review each item to see how it will affect what you write.

An even more structured way to explore an audience is to use a set of questions like the one shown below.

QUESTIONS FOR STUDYING AUDIENCE

1. What is the personal background of this audience (age, sex, social status, education, religious and political affiliation, professional or work experience, etc.)?
2. How much does this audience already know about the subject of my writing?
3. What else does this audience particularly need to know about this subject?
4. How favorably or unfavorably does the audience feel about this subject? Or is the audience neutral on this subject?
5. What is the audience's relationship to me, the writer? Am I writing to my peers or to those superior or inferior to me in some way (older/younger, more/less educated, more/less experienced)? Does the audience know me personally?
6. In general, what response do I want from this audience?

Again, your answers to these questions can help you determine, throughout the writing process, which ideas you will emphasize or de-emphasize in your writing, what kind of language you will choose, and how you will organize the material.

EXERCISE B

Assume that you are writing about your initial reactions to a traffic light installed on your corner. Using any of the techniques suggested above, explore each of the following potential audiences. After your exploration, list the three factors you consider most significant about this audience. Be prepared to explain how these factors might affect your writing in this situation.

1. The mayor of your city
   Most significant factors:

   A. _____

   B. _____

   C. _____

2. Your parents
   Most significant factors:

   A. _____

   B. _____

   C. _____

3. Your best friend
   Most significant factors:

   A. _____

   B. _____

   C. _____

4. Your nine-year-old sister
   Most significant factors:

   A. _____

   B. _____

   C. _____

5. Your boss
   Most significant factors:

   A. _____

   B. _____

   C. _____

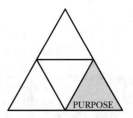

▶ ESTABLISH A PURPOSE

Closely related to your consideration of the audience for your writing is an analysis of the effect you wish to achieve with a particular piece of writing. As with audience, your purpose in writing may be given to you as part of the writing situation, or you may have some choice in what purpose you want to achieve.

Do you want members of the food co-op to understand what the term *inflation* means? Do you want to show them some ways they can get the most for their money? Do you want to convince them that inflation is not really a serious problem? Do you want them to support some piece of legislation designed to curb inflation? Each of these possible purposes for an article on inflation would demand a different selection and arrangement of material on the subject.

Most writing is aimed at achieving one of the four purposes shown in the box below.

GENERAL PURPOSES FOR WRITING

To ENTERTAIN:	**To make the subject enjoyable for the audience.**
To INFORM:	**To fill in gaps in your audience's knowledge of the subject.**
To INTERPRET:	**To explain the meaning or significance of certain facts for your audience.**
To PERSUADE:	**To convince your audience to follow a certain course of action.**

Many poems and stories and other types of imaginative writing have entertainment as their primary purpose. Academic writing, such as term papers, and business writing, such as annual reports, often aim primarily at providing information. Movie or restaurant reviews are examples of writing that tries to interpret information. Newspaper editorials and letters to government officials frequently try to persuade their readers to perform a certain action.

Whatever your purpose is, you should understand it clearly before you begin to write. If you understand why you are writing, you can better control what you say so that the paragraph does exactly and only what you intend. Of course, it frequently happens that you have more than one purpose in writing. You may want to entertain as well as inform, or to inform as well as persuade. In cases like these, you should decide which purpose is most important so that you will be able to emphasize it in your writing.

When you are exploring your own purpose in writing, you should consider each of the four general purposes and decide whether it is appropriate for what you want to do.

Suppose, for instance, that you are a member of the local board of education. One of your tasks this year has been to study the reading program in elementary schools. Now you want to write a report for your fellow board members, none of whom is too familiar with the reading program. Your exploration of purpose might look like this:

entertain
limited entertainment possibilities here
maybe a story about kids learning to read?
use a story from one of the readers
        inform
tell them what our reading program is like
describe typical reading class
use research about reading methods
compare one method of instruction to another
        interpret
explain why our program is not effective
how did we get here—history of program
disadvantages of sight reading
        persuade
get new texts

From a list like this, you would have to choose what you thought was your most important purpose, or which purpose you should deal with first. Should you just explain the instructional method being used? Or should you attack the present method? Or should you try to get the board to act right away to solve the problems you discovered?

In a longer piece of writing, different sections of the paper may have different purposes, but your reader should be able to see how each individual paragraph contributes to the purpose of its section to the whole.

Exercise C
Here are several paragraphs that might be part of the report described above. Decide what purpose each of these paragraphs seems to aim at. Be prepared to explain your choice.

1. The phonics method of instruction seems clearly superior to the sight-reading method. First of all, students learn more vocabulary and learn it more quickly with phonics instruction. While a year of sight-reading training develops an average vocabulary of 350 words, a year of phonics gives students a reading vocabulary of over 5,000 words. Even more important, though, phonics instruction gives students the ability to learn new words independently. Once students have mastered the basic sounds of the language, they can figure out unfamiliar words on their own. Sight-reading students, on the other hand, remain dependent on the teacher to identify new words for them, and they may be completely baffled by a letter combination they have not seen before. Because phonics produces better results both quantitatively and qualitatively, the board should implement phonics instruction in all elementary schools.

Purpose: _____

2. In implementing this change, the board needs to provide for an orderly transition from one method of instruction to another. First, the superintendent of schools should inform all principals of the board's decision. Then, a committee of reading teachers should prepare a plan for phonics instruction. Money should be set aside in next year's budget for the purchase of new textbooks. Finally, the board should hold a series of informational meetings for parents and taxpayers to explain the reasons for the change in emphasis. With careful planning, the new instructional program can be introduced with minimal difficulty.

Purpose: _____

3. Most children are taught to read by one of two basic methods: sight-reading or phonics. With sight-reading, children learn to read by reading. They are given short stories containing the most common English words. Gradually, through repetition, the students begin to recognize certain words. A sight-reading text might contain a sequence like this: "Here is Bob. Here is Rosa. Bob runs. Rosa runs. Run, Bob, run! Run, Rosa, run!" At the end of the year of sight-reading instruction, children should have a reading vocabulary of about 350 words. With the phonics system, on the other hand, children begin with letters rather than words. Children learn the twenty-six letters of the alphabet and the forty-four sounds those letters stand for. The letters and sounds are taught in a planned order, and students see only those words whose sounds they have already mastered. A beginning phonics reader who knew some basic consonant sounds plus the short *a* sound might be given a sentence like: "Dan can fan the man." At the end of a year of phonics instruction, children should have a reading vocabulary of about 5,000 words. Sight-reading and phonics are the basic choices the board of education has when it establishes a reading program.

Purpose: _____

▶ **SELECT A VOICE**

In every writing situation, as in every speaking situation, you use a certain voice to communicate with your audience. You try to sound a certain way to achieve a certain effect. If this quality of voice is based on your analysis of the audience, purpose, and subject of your writing, you are more likely to achieve the effect you intend.

For example, suppose that an automobile accident has occurred. One car is badly damaged. The other has only a small dent. No one has been injured. If you were a police officer writing a report on this accident, you would choose a voice that was impersonal, unemotional, and serious. You would know that your purpose was to record the factual details of the accident as clearly as possible and that your audience (for instance, your superior officer, the participants, insurance claim adjusters, the courts) would not be interested in your personal feelings about the accident. In fact, allowing emotion to show in your report might obscure the facts or lessen the degree of confidence the audience could place in your observations. So your report might sound like this:

At approximately 9:10 p.m. on Sunday, January 29, the first car, a tan 1996 Honda station wagon, approached the traffic signal at Howard and Monroe Streets at a speed of approximately 30 mph. . .

However, if you were the driver of the damaged car and you had to write your brother, who is the car's owner, explaining the accident, you would probably want a different voice to suit your purpose and audience. In this situation, a more personal and emotional voice might be more appropriate. Here, it is your interpretation of events and your relationship with your brother that will determine the effectiveness of the writing. So your letter might sound like this:

Chung-ping, I'm sorry, but I have some bad news. Your Honda has been damaged in an accident. Last Sunday, as I was going home after I had visited Dad in the hospital, some crazy driver ran the red light at the corner of Howard and Monroe . . .

In the actual writing process, voice is created by such things as sentence structure (see Chapters 2–5) and word choice (see Chapter 11). But consciously thinking about voice *before* you write can help you choose the most effective voice possible.

QUESTIONS FOR CHOOSING VOICE

DO YOU WANT: **A personal voice (I, you, we, us) or an impersonal voice (he, she, it, they)?**
An emotional voice or an unemotional voice?
Which emotion—anger, sadness, joy, excitement?
A serious voice or a light voice?
A formal voice or an informal voice?
A knowledgeable voice or a questioning voice?

EXERCISE D
For each of the following writing situations, you are given several possible opening sentences. Decide which voice is best suited to the audience, purpose, and subject in each case, and be prepared to explain your choice.

1. The editor of the Hometown Senior Citizens Newsletter has asked the president of the Hometown Historic Preservation Society to write her a short piece explaining some of the problems of preservation. Which of these openings seems most promising?
   A. Ten dollars is a small price to pay for the many benefits of membership in the Hometown Preservation Society.
   B. The current attempt to save the Sullivan Building on Crane Boulevard illustrates many of the difficulties, legal and financial, that historic preservationists have to deal with.
   C. I am very concerned about historic preservation.

2. The adult education group at your church has asked each member to write a definition of *church* for the next meeting. Which of these definitions seems more appropriate?
   A. The church is a building in our community of which we can be proud.
   B. To me, the church is not a building of brick or wood, but rather the people caring for each other in God's love.

3. Your daughter's third-grade teacher has asked each parent to write a paragraph or so about his or her work for the students' unit on careers. You are a veterinarian. Which opening would be most suitable for your daughter's class?
   A. If you like helping animals and don't mind working at some unusual hours of the night, you could be a good veterinarian.
   B. Veterinary medicine is a good career for people who have a strong sense of other-directedness and the intellectual ability to master advanced principles of anatomy and physiology.
   C. Dogs can have some unusual health problems.

4. Your credit card company has just billed you for the fourth time for a round-trip ticket to Iquitos, Peru. You feel there has been a mistake and you want it straightened out. Which of these openings would be most effective?
   A. I know your efficient computers hardly ever make mistakes, but I should respectfully like to suggest that there is (maybe) a possible error in the bill you recently sent me, although I must admit you have given me fine service for the last three years and I am reluctant to believe that you are mistaken, but I'm pretty sure I never spent that money.
   B. On June 17, 1984, you billed my account #A-300-166 for $748.18 for a round-trip ticket to Iquitos, Peru; however, I believe this billing is in error.
   C. You guys had better do something about this foul-up with my credit card account #A-300-166.

5. Your final exam in American history asks you to discuss the major causes of the Civil War. Which of these openings will be the most impressive to your history professor?
   A. The Civil War has always fascinated me.
   B. Although it is difficult to pin down exact events that caused a major historical phenomenon like the Civil War, we can see general causes of the

war in the economic conditions of the North and the South and in the
relative political power of the two areas.

C. Basically the Civil War was fought by infantry and cavalry troops who each
performed a distinct military function.

WRITING PRACTICE:

1. From the journal entries you did for Exercise A in this chapter, choose an item
to develop into a 250-word letter. Use the strategies discussed in this chapter to
generate some ideas and explore the other aspects of this writing situation:
audience, purpose, and voice. Hand in your exploration sheets with your letter.

2. The mayor of your town has encouraged community college students to
communicate with her about the things they like or don't like about their
community. Write a 250-word letter to the mayor about what you consider to be
your community's greatest strength or its greatest weakness. Before you write
the letter, use the strategies discussed in this chapter to generate some ideas
and explore the other aspects of this writing situation: audience, purpose, and
voice. Hand in your exploration sheets with your letter.

3. When you mention to your friend who works for the local paper what you have
written to the mayor, he is very impressed with your idea. He asks you to write it
up as an editorial for the paper. Before you prepare the article, use the
techniques presented in this chapter to explore this writing situation. Hand in
your exploration sheets with your article.

◀ *Chapter 10* ▶

Drafting

• • • • • • • • • • •

▶ NARROW THE FIELD
▶ RELATE IDEAS AND FILL IN GAPS
▶ REVIEW STRATEGIES
▶ ARRANGE GROUPS LOGICALLY
▶ STATE THE FOCUS
▶ DISPLAY ORGANIZATION

• • • • • • • • • • •

When you have spent some time exploring each of the factors in a writing situation—subject, audience, purpose, voice—your mind really starts to become engaged with this problem. You have churned up lots of ideas, and now you can begin to sort through them and select the ones you want to use.

An incubation period can be very useful now. If you have enough time (and this is one reason for allowing plenty of time for a writing project), you should let your ideas simmer for a day or two and see which ones seem to float to the top. Your subconscious mind can do a lot of work for you if you give it the time and the material to work with.

Although this chapter is going to give you some suggestions for shaping this welter of ideas into a semicoherent whole, keep in mind that the writing process doesn't always happen in a nice, orderly progression. You may not do things in the same order in which they are presented in the text. You may find several of these operations happening at once. You may find yourself ready to go right into a draft of your paper without performing all these preliminary steps. So stay flexible and be willing to try new strategies.

▶ NARROW THE FIELD

If you are lucky, your mind will already have begun the process of narrowing the field by the time you start reviewing your exploration sheets. One or two ideas will "grab" you as promising material. If you aren't already conscious of an emerging focus for your ideas, look at your exploration sheets to see what material is repeated. Are there any ideas that seemed to crop up in several different ways? Quite often, those are the ideas that you think are important. If none of the ideas particularly inspires you, go back anyway and circle two or three that you think you might be able to work with. (Face it: not every piece of writing will be inspired!)

EXERCISE A

Study the writing situations below. Narrow the field to two or three aspects of the subject that seem promising.

EXAMPLE:

Choosing a Day-Care Facility

Situation: A mother is evaluating a day-care facility for her second child.

Writing Possibilities (based on explorations shown in Chapter 9):

1. *the importance of discipline and order at Tiny Tots*

2. *the characteristics of the teaching staff*

3. *first child's experiences at Tiny Tots*

1. Sports

   Situation: You want a local company to sponsor a community athletic program.

   Writing Possibilities:

   1. _____

   2. _____

   3. _____

2. Senior Citizens

   Situation: The American Association for Retired Persons Scholarship will be awarded to the writer of the best essay on ways senior citizens and preschoolers can interact.

   Writing Possibilities:

   1. _____

   2. _____

   3. _____

3. Civic Pride
   Situation: You are concerned and want to write a letter to the editor of your local newspaper about the lack of pride people take in your community.
   Writing Possibilities:

   1. _____

   2. _____

   3. _____

4. School
   Situation: You are working on a letter to your former principal about stories you hear about current racial tensions at your alma mater.
   Writing Possibilities:

   1. _____

   2. _____

   3. _____

5. Community
   Situation: Your sociology professor's first assignment asks you to define the term *community.*
   Writing Possibilities:

   1. _____

   2. _____

   3. _____

▶ RELATE IDEAS AND FILL IN GAPS

When you have narrowed your field to a topic, go back over your exploration sheets and look for connections among ideas. Which details or ideas seem to relate to each possible approach? Within the ideas for each narrowed topic, can you see any natural groups? What ideas seem to belong together?

One student, for example, was working on a definition of *community* for his sociology class. In reviewing his initial exploration sheets, he found the following details related to that topic. The lines show some of the initial connections he made.

to commune

to communicate

to live with others ←
→ *to have a sense of belonging*
others know me ←
common concerns
interested in safety ←
interested in keeping up property ←
small parties
network to work world
car pools
→ *identity*
→ *where I'm from*
values
quality (or lack thereof) of life ←
tone
together but private
→ *a shared sense*

As he looked at these connections, he saw a pattern. He had details relating to two of the three different aspects of community-identity and quality of life. He added the third aspect—allow differences—to his list and filled in some other ideas. Eventually, he came up with a rough grouping that looked like this:

Identity	Quality of Life	Allow Differences
sense of belonging	maintain property	Mastmanns = British, Protestant
own identity	want safety	Costellos = Italian, Catholic
where I'm from	block parties	Tidwells = African, Muslim
cohesiveness	bonding for tragedies	Stroebels = German, Lutherans
when meet outsider	community boundaries	
team T-shirts	marked	

All Communities

function
dysfunction
tone

As this writer's experience shows, in grouping ideas, you will probably leave out some things from your exploration sheets and add other ideas to fill in gaps. You may also uncover places where you need to go out and find additional information.

▶ REVIEW STRATEGIES

As you begin to establish connections between your ideas, you may see a clear pattern developing, as the writer of the *community* definition did. At other times, you may need to consciously review various strategies (such as the five shown in Chapter 8: telling a story, describing, listing examples, breaking down into categories, and comparing or contrasting) to decide on an appropriate way to develop your narrowed topic so that it suits your audience and purpose.

For example, the student evaluating the day-care center for her child listed the influence of the teachers on her son as one possibility for approaching her writing project. In order to discuss her son's experience with the teachers who were at the facility when he attended, she might tell the story of one particular incident that sums up his feelings about the teachers. Or she might list several examples of ways the teachers influenced him. Or she could categorize the kinds of teachers her son had at the school.

In trying to move your writing to completion, look for a strategy that seems to suit your material. Again, if you are lucky, one strategy may stand out to you as absolutely right for this situation. If none seems particularly better than another, choose any one that you think you can work with. You can always revise if inspiration strikes later in the process.

EXERCISE B

Study each of the following lists of details. What connections can you see among the ideas on each list? For each list, suggest a possible set of groupings. Label each group of ideas. Feel free to add more ideas to any group.

When you have established a set of groups, consider possible strategies for developing this topic and choose the one that seems most appropriate for this subject, audience, and purpose. Be prepared to explain your choices.

EXAMPLE:

Writing Situation: Your local chamber of commerce wants to persuade people living in nearby counties to visit your community more often.

Topic: Things to Do in My Community

zoo	little restaurants	neighborhood bars
museum	symphony	specialty stores
parks	major-league sports	theaters
ethnic food	historical sites	historic district

Groups:

I. *Stretch the Mind*	II. *Relax Outdoors*	III. *Eat*
*museums	*zoos	little restaurants
*symphony	parks	neighborhood bars
*theaters	*major-league sports	*ethnic food
*art galleries (added)	*tour historic sites	*elegant restaurants (added)
*indicates unique		gourmet food (added)
city attractions		

Strategy: Compare community attractions to suburb attractions.

1. *Situation:* You want a local company to sponsor a community athletic program.

Topic: Reasons for the Support

no after-school programs	teenagers just hang out	neighbors concerned
increase in drug use	not enough jobs	athletic talent
increase in teenage pregnancy	informal survey	relationship to area
increase in crime rate	willing coaches	good politics
help police	schools underfunded	leadership available

Groups:

I.   II.   III.

Strategy:

2. *Situation:* You are concerned and want to write a letter to the editor of your local newspaper about the lack of pride people take in your community.

Topic: Signs of Disgrace

graffiti	peeling paint	boarded-up buildings
abandoned cars	sidewalks not swept	and homes
small children out late	trees unpruned	crack dealers
loud music	uncovered trash cans	people afraid

Groups:

I.   II.   III.

Strategy:

3. *Situation:* The AARP Scholarship will be awarded to the writer of the best essay on ways senior citizens and preschoolers can interact.

Topic: Ways to Interact

reading stories	attend church	help pick up things
sitting while sick	take to movie	push wheelchair
take on visits to doctor	writing letters as dictated	carry important objects
invite for holidays	play Santa	change diapers
feed infants	sing songs	play musical instruments
make things	build sandcastles	blow bubbles

> *Groups:*
> I.   II.   III.

> *Strategy:*

▶ ARRANGE GROUPS LOGICALLY

When you have a sense of strategy for your writing and you have set up some groups within your list of ideas, you need to consider the arrangement of those groups. Which details should come first in your paper? Which should come later? Which should you end with?

The writer of the definition of *community,* for instance, used the strategy of showing different categories of community, and the writer had broken his material into three general groups.

One logical way to arrange the three points would be to use the information about community in general as an introduction and then present the three aspects of community in an orderly pattern.

I. All Communities	arranged by size from specific
II. Personal Identity Enhanced	→ to general
III. Differences Accepted	
IV. Quality of Life Maintained	

or

I. All Communities	
II. Differences Accepted	→ arranged in order of importance
III. Quality of Life Maintained	
IV. Personal Identity Enhanced	

Logical patterns of arrangement can be based on *time* (earliest to latest event), *space* (farthest away to closest, top to bottom, left to right), or *size* (smallest to largest). If no other pattern of arrangement seems obvious to you, you can arrange points in order of *importance,* always beginning with the least important and ending with the most important. Writers call this "saving your big guns for last."

Of course, the order in which you present your ideas depends, to some extent, on your audience and purpose. For instance, in the example shown above on community, an arrangement from specific to general would be suitable for an audience whose knowledge of community was not very specialized. The arrangement for order of importance would be suitable if your audience had more of a philosophical understanding or if your purpose were to explain *community* as it relates to a sociological theory.

Knowledge of audience is particularly critical when you arrange items in an order of importance. The most important point to one audience may not be the most important point to another. Suppose, for instance, that your employee group has three complaints about the job: low pay, poor working environment, and the difficulty of the work. If you were writing to the supervisor about these complaints, you might choose to end with (that is, emphasize) poor working environment because that is the area that the supervisor can do the most about. A letter to fellow workers, on the other hand, might make low pay the item of greatest importance.

Whatever pattern of arrangement you choose, be sure that it is as clear to your reader as it is to you. This may require some use of signals in your writing to tell your reader what the organizational structure is. In the example about community, you could say, "Quality of life, which is the most written about aspect, . . ." and "a critical aspect is whether differences are accepted." Phrases like these would indicate to your reader the direction in which you were moving. (The section on Coherence in Chapter 11 presents a full discussion of connectives between major ideas.)

Exercise C

Arrange each of the following lists of major supporting points in logical order and explain briefly what principle you have used to organize them. For what audience and purpose would your arrangement be best suited?

1. Drinking water in your community
   availability   I.
   taste   II.
   clarity   III.
   chemical analysis   IV.
   smell   V.
   intestinal diseases   VI.

   Explanation: _____

   _____

   Audience: _____

   Purpose: _____

2. Need for jogging and bicycling paths
   accidents   I.
   new interest in exercise   II.
   fatalities   III.
   future road design   IV.
   traffic patterns   V.
   jogging and biking for charities   VI.

   Explanation:

   _____

   _____

   Audience: _____

   Purpose: _____

3. Increased building in your community
   impact on social services   I.
   increased crime rate   II.
   impact on sanitation   III.
   impact on traffic   IV.
   increased tax base   V.
   impact on school populations   VI.

   Explanation: _____

   _____

   Audience: _____

   Purpose: _____

4. Need for a neighborhood watch program
   increase in drug abuse   I.
   fear among elderly people   II.
   increase in crime rate   III.
   cutbacks in number of police   IV.
       officers

   Explanation: _____

   _____

Audience: _____

Purpose: _____

5. Description of neighborhood
    buildings   I.
    traffic   II.
    shrubbery   III.
    overall impression   IV.
    families   V.
    ethnicity   VI.
    ages   VII.

    Explanation: _____

    _____

    Audience: _____

    Purpose: _____

When the major groups have been arranged satisfactorily, you can arrange any supporting detail within each category. For instance, look at the details you saw listed earlier under *community*.

Identity	**Quality of Life**	**Allow Differences**
sense of belonging	maintain property	Mastmanns = British, Protestant
own identity	want safety	Costellos = Italian, Catholic
where I'm from	block parties	Tidwells = African, Muslim
cohesiveness	bonding for tragedies	Stroebels = German, Lutherans

The supporting points under quality of life could be arranged into two groups: physical needs and human needs. The supporting points under differences could be arranged similarly: ethnic and religious differences. Sometimes topics like types of community organizations will allow you to have the same categories (membership and functions) so that the organization of supporting details ensures that you will cover the same points for each aspect of community.

▶ STATE THE FOCUS

At some point in this organizing process, you should be ready to state the focus of your paper. You may do this after you have chosen a strategy and begun to arrange supporting details or even after you have worked out a draft of the paper. Or you may choose to do this early in the process.

The focus statement, whenever you compose it, helps to clarify in your mind the main point you want to make in this piece of writing. It serves as the basis for a topic sentence and/or a thesis statement in your finished paper.

For instance, suppose your job in retail requires you to advise professionals on different images created by clothing. You have decided that certain hints in conversation and perhaps a newsletter will help boost your sales. You have this list of details on the "real estate" look:

> *nautical look*
>
> *white slacks*
>
> *penny loafers*
>
> *light blue Gant shirt*
>
> *blue blazer*
>
> *gold bracelet*
>
> *short haircut*
>
> *suntan*
>
> *sunglasses on string*

Now, looking at this list, you can try to decide on one word that most clearly defines the central impression you want your customers to have in mind. Brainstorming can be useful in this process. Just list the words you think might fit:

> *competent*
>
> *open*
>
> *freedom*
>
> *confident*
>
> *professional* √

Then consider your audience. Which word will your customers respond to most favorably? Try creating a focus statement that will emphasize whatever word you have chosen. Try using the key idea in several different positions in the sentence:

Subject —Professionalism is the key to clothing style.

Verb —

Complement —The image projected by this clothing style will be the consummate professional.

Exercise D

Choose one topic from each subject you developed in Exercise A. After doing whatever grouping of details you can, select an appropriate strategy for your topic and compose a focus statement that will show the main point you would try to get across in this paper.

<u>EXAMPLE:</u>

Subject: Scouts

Topic: *The Influence of My Leaders*

Strategy: *Tell a story about one influential event*

Focus Statement: *More than anything else, Mrs. Halla's patient work with me on my entry for the Girl Scout Writing Competition taught me to think of myself as a creative person.*

1. *Subject:* Athletic program

   Topic: _____

   Strategy: _____

   Focus Statement: _____

   _____

2. *Subject:* Senior citizens

   Topic: _____

   Strategy: _____

   Focus Statement: _____

   _____

3. *Subject:* Community pride

   Topic: _____

   Strategy: _____

   Focus Statement: _____

   _____

4. *Subject:* Your alma mater

   Topic: _____

   Strategy: _____

   Focus Statement: _____

   _____

5. *Subject:* Community

   Topic: _____

   Strategy: _____

   Focus Statement: _____

   _____

▶ DISPLAY ORGANIZATION

You have three ways to highlight the organization of a piece of writing: (1) the advanced organizer, (2) use of fonts and computer graphics, and (3) the traditional outline. In the drafting stage of a long piece of writing, you can use these techniques to clarify the planning you have done, clearly showing the coordinate and subordinate relationships among your ideas. Later, these techniques can also be useful to your readers, especially for a long piece of writing, by showing them the logic of your organization of ideas.

The Advanced Organizer: At the beginning of each chapter of this book, you see the focus of the chapter—a list of the items to be covered. This technique is helpful to readers as a preview of what will be discussed. It gives readers a framework on which to attach the information in that chapter. You may use this idea as a preface in a long paper or letter.

Use of Fonts and Computer Graphics: To some extent, readers are affected by the layout of text on a page. Companies spend millions of dollars to market their products, and they pay for people's expertise in coining slogans and laying out eye-catching advertisements for the print media. Your reader is also affected by the visual impression of the page along with the content of the message. Your careful use of bullets, fonts, and graphics can help the reader follow the progression of your thinking.

The Outline: Traditionally, writers have used the formal outline to help organize their own thinking and to help the reader preview their intent. An outline uses Roman numerals (I, II, III) to show major points. Capital letters (A, B, C) show supporting details for each major point. Arabic numerals (1, 2, 3) show any further examples under A, B, C.

Here is an outline of the paper on community:

Topic Sentence: My definition of *community* comes from my experience of growing up in Richmond Hill.

   I. All communities
      A. Function
      B. Composition
  II. Differences accepted
      A. Many ethnic groups represented
      B. Many religious differences
         1. Protestants
         2. Catholics
         3. Muslims
      C. Food preferences
 III. Quality of life maintained
      A. Block parties
         1. Fourth of July
         2. Military homecoming
      B. Landscaped yards
      C. Safe environment
      D. Bonding for tragedies
 IV. Personal identity enhanced
      A. Pride in community
      B. Sense of belonging

Conclusion: Because of these positive aspects of community, my experience of growing up in Richmond Hill was a happy one.

Notice that an outline moves from the most general idea, expressed in the topic sentence, to the most specific idea, here expressed as Arabic numerals 1, 2, and 3. In an outline that goes only as far as Arabic numerals, you usually will not have a I without a II or an A without a B. Sometimes, if you are using only one example, there may be a 1 without a 2, but this is not the norm.

Be careful that your outline accurately reflects the weight to be given to each point. All Roman numeral items should coordinate. Similarly, all capital letter items should be of equivalent weight but subordinate to the Roman numeral points. (For coordination, see Chapter 4. For subordination, see Chapter 5.)

What is wrong with the following outline?

Topic Sentence: All community residents should take pride in our neighborhood by listening to people who live in fear, by fixing up homes and businesses, and by working with the police to lessen crime.

    I. Deteriorated buildings
       A. Boarded up
   II. People who are afraid
       A. Elderly
       B. Children
  III. Crack dealers are selling

Conclusion: Residents need to take back the neighborhood and be proud again of their community.

For one thing, III. *Crack dealers are selling* is not coordinate with I and II and shouldn't get a Roman numeral in this outline. *Crack dealers are selling* is really a supporting example subordinate to a general category of *crime.* Another problem with this outline is the order in which the major points are presented. The topic sentence gives them in one arrangement, but the outline does not follow that pattern. Finally, coordinate points should be phrased in a similar way to emphasize their relatedness. So *people who are afraid* should be *scared people* to emphasize its coordination with *deteriorated buildings* in I.

    Here is a more accurate version of this outline:

Topic Sentence: All community residents should take pride in our neighborhood by listening to people who live in fear, by fixing up homes and businesses, and by working with the police to lessen crime.

    I. Deteriorated buildings
       A. Boarded up
       B. Graffiti filled
       C. Proposed
   II. Scared people
       A. Elderly
       B. Children
       C. Solutions
  III. Crime level
       A. Increase in drug abuse
       B. Increase in robberies
       C. Decrease in crime

Conclusion: Residents need to take back the neighborhood and again be proud of their community.

    Outlining, then, can be a way to help you (and your reader) see the various levels of generalization in your writing and visualize the coordinate and subordinate relationships among your ideas.

EXERCISE E

Put the following list of details into outline form. You may wish to do a rough grouping first, then a more formal outline.

1. a. Eskimos in the Arctic
   b. Build spacecraft
   c. Protect orphans
   d. Construct radio telescopes
   e. Tuaregs in the Sahara
   f. Live anywhere
   g. Make marvelous tools
   h. Computers
   i. Altruistic
   j. Provide for the helpless
   k. Mourn the dead

   Topic sentence: Human beings are amazing.

   I. _____

      A. _____

      B. _____

      C. _____

   II. _____

      A. _____

      B. _____

      C. _____

   III. _____

      A. _____

      B. _____

   Conclusion: Human beings are astonishingly complex.

WRITING PRACTICE:

1. Choose any one of the writing projects you worked on in Exercises A and C of this chapter and produce a finished version of it. If you wish, have someone else review a draft of your writing and make suggestions for revisions or corrections.

2. You are a member of this year's Fourth of July committee, working on the selection of a speaker for the event. Using whatever methods of exploring, focusing, and organizing you like, choose an appropriate candidate and write a report to the committee nominating your chosen speaker.

You may check with your instructor or a librarian for assistance in getting background information about possible speakers. Speakers may come from any field so long as you think they will have something interesting to say to those attending the Fourth of July celebration.

Chapter 11

Revising

• • • • • • • • • • •

- ▶ UNITY
  - Relating Support to Topic Sentence
  - Unifying through Subordination
- ▶ COHERENCE
  - Sentence Combining
  - Transition Signals
  - Parallel Structure
  - Repetition of Key Words
- ▶ WORD CHOICE
  - Level of Generality
  - Connotative Value
  - Degree of Formality
  - Degree of Conciseness

• • • • • • • • • • •

Since writing involves so many considerations—audience, purpose, organization, sentence structure, word choice—it is almost impossible for any writer to keep all these factors in mind at once. Because of this complexity, most writers will do some planning before writing, then write a draft of the paper, then work on revising that draft.

Re-vision means *seeing again*. In revising a piece of writing, you go back to it, perhaps several times, looking at it from different perspectives. One time, you might be looking to make sure you have stayed with your main idea. On another reading, you might be checking to see that connections have been established between ideas. Looking a third time, you might concentrate on whether the particular words you have chosen are suitable for your audience and purpose.

During the revision process it is often helpful to have someone else read your paper: your roommate, your professor, your English lab instructor, a friend, a classmate. Someone else may see problems in organization or wording that you have overlooked because you are so familiar with the ideas you are writing about. Basically, you want feedback on whether all parts of the paper make sense to someone else.

A final version of your paper may come only after several revisions. There is nothing out of the ordinary about this. No writer sits down and produces a perfect letter, paragraph, essay, or report on the first try. It's important, then, that you allow yourself plenty of time for revision. That way, your final copy will present your idea as accurately and convincingly as possible. Time spent in revising your writing is time well spent.

▶ UNITY

One way to begin the revision process is to evaluate the unity of your writing. How well does this piece of writing stick to the main idea?

REVISING TO HELP READERS SEE UNITY
RELATING SUPPORT TO TOPIC SENTENCE
UNIFYING THROUGH SUBORDINATION

By the time you have finished your first draft, you should have pretty well committed yourself to dealing with a particular, limited subject in a particular, limited way.

● Relating Support to Topic Sentence

The topic sentence of your paragraph is your written commitment to your audience of what you will do in a certain piece of writing. For instance, if your topic sentence has told the audience that you are going to write about the costs of electing a prime minister, you can't turn around and discuss the rewards of being a prime minister. You must deliver to your reader what you promised in the topic sentence.

Look at this paragraph:

Mohandas Gandhi's plans for nonviolence worked. First, he taught the Indians to spin and weave their own cotton cloth. By buying cloth from themselves instead of from the

English, the Indians gained financial power. Gandhi suggested another way to fight back without guns and violence. He told the people they should disobey unfair laws and then go peacefully when arrested and taken to jail. Sometimes Gandhi even fasted for days in order to call attention to an injustice. As the harshness of the English was seen by more and more people, the Indians slowly but peacefully won their freedom from England.

What does this paragraph promise the reader? How does it keep that promise?

Well, the topic sentence limits the discussion to Mohandas Gandhi's plans. The topic sentence also requires that the paragraph discuss only the plans for non-violence, not the Indians' social status or their divisions among themselves. In addition, the topic sentence suggests that his plans worked.

The topic sentence's promise is kept by the writer's giving three strategies Gandhi used and how the strategies were employed. So the paragraph does stick to the subject and focus set up in the topic sentence.

Because the focus part of the topic sentence exerts such control over what happens in the rest of the paragraph, it is frequently referred to as the controlling idea of the paragraph. Thus, a paragraph in which the support fits the topic sentence is said to have *unity*. In a unified paragraph, all the supporting sentences relate directly to the subject and the controlling idea presented in the topic sentence. Computers offer writers easy ways to move supporting sentences into isolation onto a list. Writers can then check supporting sentences, sentence by sentence, to check visually whether the supporting sentences actually relate directly to the controlling idea.

Exercise A

In each of the following exercises, you are given a topic sentence and some possible supporting details. In each case decide which details would fit in a unified paragraph and be prepared to explain why.

1. Yo-Yo Ma is one of the finest cellists in the world.
   a. He was born in Paris, France, to Chinese parents.
   b. Both his mother and his father are musical and well-educated.
   c. When Yo-Yo was seven, his family moved to New York City.
   d. Many musicians study only music.
   e. Yo-Yo Ma decided to go to Harvard University to study music and other subjects.
   f. At the Marlboro Music Festival, he met Jill Horner, with whom he fell in love.
   g. Certain old cellos made by great craftsmen sound better than newer cellos.
   h. One of Yo-Yo Ma's favorite musicians is the German composer Johann Sebastian Bach who wrote beautiful music for the cello.
   i. As his father advised him, Yo-Yo plays a little of Bach's music each night before bed.
   j. Yo-Yo Ma continues to practice many hours every day.
2. Winston Churchill helped save England from Hitler's Nazis.
   a. As a young boy, Winston Churchill did poorly in school.
   b. Adolf Hitler attacked England after taking over Poland, Denmark, Norway, France, and Holland.

    c. As prime minister—the chief government leader of England—Winston Churchill spoke to his people on the radio.

    d. Churchill's speeches were magnificent, for he helped the English feel brave.

    e. He said, "We shall fight on the beaches, we shall fight on the landing grounds, we shall fight in the fields and in the streets, we shall fight in the hills; we shall never surrender."

    f. When German pilots dropped bombs on London, Winston Churchill visited frightened people in factories, stores, and homes.

    g. Churchill asked his people to fight hard.

    h. Churchill helped his country along with the other Allied countries defeat Nazi Germany to end World War II.

    i. Winston Churchill's family has a beautiful home in Blenheim.

    j. A prime minister is much like the president of the United States.

3. Katsushika Hokusai always wanted to do better as an artist.

    a. Katsushika Hokusai was born near Tokyo, Japan.

    b. During his lifetime he made 40,000 drawings and over 10,000 woodcuts.

    c. A woodcut is a print made by pressing a piece of paper onto a carved and inked block of wood.

    d. Hokusai was born poor and stayed poor for most of his life.

    e. Hokusai was always excited about the next drawing he was going to do or the next woodcut he was going to make.

    f. Because he liked to change what he drew and how he drew, each time he changed his drawing style, he changed his name.

    g. He changed his name more than thirty times, but the name he used most was Hokusai.

    h. At the age of seventy-five, Hokusai wrote about his life's work.

    i. His famous pictures are of people, animals, ocean waves, and Mount Fuji.

    j. He also published drawing books that showed how to draw animals and people.

● Unifying through Subordination

In the exercise you just worked on, you deleted any details that did not refer directly to the topic and controlling idea set up for the paragraph. There is, however, another way of dealing with such material. Some details that are interesting but not directly related to the controlling idea may be included in your writing through the use of subordination.

For example, you are writing to your parents about some research you are doing in college on Gandhi. Perhaps your topic sentence is: *I have discovered that Gandhi won power without fighting.* You have three facts you want to report:

> **Gandhi fasted for days in order to call attention to an injustice.**
>
> **Gandhi peacefully went to jail many times for good causes.**
>
> **Gandhi was shot and killed by a fellow Indian.**

If you just leave out all mention of his being killed, you're not giving an entirely accurate picture of Gandhi's life. On the other hand, his being killed by a fellow Indian doesn't really support the impression of success you want to create.

One way of handling this difficulty is to emphasize his success by putting those strategies into the base sentence and to de-emphasize his death by putting that in a subordinate word group.

> **Even though Gandhi was shot and killed by a fellow Indian,** *he inspired people around the world by fasting for days in order to call attention to an injustice and then peacefully going to jail many times for good causes.*

Here is another situation that calls for the use of subordination. Suppose you are intrigued by Hokusai's woodcuts. In your opening sentence, you want to convey your favorable impression of his work and you also mention where he was born. Since the main purpose of your paper is to give your opinion, you don't want to give too much importance to his birthplace. However, the location is certainly relevant information to your readers. The solution is to subordinate the location.

> **Katsushika Hokusai,** born near Tokyo, Japan, *always wanted to do better as an artist.*

The techniques of subordination are presented in Chapter 5; you may want to review them before doing the exercises that follow.

Exercise B

Each topic sentence below suggests a unifying idea. Use subordination to make the supporting sentences fit that controlling idea.

Example:

    T.S. Walt Disney revolutionized animated cartoons.
        Pre-Disney cartoons featured simple, two-dimensional pictures.   Disney insisted on humanized figures.   Earlier cartoons were based on slapstick comedy.   Disney wanted humor that developed out of personality.

While pre-Disney cartoons featured simple, two-dimensional pictures, Disney insisted on humanized figures. Disney wanted humor developed out of personality rather than the slapstick comedy of earlier cartoons.

1. *T.S.* "Babe" Didrickson was the greatest female athlete of modern times. She excelled in basketball.   She excelled in track and field.   She excelled in golf.   Most athletes specialize in one sport.

_____

_____

_____

2. *T.S.* Frederick Douglass, once a slave himself, became a famous antislavery speaker.
   He practiced reading.   He practiced writing.   He managed to learn as a slave.   The education of slaves was illegal.

   _____

   _____

   _____

3. *T.S.* George Balanchine is respected as one of the world's greatest choreographers.
   Some of his ballets tell stories.   Others express the music and do not tell stories.   He created a version of Stravinsky's *Firebird* for his wife Maria. In this ballet, she danced the part of a magical wild bird.

   _____

   _____

   _____

4. *T.S.* Elizabeth Cady Stanton wanted women to have the same rights as men.
   Elizabeth Cady Stanton, along with Lucretia Mott, organized the first women's rights convention ever held.   In the *Declaration of Sentiments*, she wrote that "all men *and women* are created equal."

   _____

   _____

   _____

5. *T.S.* Martin Luther King, Jr., helped launch the Civil Rights movement.
   Reverend King led the Montgomery bus boycott.   Black people in Montgomery walked to work.   Some rode bicycles.   Others drove cars. They refused to pay to support an unfair bus company.

   _____

   _____

   _____

REVISION PRACTICE:

Identify the controlling idea of each of the following student paragraphs. Then, using a separate sheet of paper, revise the paragraphs for unity by eliminating any details not pertinent to the focus and by making sure that each base sentence relates directly to the controlling idea of the paragraph.

1. Wye Castle has a sinister reputation. The castle, which is featured in many legends of dark deeds, sits on a hill in Shropshire near the Welsh border. Of all the great mansions in the area, Wye Castle is the largest and grandest. According to one tale, moonlight shines where a bloodstain appears on the stone floor of the Duke's bedroom. Esmerelda, whose blood supposedly stains the floor, was a beautiful peasant whom the Duke set above his family. She was the youngest of five daughters. A mirror stands in the bedroom where one can allegedly see the Duke's sons stabbing Esmerelda while their mother looks on. The mirror has an elaborately carved mahogany frame that matches the other rich furnishings in the room. There is also the cellar door where, every New Year's Day, someone taps, asking to be let in. But although there is no one there, someone always opens the door. While no one lives there now because of its dark secrets, the castle is quite attractive by daylight.

2. Homer celebrates cleverness and cunning in *The Odyssey.* The figures of Athena and Odysseus, who are extremely intelligent, dominate the poem. Odysseus, who is the cleverest man alive, is trying to get home to his wife and son. Odysseus is married to a patient and faithful woman named Penelope. While Odysseus, whom Homer calls "the man who is never at a loss," conquers Troy by using a clever stratagem, other heroes have fought for ten years without taking the city. The war over Troy begins with the kidnap-  ping of the beautiful Helen. Although Odysseus finally manages to get home, on the way there his crew is disobedient, and several gods are against him. Athena is the courageous goddess of wisdom who is Homer's second example of cunning. Her father, whom she tricks, is the chief of gods, and her uncle, whom she outwits, is the sea-god. Many of the Greek gods seem as petty as the mortals whose lives they supposedly rule. Athena meets Odysseus and they argue in a battle of wits. Because of Odysseus' craftiness and Athena's cleverness, there is peace at last in the world of the poem. Homer admires honesty and respects courage, but he feels intelligence is greater. Other ancient writers put more value on courage than on cleverness.

▶ COHERENCE

To communicate an idea clearly to an audience, a paragraph should certainly be unified around one central idea. But unity is not always enough to ensure clear communication. Research has shown that readers have very short memories and need constant reminders to help them keep the message in mind.

Therefore, your paragraph may be unified and well-organized but still be difficult to follow because you haven't provided the clues that will help your reader establish the connections between your ideas. In revising a piece of writing, you need to pay special attention to showing the relationships between and among your sentences. This quality of showing relationships is called *coherence,* making sure ideas stick together.

REVISING TO HELP READERS SEE CONNECTIONS
SENTENCE COMBINING
TRANSITION SIGNALS
PARALLEL STRUCTURE
REPETITION OF KEY WORDS

Look at the two paragraphs below. Which one is easier to follow?

A. Henry Ford experienced several setbacks in establishing his company, but he eventually contributed significantly to the automobile industry. After running off to work in a machine shop at the age of sixteen, he built himself a steam car which he discarded as unsafe. Even though he developed a better model car by working at night in his shed, he later had two failed attempts at companies. In 1901, a Ford model car won a race, and he attracted a new group of backers for a third try. This time he had an uninterrupted upward climb. Some observers were impressed that he was able to bring together mass production and central assembly so that he could keep his costs low enough to price his product for the largest possible mass market. Others in the industrial world were shocked by his cutting working hours and raising the minimum wage. If higher pay could give him more production and better workmanship, the benefits were worth the costs. Besides, more Americans would be able to afford his cars.

B. Henry Ford experienced several setbacks. He had difficulty establishing his company. He contributed significantly to the automobile industry. He ran off to work in a machine shop at the age of sixteen. He built himself a steam car. He discarded it as unsafe. He developed a better model car by working at night in his shed. He failed twice at companies. In 1901, a Ford model car won a race. He attracted a new group of backers for a third try. This time he had an uninterrupted upward climb. He brought together mass production and central assembly. He was able to keep his costs low enough to price his product low. He could get to the largest possible mass market. The industrial world was shocked. He cut working hours and raised the minimum wage. Higher pay gave him more production and better workmanship. The benefits were worth the costs. More Americans would be able to afford his cars.

Paragraph B is unnecessarily hard to read. To understand it, you may have to reread the paragraph several times, working to tie the ideas together. In Paragraph B, the relationships between one sentence and another and between one part of the paragraph and another are not clear. In this version, for instance, you may not have realized that the writer intends to emphasize one attempt or one contribution more than another. Paragraph B lacks coherence—that is, the ideas do not stick together (cohere) well.

In Paragraph A, on the other hand, four specific writing techniques have been used to show the relationships between ideas. First, some sentences have been combined using methods familiar to you from exercises in previous chapters.

> **Even though he developed a better model car by working at night in his shed, he later had two failed attempts at companies.**
>
> **In 1901, a Ford model car won a race, *and* he attracted a new group of backers for a third try.**

Second, some sentences have been tied into the paragraph by the addition of transition signals that explain their relationships either to the preceding sentence or to the topic sentence.

> ***Besides*, more Americans would be able to afford his cars.**
>
> ***After* running off to work in a machine shop at the age of sixteen, he built himself a steam car which he discarded as unsafe.**

Third, some sentences have been rewritten to give them parallel structures emphasizing their parallel functions in the paragraph.

> ***Some observers* were impressed that . . .**
>
> ***Others in the industrial world* were shocked . . .**

Finally, the wording of some sentences has been changed so that key words and phrases are repeated to help the reader follow the discussion.

> **. . . a *steam car* which he discarded as unsafe. Even though he developed a *better model car* . . .**
>
> **. . . he had *two* failed attempts at companies . . . he attracted a new group of backers for a *third* try.**

Exercise C

In each of the following paragraphs, identify the methods the writer has used to achieve coherence.

1. Like other rulers of the late eighteenth century, Empress Catherine the Great of Russia is often referred to as an "enlightened despot." On the one hand, she helped Russia by establishing closer diplomatic ties with European nations. She also founded hospitals, schools, and the St. Petersburg Public Library to benefit the Russian people. She even introduced some progressive legal ideas such as the abolition of torture. On the other hand, Catherine had no qualms about murdering her husband to gain his throne. In addition, she extended the appalling system of serfdom into vast areas of Russia when it suited her fiscal policies. Finally, in her foreign policy, she unscrupulously took advantage of neighboring countries' difficulties to seize their land. Poland, for example, was swallowed up during her reign. Because of the glaring contrasts in her actions, some historians find it hard to decide whether Catherine was more enlightened or more despotic as a ruler.

2. Ralph Bunche made a statement with his life that no problem of human relations is ever insoluble. In 1950, Dr. Bunche brought about a truce between warring Jews and Arabs in Israel. Although fighting in the Middle East still breaks out, the truce was a major accomplishment because it brought temporary peace to the area and showed that the newly created United Nations was capable of acting firmly to end conflict. He was called on again in  1960 when Belgium withdrew its control over the Congo (now called Zaire). Fighting had broken out, and Dr. Bunche was sent to bring peace to the area. At that time, his actions helped prevent a major war in central Africa and gave the new government a chance to survive. During the next few years, Dr. Bunche continued his diplomatic activities working to end fighting on the island of Cyprus, supervising peacekeeping troops at Egypt's Suez Canal, and serving as a mediator in a dispute between India and Pakistan. In short, his life was a testimony to attempting to gain peace in our time.

● Sentence Combining

You have been learning the technique of sentence combining since you began speaking, and you have been working at it pointedly ever since you opened this book. It is one of the most useful tools in achieving coherence because it employs the most common devices in the language for bringing out the relationships between ideas. Every time you modify a word, coordinate two ideas, or subordinate one idea to another, you are creating and explaining relationships. So fundamental are these devices that you could say the invention of the conjunctions (*so, or, and* and others) was one of humanity's giant steps forward.

Careful combining of sentences helps readers see precisely the connections you want them to see. For instance, compare these examples:

> **Henry Ford experienced several setbacks. He had difficulty establishing his company. He contributed significantly to the automobile industry.**
>
> **Henry Ford experienced several setbacks in establishing his company, but he eventually contributed significantly to the automobile industry.**

In the first version, the reader is presented with unconnected statements about Henry Ford. By using coordination, the second version helps the reader to see the relationship of the contrasts. Henry Ford experienced several setbacks; *however,* he eventually contributed significantly to the automobile industry.

If you used subordination, your reader would expect a different emphasis in the paragraph:

> *Although* Henry Ford experienced several setbacks, he eventually contributed significantly to the automobile industry.

By using subordination, you allow the reader to see immediately that the real emphasis of the paragraph will be on Henry Ford's contributions to the automobile industry and not on his failed attempts. *Although* clearly suggests contrast, not example. Sentence combining, then, is the basic stuff of coherence. (If you need to review any of the techniques of sentence combining, refer to Chapters 4 and 5.)

● Transition Signals

This technique is closely related to sentence combining. You add a word or phrase to a sentence to make its connection to the preceding or following sentences clear. Words like *thus* or *in addition* serve as signs to your reader of the way in which one sentence relates to another. Transition signals can help your reader follow more easily the pattern of your thinking. For instance, in the paragraph shown in the last exercise, the last sentence begins with the word *in short,* which lets the reader know that a conclusion is about to be drawn from what has been said before. Without that signal, the reader might be unprepared for a conclusion and might have to go back and reread the sentence.

Each transition signal sets up a different kind of relationship between ideas. Here are some of the most common transition signals, grouped according to the kind of connection they establish between ideas.

TRANSITION SIGNALS	
Adding on:	also, besides, first, second, furthermore, in addition, moreover, next, then, after, finally, last, and
Comparing:	similarly, likewise, in the same way
Contrasting:	however, on the other hand, nevertheless, instead, otherwise, yet, but, on the contrary
Giving examples:	for instance, for example, specifically, in fact, in particular
Showing result:	thus, therefore, consequently, as a result, accordingly, so
Summing up:	in conclusion, in short, on the whole, in general, in summary, in other words
Moving in time:	then, shortly, afterward, in the meantime, soon, at last, now, later, meanwhile
Moving in space:	nearby, overhead, opposite, on the left, on the right, there, here

Transition signals usually require punctuation since they are interrupting or preceding the base sentence:

We listened to two senators at the hearing. *Afterward,* **we went to dinner.**

The president has accomplished many political goals; *therefore,* **I will vote for him again.**

Their local constituencies are loyal. Campaigning, *as a result,* **takes place in other cities.**

Exercise D

Use appropriate transition signals to show the relationships between the sentences in each of the following sets. Punctuate as needed.

1. Neil Armstrong was born in a farmhouse.   He lived in many homes in a short period of time. His father was an itinerant auditor.

_____

_____

2. Neil enjoyed building model airplanes.   He powered his planes with rubber bands.   He sought to make his games a reality.

_____

_____

3. He flew solo at the age of fifteen.   At sixteen, he was granted a student pilot's license.   Two years later he joined the United States Navy.   He reported to Pensacola in Florida for training as a fighter pilot.

_____

_____

4. The space age opened on October 4, 1957.   The Russians launched Sputnik.   Sputnik was the first artificial earth satellite.   Sputnik bleeped its way in orbit around the earth for three weeks.

_____

_____

5. President Kennedy announced that the United States would commit to landing a man on the moon.   This announcement did not stir a response

from Armstrong.   He was a civilian test pilot.   He thought Kennedy's decision might cut funds for the winged rocket program.

_____

_____

6. In 1962, John Glenn became the first American to orbit the earth in space. Armstrong and other test pilots began to consider the possibility of joining the NASA team.

_____

_____

7. He began physical and psychological training.   He was now involved in the space race.   On March 16, 1966, he was co-pilot of Gemini 8 spacecraft. They successfully made the first docking in outer space.

_____

_____

8. NASA announced the three astronauts for the Apollo 11 mission to the moon. Armstrong would be in command of the flight.   Michael Collins would be the pilot of the command module.   Edwin Aldrin would be the pilot of the lunar module.

_____

_____

9. They had to study the evidence accumulated from exploratory flights by manned and unmanned spacecraft.   They had to examine an extensive photographic program by the lunar orbiters.   They had to learn from the team that had orbited the moon ten times in the *Apollo 8* spacecraft.

_____

_____

10. Armstrong and Aldrin lowered the ladder to the lunar surface.   Armstrong set foot on the moon.   Millions of people around the world watched.   He commented, "That's one small step for a man, one giant leap for mankind."

_____

_____

● Parallel Structure

When you want to show that two sentences do the same work or hold the same relationship to the topic sentence, arrange them in the same (or **parallel**) pattern.

For example, in the second version of the paragraph that opened the section on coherence, Ford's actions were described this way:

> **He brought together mass production and central assembly.**
>
> **The industrial world was shocked.**

These two sentences are doing the same work, presenting information about Henry Ford, but their structure is not parallel, and the reader is not helped to see the similarity of their function.

In the more coherent version, the same sentences read:

> **Some observers were impressed that he was able to bring together mass production and central assembly so that he could keep his costs low enough to price his product for the largest possible mass market.**
>
> **Others in the industrial world were shocked by his cutting working hours and raising the minimum wage.**

Both these sentences follow the same pattern: they begin with the persons who reacted and end with what they reacted to. Here the parallel structure signals the parallel function and helps the reader see the underlying sameness of the sentences.

In the combining exercises given earlier, you practiced all the major sentence patterns in English. You can apply your skill to create parallel structures when you want to give your reader a clearer sense of the underlying relationships within your paragraphs.

This device of parallelism can be used to stress the similarity of ideas within one sentence as well as between sentences:

> **In the evening, Henry Ford liked *to read the newspaper, to drink a glass of wine,* and *to snooze before the fire.***

In this sentence, the three things that Ford liked are phrased in parallel ways—all using the *to + verb* construction.

● Repetition of Key Words

This important device consists of weaving the ideas of the paragraph together by repeating the words related to the topic and/or the controlling idea of the paragraph. Weaving is an appropriate image since this technique does not show relationships or organization; instead, it focuses the reader's attention on the "threads," the important ideas, as they move through the paragraph to make up the fabric of the discussion.

For example, in the paragraph on Henry Ford, the key words *car* and *production* appear several times, along with other significant words like *costs*. These repetitions help the reader to see the main ideas and look for important connections.

Part of the technique of repetition is the correct use of pronouns to help tie the paragraph together. For instance, proper use of *this* and *that* with words referring back to the key words helps the reader see the "threads" of your paragraph. Similarly, proper use of a pronoun like *it* to refer back to a key word creates coherence. However, using *this, that,* or other pronouns without clear reference back to the key word can destroy coherence:

> **Some of Ford's workers were always late to work, and they could not seem to be punctual for any appointment. This caused problems on the assembly line.**

In this example, the use of *this* hurts the coherence. What specifically does *this* refer back to? You can answer only with some awkward phrase like "their being late to work and for appointments." When you have this kind of situation in writing, pick a word that sums up what you are trying to say and use it with the *this* or *that* to make the meaning clear:

> **Some of Ford's workers were always late to work, and they could not seem to be punctual for any appointment. This *tardiness* caused problems on the assembly line.**

The same problem can exist with the use of any pronoun. When the pronoun does not refer back to any specific word before it, be careful! Replace the pronoun with a word or phrase that says exactly what you mean.

> **Henry Ford took on the titles of designer, master mechanic, superintendent, and general manager. They were helpful in his development of a simple, standard model.**
>
> **Henry Ford took on the titles of designer, master mechanic, superintendent, and general manager. *These roles* were helpful in his development of a simple, standard model.**

Using pronouns is discussed in more detail in Chapter 6.

EXERCISE E

Revise the following sets of sentences as appropriate to repeat key ideas. Several of the original sentences are famous quotes. You may also use parallel structures or transition signals if you feel these would enhance the coherence of the sentences.

EXAMPLE:

> **Open-mindedness characterizes most world leaders' approaches.   Lack of narrow focus rules their opinions.**

Open-mindedness characterizes most world leaders' approaches. Open-mindedness rules their opinions, too.

1. Ask not what your country can do for you.   Inquire about what actions you can take for the benefit of the nation.

___

2. The gods help some people.   Others have to come to their own assistance.

___

3. When in Rome, do as the people in that area do.

___

4. My mother didn't allow us to play with guns.   We couldn't even pretend we had any sort of firearms.

___

5. People who try to prove too much sometimes wind up giving a demonstration of nothing.

___

6. Money can't buy happiness.   Contentment comes easier with a little wealth.

___

7. Peter was the original "organization man."   His life was arranged so
   carefully that he drove the rest of us, who were slobs without any sense of
   order, crazy.

   _____

   _____

8. Spring has a special fascination for me.   Everything seems full of potential.
   Nothing seems impossible.

   _____

   _____

9. No one is more laid-back than a New Yorker.   Cabbies don't look twice at a
   passenger in a mermaid costume.   Shop clerks don't bat an eye when
   mink-wearing customers fight over a $1.50 tube of lipstick.

   _____

   _____

10. Smart buyers shop as carefully for the loan as they do for the car.   People
    should not automatically let the dealer arrange the details.   People should
    consider banks, credit unions, and life insurance policies as sources for money.

    _____

    _____

REVISION PRACTICE:

Using a separate sheet of paper, revise the following student paragraphs so that
they establish connections between ideas more clearly. Use any of the coherence
and unity techniques presented in this chapter.

   1. America's attitude toward people with disabilities has been undergoing a
slow but definite change. There have been benefits from a general shift in peoples'
expectation of government. Since the Depression, there has been an assumption
that people in trouble should be helped with public funds. The disabled have followed the lead of other minorities in demanding not just public assistance, but
their full rights as citizens. Increased visibility is a reason for the different attitude.
The population is growing older. More people are more subject to crippling diseases and injuries. Changes in medicine and technology have vastly increased the
number of people, both young and old, who survive an accident or disease. People with disabilities are moving out of hiding and into the mainstream of life.

2. That two-minute interview with the expert on Soviet military planes that you saw on the network news last night probably took some associate producer weeks to line up. The "booker" has the job of finding interviewees. The booker has to maintain a long list of people who are knowledgeable in subjects ranging from Middle Eastern oil policies to urban soup kitchens. The booker needs phone numbers that will reach them at any hour. The booker may need a person on short notice. The booker interviews each person ahead of time. The booker must determine if the person has the right information and be sure the person will come across well in front of the camera. Some guests are invited to appear. Finding people for news shows is a demanding process.

▶ WORD CHOICE

As you have seen in the previous sections on revision, one way of writing a sentence does not have the same effect on a reader that another way has. Different structures can convey different meanings. The same principle holds true with word choice. One word does not have exactly the same effect on a reader as another.

In drafting a piece of writing, you may not be too concerned about your individual word choices. As has been mentioned in earlier discussions of revising, you often need to get a feel for the shape of the whole piece of writing before you begin to focus on details of sentence structure and word choice. However, once you have a draft you feel comfortable with, you can look for ways to make your point more effectively by substituting a more exact word or eliminating some unnecessary words.

In revising your writing, you have to be as careful to choose the right words as you are to choose the right sentence structure, the right supporting examples, and the right pattern of arrangement for your subject, audience, and purpose. In evaluating the appropriateness of your language, you need to look at several different aspects: its level of generality, its connotative value, its degree of formality, and its degree of conciseness.

REVISING TO HELP READERS SEE APPROPRIATE MEANING
LEVEL OF GENERALITY
CONNOTATIVE VALUE
DEGREE OF FORMALITY
DEGREE OF CONCISENESS

● **Level of Generality**

Earlier in the book, when you were looking at paragraph structure, you saw that paragraphs and longer pieces of writing often move among ideas on several levels of generality. That same scale of generality operates at the level of individual words and phrases. *Leadership,* for example, is a more general word than *leaders; Kennedys* is more specific than *leaders* while *John F. Kennedy* is even more specific.

In revising your word choice, you want to make sure that your language is specific enough to suit your purpose and meet the needs of your audience. For example, if you are trying to show your readers that you respected the influence your grandfather had but that he was a messy housekeeper, then a detail like "His dining room table was covered with books" may be specific enough to establish your point. But if you are trying to demonstrate your grandfather's intellectual curiosity, you may need to move to a more specific level of language and name the kinds of books that are on his table, or even give some specific titles.

"My grandfather read a lot of books" doesn't convey his curiosity as well as "My grandfather read everything from Aristotle's *Poetics* to Darwin's *Origin of Species.*"

EXERCISE F
Revise each of the following sentences by making the underlined language more specific.

1. I didn't like the senator's <u>looks</u>.

   _____

2. I have been in the Senate chambers <u>for a long time</u>.

   _____

3. A group of them <u>walked</u> across the yard.

   _____

4. <u>A vehicle</u> roared down the street.

   _____

5. The street looked <u>strange</u>.

   _____

6. Actually, <u>the event</u> was dull.

   _____

7. Someone then <u>communicated with</u> the president.

   _____

8. Recently, <u>some people</u> accused him of being in Chicago on business.

_____

9. During the investigation, <u>the weather was not good</u>.

_____

10. The legislative aide <u>did well</u>.

_____

● Connotative Value

The words in the list below are all related to the word *small,* and they are all at roughly the same level of generality. (You can find related words like this in a thesaurus.)

little	trivial
tiny	unimportant
short	petty
wee	puny
dwarfish	slight
undersized	weak
stunted	mean
minute	paltry
infinitesimal	pygmy
dainty	Lilliputian
petite	

Now, because all these words are related to *small,* does that mean you can freely substitute one for another? No.

How would you feel if someone described your brand-new baby daughter as *undersized?* Would you feel different if she were described as *tiny?* What is the difference between the two words? The distinction lies mainly in the feelings that are associated with each word. These feelings are called *connotations. Undersized* has negative connotations while *tiny* has positive connotations.

Here are some other examples of difference in connotation.

Neutral	Positive	Negative
inexpensive	thrifty	cheap
worker	craftsperson	drudge
slowly	leisurely	sluggishly

In choosing words, then, you need to be sure that a word carries the right feelings for the subject, audience, and purpose you have chosen. For instance, if you were trying to give an unbiased report, you would choose words that do not have strong favorable or unfavorable connotations:

Astronaut Edwin Aldrin had six months of NASA training.

If you were trying to criticize, you would choose words that have an unfavorable connotation:

Edwin Aldrin was a raw beginner in NASA training.

If you were trying to praise, you would choose words with favorable connotations:

Edwin Aldrin brought a fresh, new approach to NASA training.

EXERCISE G

In each of the following paragraphs, you are given two controlling ideas in the topic sentence. You must choose one by underlining it. Then, in the supporting sentences, choose from each pair of words in parentheses the one whose connotations fit your controlling idea. Cross out the word whose connotations don't fit. Use a dictionary for unfamiliar words.

<u>EXAMPLE:</u>

The setting for the Nobel Prize ceremonies was a (<u>pleasant</u>, dull) winter afternoon. The sun cast a (soft, ~~feeble~~) glow on the (white, ~~pale~~) landscape.

1. Gabriela Mistral, the Chilean poet, glanced up to see a rather (sinister, appealing) figure enter her courtyard. He was (obese, plump); his (graceless, awkward) body filled the archway. He had tiny, (half-closed, squinty) eyes like a scared (rat's, fieldmouse's). Even at this distance, his skin appeared (creased, wrinkled), as though he had slept in it badly. Fittingly, his hair was (wild, mussed) and stood up in stiff (spikes, cowlicks). When he spoke, his voice was (high, shrill) and had a nasal (twang, whine). Gabriela Mistral walked toward him and shook his hand. The palm was (moist, clammy), his grip (hard, firm). Gabriela Mistral wanted to (help, get rid of) him.

2. Cesar Chavez is remembered as a (humanitarian, troublemaker). By the time Cesar was in eighth grade, he had (gone to, left) more than thirty schools. His family was (poor, destitute) and lived in tiny (cottages, shacks) with no running water. When Cesar Chavez grew up, he (became a leader of, riled up) the (disgruntled, dissatisfied) migrant workers. He (helped, coerced) them to form a union called the National Farm Workers' Association. In 1965, the grapeworkers (went on strike, refused to work). Cesar Chavez and the union (asked, pleaded with) the people across the United States to  (help, support) the strike by not buying grapes. Through his (hard work, revolutionary activities), Cesar Chavez helped migrant workers gain better housing, higher pay, more schooling, and respect for their union. In short, he is one of the (heroes, rabble-rousers) of his time.

● Degree of Formality

In choosing language appropriate for your subject, audience, and purpose, you also need to consider how formal the diction should be. *Male progenitor, father, daddy,* and *my old man,* for example, could all refer to the same person. But these word choices would not be equally suitable for different writing situations. Which word would you choose if you were writing a safety pamphlet for young children? Which language would be appropriate for an academic paper in science or social science? Which language would you use in a satiric skit about family life for an audience of your friends?

Formal language often uses multisyllable words (*expeditiously* as opposed to *fast*), highly specialized terms (*regulated liability product* as opposed to *savings account*), or foreign words (*coiffure* as opposed to *hairdo*). Such formality may be appropriate for highly educated audiences, for experts in a particular field, or in important public situations such as a graduation speech or an inauguration address.

Informal language tends to be more conversational, more relaxed than formal language. In informal writing situations or in writing to young audiences or audiences without a great deal of education in your subject, you would choose more everyday words, shorter words, words that don't demand knowledge of a second language. In a very informal writing situation, you might use slang words like *wheels* instead of *car,* or *jammin'* instead of *doing it quickly,* or *kick it* instead of *leave.*

Whatever level of language you choose, it should fit the subject, audience, and purpose of your writing, and it should stay consistent throughout a particular piece of writing. Shifts in the level of formality can destroy the unity of a paragraph.

Exercise H

Arrange each of the following lists of words in order from the most formal to the most informal language.

<u>Example:</u>
  inconsiderable, petty, small-time, dinky

1. scare the pants off of, arouse trepidation, frighten

2. antithesis, a horse of a different color, opposite

3. car, passenger-carrying automotive vehicle, automobile, clunker

4. uncertain, fishy, questionable, dubitable

5. mistake, unintentional deviation, boo-boo, slip-up

EXERCISE 1

From the following list of words and phrases, choose the ones appropriate to each audience or situation described below. Some language may fit more than one situation. Use your dictionary to check the meaning of any unfamiliar words.

speak	articulate	verbalize	converse
jabber	talk	proclaim	sound off
flap your tongue	yak	state	affirm
phonate	announce	run off at the mouth	chew the fat
say	tell		

1. Which words would be appropriate for an audience of elementary school children?

   _____

2. Which words would be appropriate for a speech therapist's records of a client's progress?

   _____

3. Which language would be appropriate for a humorous description of a friend who likes to talk?

   _____

4. Which language would be appropriate for a newspaper account of the governor's speech?

   _____

5. Which language would be appropriate for a college speech teacher's instructions for a speaking assignment?

   _____

● **Degree of Conciseness**

Finally, in choosing appropriate language, you want to use your words efficiently. Every word should be necessary to convey your meaning. In revising a draft, then, you might look at it as though you had to pay a dollar for each word. Be sure each word is worth paying for. Wordiness may leave your readers feeling that you are not quite in control of your writing, or even worse, that you are wasting their time by not getting to the point.

Look at these sentences. Which version is more concise?

A. As a young man, Dag Hammarskjold lived in an intellectual climate at home as well as at the University. He would often ask his father, then the prime minister of

B. When Dag Hammarskold was a young man, in his teens, he lived at home and was intellectually stimulated or obliged to think through problems. Also, he experienced a

Sweden, for answers to problems in international relations and he'd receive answers few other fathers could give.

similar climate at the University. Dag's father was the prime minister of Sweden, so Dag felt comfortable asking him about solutions to some of the international or global problems the planet faced. His father gave him his answers, but probably other fathers were not able to have such insights into the problems.

Paragraph B shows several of the problems that can lead to wordiness. For one thing, the writer has frequently used a long phrase where a simple phrase or one word would have conveyed exactly the same information: *intellectually stimulated or obliged to think through problems* instead of *lived in an intellectual climate; other fathers were not able to have such insights into the problems* instead of *answers few other fathers could give.* Second, the writer has repeated herself: *international or global.* Nothing is gained by this unnecessary repetition.

In writing, more words are not necessarily better than fewer words. What matters is not so much the number of words as the fact that each word does its fair share of work in the sentence or paragraph.

You can often spot wordiness in your writing by looking closely at your verbs. For example, what do you notice about the verbs in the following paragraph?

People who are world leaders have many motivations that are different. One reason they are world leaders is that they are interested in power and prestige. Acquiring power, for example, is one step toward being on the front page often. Other world leaders who are interested in power but are not motivated by personal prestige are those who are desiring political change. Another motivation of world leaders is rather selfless. Even though there is a need for power in this person, their goal is to make changes that are going to help humanity. The truth of the matter is that all these motivations are probably found to some extent in all people who are at that level of prominence.

The verb *to be* occurs seventeen times in seven sentences. The *to be* verbs *(am, is, are, was, were, be, been)* carry little meaning of their own. When you use them, therefore, you often have to add a few extra words to get the meaning across.

If you find your writing leaning too heavily on these verbs, look for other words in the sentence that you can make into verbs. For example, "they are interested in power and prestige" can become simply "they desire power and prestige."

Here is the same paragraph revised to use fewer *to be* verbs.

World leaders have many motivations. For one thing, they desire power and prestige. Acquiring power, for example, puts them on the front page. Other world leaders want power, not personal prestige, to enable political change. Some world leaders remain selfless. They need power only to make changes that will help humanity. In actuality, most world leaders probably have all these motivations in different degrees.

By eliminating most of the *to be* verbs and the extra words they dragged along with them, the revision covers in 64 words what it took the original version 119 words to say. (If you were paying for this paragraph, you would now be $55 richer.)

Besides getting rid of *to be* verbs, you can also make your writing more concise and more forceful by building your sentences with the most *meaningful* words, that is, with words that convey your meaning most directly.

For example, look at the base sentence buried here:

> In order for Dag Hammarskjold to keep perspective when he was the secretary general of the United Nations, *it was required* that he do several things: listen to music, translate the works of revered authors, and commune with nature.

This whole thirty-nine-word structure rests on a vague pronoun and a weak verb. To revise a sentence like this, you first need to mark the words that carry the main ideas. If the sentence is long, you may need to break it into smaller units and find the meaning-bearing words in each section of the sentence:

In order for Dag Hammarskjold / to keep perspective when he was the secretary general of the United Nations /, *it was required* that he do several things: / listen to music, / translate the works of revered authors, / and commune with nature.

Then you can rebuild the sentence to emphasize the *meaningful* words:

> As secretary general of the United Nations, Dag Hammarskjold kept perspective by listening to music, translating works of revered authors, and communing with nature.

This sentence now weighs in at a trim twenty-four words—a mere one-third of its former flabby self—and virtually every word carries its share of the weight of the sentence.

EXERCISE J

The following paragraphs contain many examples of wordiness. On a separate sheet of paper, rewrite the paragraphs using the fewest possible words. Be ruthless.

1. As an artist, Picasso went through several different periods in his paintings. In 1901 or thereabouts, Picasso discovered Paris for the first time. Also, during this time period, he started on what was referred to as his "blue" period. In all actuality, the color of blue became the one on his palette that he used to portray and show human misery experienced by people, not actually feeling good, being lonely, and also he used the blue to show poverty. The next period of his life we need to discuss was the "rose" period of his painting. He became really interested in and fascinated by the people who worked in the circus, actual characters and harlequins from the circus ring. From both these periods and time frames, the blue period and the rose period, the world has received for our time and the future many great masterpieces from this great painter.

2. Eleanor Roosevelt used her position and role as first lady to help people in her family and outside her immediate circle. First of all and primarily in her mind, was her need to help her husband, Franklin, who had contracted and become a victim of polio and could no longer get around at all without leg braces for both legs, a wheelchair, and crutches. In addition to doing traveling for him, she also worked on her own to help young people who often had nobody who cared about them and poor people who needed her help. When she finally lost her husband and he died, Eleanor Roosevelt was appointed to and became and served as the U.S. delegate to the United Nations. It was at the very important time in history, 1948, that she helped draft and write the Universal Declaration of Human Rights. This document, for example, stated clearly and in writing by getting said that all people around the world are born free and equal. Eleanor Roosevelt managed in her lifetime to help her own family (she had five children) and other human beings who lived all over the entire world.

Revision Practice:

Revise the following student paragraph so that its language is appropriate in its level of generality, its connotative value, its degree of formality, and its degree of conciseness.

Those of us who live in America have a tendency to undervalue the idea of friendship. We are often guilty of the use of the term in such a loose way that we don't give much real thought to what behaving in an amicable way means. We call other members of the human species our good buddies when we have been introduced to them on only a few social occasions. Such free and easy utilization of this verbal utterance makes it seem trivial instead of a description of one of the greatest things that can happen to us. The word *friend* should be reserved for someone with whom our hard work has been shared and perhaps even our hard times, someone who is aware of what is going on in our noggins or is able to bring to his recollection the same events we do, a childhood chum or a colleague from the time of our service in the armed forces of our country. We may be acquainted with lots of people, but we really have only a couple of friends.

Writing Practice:

1. Your campus organization or a group or team off-campus has decided to raise money by writing and selling a student guide to local restaurants. Using whatever techniques of exploring, focusing, and organizing you like, choose one restaurant that might be included in such a guide and write a 300-word entry for it in the guide.

In a writing situation like this, the format of your entry can also be an important tool for coherence. Be sure you lay out the information on the page in such a way that it is easy to follow. Perhaps you and some classmates could design a standard format for restaurant-guide entries.

When you have written a draft of your entry, review it for its unity, coherence, and word choice and make whatever revisions you feel are necessary. On your own, or with help from someone else, check your entry for problems with punctuation, spelling, or sentence structure and make whatever corrections are necessary before turning in your final version.

2. In an effort to attract new listeners, the campus radio station, where you work, is planning a special celebration of one musician or one style of music. Prepare a proposal of 300 to 500 words for the station manager explaining which musician or style of music you would like to see featured. Use whatever methods of exploring, focusing, and organizing you like as you prepare your proposal.

When you have a draft of your proposal, review it for unity, coherence, and word choice and then for any problems in punctuation, spelling, or sentence structure. Make whatever revisions or corrections are necessary before turning in your final version.

3. A. You have just moved into your neighborhood/apartment/dorm, and you want to describe it to a friend back home. Since you are feeling a bit lonely this particular evening, everything about the place seems unappealing. Using the techniques you have learned for the various stages of the writing process, compose a description of about 200 words that will convey your negative impression. When you are revising, check for unity and coherence and then focus on checking the connotations of the descriptive words you have chosen.

B. A few weeks later, your outlook has brightened as you have gotten involved in more activities and met your neighbors. Write another description that makes the place seem more attractive. If possible, use some of the same details that previously seemed unappealing, but describe them in positive language this time.

◀ Chapter 12 ▶

Editing

• • • • • • • • • • •

continued

continued
- ● **Misplaced Modifiers**
- ● **Dangling Modifiers**
- ● **Shifts in Verb Tense**
- ● **Shifts in Point of View**
- ● **Passive Verbs**
- ▶ **PUNCTUATION**
  - ● **Basic Sentence Patterns**
  - ● **Comma Splices and Run-on Sentences**
  - ● **Commas**
    - ■ *Commas with Coordinate Ideas*
    - ■ *Commas with Subordinate Ideas*

● ● ● ● ● ● ● ● ● ● ●

In the revision process, you are looking for ways to clarify your ideas through improved unity, coherence, and word choice.

In the editing process, which should be the last step before preparing a final copy, you are looking for errors that may distract your reader from your idea.

Misspelled words, sentence construction errors, or improper punctuation can give your reader a negative impression of a piece of writing. These errors may be so annoying to a reader that he or she will not really pay attention to your carefully organized, well-supported, beautifully worded paper. In fact, Mina Shaughnessy in *Errors and Expectations* went so far as to say this about spelling: "The ability to spell is viewed by many as one of the marks of an educated person, and the failure of a college graduate to meet that minimal standard of advanced literacy is cause to question the quality of his education or even his intelligence."

So, teach yourself to recognize the errors you know you are prone to, and check your writing very carefully for those kinds of mistakes.

In writing, one of the most important impressions you want to create for your reader is the feeling that you are in control. No matter how exact or how concise your word choices, the impression of being in control of your material can be destroyed by a series of misspelled words. One spelling error might be overlooked, but a pattern of poor spelling can make even a sympathetic reader doubt the value of your ideas. Therefore, you need not only to choose the correct word for each writing situation but also to edit carefully for correct spelling.

▶ SPELLING

● Using the Dictionary and Spell-Check

The most useful all-around tool in editing is the dictionary. You may use the traditional hard-copy volume or an on-line dictionary. Both help with spelling, grammar, word choice, defining, and understanding. However, remember that word-processing spell-checkers can catch most but not all spelling errors. Computers are not smart enough yet to know whether a correctly spelled word is appropriate for

limp² (limp) ***adj.*** ⟦< base of prec., akin to MHG *lampen,* to hang limply⟧ **1** lacking or having lost stiffness or body; flaccid, drooping, wilted, etc. **2** lacking firmness, energy, or vigor **3** flexible, as the binding of some books —**limp'ly** ***adv.*** —**limp'ness** ***n.***

lim·pet (limp'it) ***n.*** ⟦ME *lempet* < OE *lempedu* < ML *lempreda,* limpet, LAMPREY⟧ a gastropod mollusk of various families, mostly marine, with a single, low, cone-shaped shell and a thick, fleshy foot, by means of which it clings to rocks, timbers, etc.

lim·pid (lim'pid) ***adj.*** ⟦Fr *limpide* < L *limpidus,* altered (? from *liquidus,* LIQUID) < OL *limpa, lumpa,* water: see LYMPH⟧ **1** perfectly clear; transparent; not cloudy or turbid *[limpid* waters*]* **2** clear and simple *[limpid* prose*]* —**lim·pid'i·ty** or **lim'pid·ness** ***n.*** —**lim'pid·ly** ***adv.***

☆**limp·kin** (limp'kin) ***n.*** ⟦LIMP¹ + -KIN: from its walk⟧ a gruiform bird (*Aramus guarauna*) of a family (Aramidae) with only one species, found in Florida, Central America, the West Indies, and South America

Lim·po·po (lim pō'pō) river in SE Africa, flowing from Transvaal, South Africa across Mozambique into the Indian Ocean: *c.* 1,000 mi. (1,609 km)

limp·sy or **limp·sey** (limp'sē) ***adj.*** **-si·er, -si·est** [Dial.] limp, as from exhaustion or weakness

lim·u·lus (lim'yoo ləs) ***n.,*** *pl.* **-li'** (-lī') ⟦ModL < L *limulus,* dim. of *limus,* oblique + -OID⟧ HORSESHOE CRAB

lim·y (lim'ē) ***adj.*** **lim'i·er, lim'i·est** **1** covered with, consisting of, or like birdlime; sticky **2** of, like, or containing lime —**lim'i·ness** ***n.***

lin·ac (lin'ak') ***n.*** *short for* LINEAR ACCELERATOR

lin·age (līn'ij) ***n.*** **1** the number of written or printed lines on a page or in an article, advertisement, etc. **2** payment based on the number of lines produced by a writer

lin·al·o·ol (lin al'ō ōl', -al'ə ōl'; lin'ə lōōl') ***n.*** ⟦< MexSp *linaloa,* an aromatic Mexican wood (< Sp *lináloe* < ML *lignum aloës:* see LIGNALOES) + -OL¹⟧ a terpene alcohol, $C_{10}H_{17}OH$, in several essential oils, used in perfumery

linch·pin (linch'pin') ***n.*** ⟦ME *lynspin* < *lyns* (< OE *lynis,* linchpin, akin to Ger *lünse* < IE base **(e)lei-* to bend > ELL², Sans *āṇīh,* linchpin) + *pin,* PIN⟧ **1** a pin that goes through the end of an axle outside the wheel to keep the wheel from coming off **2** anything serving to hold together the parts of a whole

Lin·coln (liŋ'kən), **Abraham** 1809-65; 16th president of the U.S. (1861-65): assassinated —☆**Lin·coln·esque** (liŋ'kən esk') ***adj.*** —☆**Lin·coln·i·an** (liŋ kō'nē ən) ***adj.***

Lin·coln (liŋ'kən) **1** ⟦after Pres. *Lincoln*⟧ capital of Nebr., in the SE part: pop. 192,000 **2** LINCOLNSHIRE **3** city in Lincolnshire, England: pop. 78,000 —***n.*** a breed of sheep with long wool: orig. from Lincolnshire

Lin·coln·i·an·a (liŋ kōn'ē an'ə, -än'ə) ***n.pl.*** books, papers, objects, etc. having to do with Abraham Lincoln

Lincoln Park ⟦after Pres. *Lincoln*⟧ city in SE Mich.: pop. 42,000

Lin·coln·shire (liŋ'kən shir', -shər) county in NE England, on the North Sea: 2,272 sq. mi. (5,885 sq. km); pop. 556,000

Lincoln's Inn *see* INNS OF COURT

☆**lin·co·my·cin** (liŋ'kō mī'sin) ***n.*** ⟦(*Streptomyces lincoln(ensis),* the bacteria from which derived (isolated from a soil sample collected near LINCOLN, Nebr.) + MYC- + -IN¹⟧ an antibiotic drug, $C_{18}H_{34}N_2O_6S$, used in the treatment of various bacterial diseases, esp. those resistant to penicillin or those involving an allergy to penicillin

Lind (lind), **Jenny** (born *Johanna Maria Lind; Mme. Otto Goldschmidt*) 1820-87; Swed. soprano: called the *Swedish Nightingale*

Lin·da (lin'də) a feminine name: see BELINDA

lin·dane (lin'dān') ***n.*** ⟦after T. van der *Linden,* 20th-c. Du chemist + -ANE⟧ an isomeric form of benzene hexachloride, used as an insecticide

Lind·bergh (lind'burg'), **Charles Augustus** 1902-74; U.S. aviator: made first nonstop solo flight from New York to Paris (1927)

lin·den (lin'dən) ***n.*** ⟦ME, adj. < OE < *lind,* linden, akin to Ger *linde:* popularized as n. via Ger *linden,* pl. of *linde:* prob. < IE base **lento-,* flexible, yielding > LITHE⟧ BASSWOOD —***adj.*** designating a family (Tiliaceae) of chiefly tropical, dicotyledonous trees (order Malvales), including the jutes

Lind·say (lind'zē) **1** a feminine name: also **Lind'sey** **2** **(Nicholas) Va·chel** (vā'chəl) 1879-1931; U.S. poet

☆**Lin·dy (Hop)** (lin'dē) ⟦after C. A. *Lindbergh's* ("*Lindy's*") transatlantic "hop"⟧ [*also* **l- h-**] a lively dance for couples, popular in the early 1930's

line¹ (līn) ***n.*** ⟦ME merging OE, a cord, with OFr *ligne* (both < L *linea,* lit., linen thread, n. use of fem. of *lineus,* of flax < *linum,* flax)⟧ **1** *a)* a cord, rope, wire, string, or the like *b)* a long, fine, strong cord with a hook, sinker, leader, etc. used in fishing *c)* a clothesline *d)* a cord, steel tape, etc. used in measuring or leveling *e)* a rope, hawser, or cable used on a ship *f)* a rein (*usually used in pl.*) ☆**2** *a)* a wire or wires connecting a telephone or telegraph system *b)* a system of such wires *c)* effective contact between telephones *d)* a telephone extension *[*call me on *line* 9*]* **3** any wire, pipe, system of pipes or wires, etc. for conducting water, gas, electricity, etc. **4** a very thin, threadlike mark; specif., *a)* a long, thin mark made by a pencil, pen, chalk, etc. *b)* a similar mark cut in a hard surface, as by engraving *c)* a thin crease in the palm or on the face **5** a mark made on the ground in certain sports; specif., *a)* any of the straight, narrow marks dividing or bounding a football field, tennis court, etc. (often used in combination) *[sideline]* *b)* a mark indicating a starting point, a limit not to be crossed, or a point which must be reached or passed ☆**6** a border or boundary *[*the State *line]* **7** a division between conditions, qualities, classes, etc.; limit; demarcation **8** [*pl.*] outline; contour; lineament *[*built along modern *lines]* **9** [*pl.*] [Archaic] lot in life; one's fate **10** [*usually pl.*] a plan of construction; plan of making or doing **11** a row or series of persons or things of a particular kind; specif., *a)* a row of written or printed characters extending across or part way across a page *b)* a single row of words or characters making up a unit of poetry, often of a specified number of feet ☆*c)* a row of persons waiting in turn to buy something, enter a theater, etc.; queue *d)* an assembly line or a similar arrangement for the packing, shipping, etc. of merchandise **12** a connected series of persons or things following each other in time or place; succession *[*a *line* of Democratic presidents*]* **13** LINEAGE¹ **14** the descendants of a common ancestor or of a particular breed ☆**15** *a)* a transportation system or service consisting of regular trips by buses, ships, etc. between two or more points ☆*b)* a company operating such a system *c)* one branch or division of such a system *[*the main *line* of a railroad*]* *d)* a single track of a railroad **16** the course or direction anything moving takes; path *[*the *line* of fire*]* **17** *a)* a course of conduct, action, explanation, etc. *[*the *line* of an argument*]* *b)* a course of movement **18** a person's trade or occupation *[*what's his *line?]* ☆**19** a stock of goods of a particular type considered with reference to quality, quantity, variety, etc. **20** *a)* the field of one's special knowledge, interest, or ability *b)* a source or piece of information *[*a *line* on a bargain*]* **21** a short letter, note, or card *[*drop me a *line]* **22** [*pl.*] all the speeches in a play; esp., the speeches of any single character **23** [Colloq.] persuasive or flattering talk that is insincere **24** [Slang] a small quantity of cocaine sniffed at one time **25** [*pl.*] [Chiefly Brit.] a marriage certificate: in full **marriage lines** **26** *Bridge* the horizontal line on a score sheet below which are recorded points that count toward a game and above which, all other points ☆**27** *Football a) short for* LINE OF SCRIMMAGE *b)* the players arranged in a row on either side of the line of scrimmage at the start of each play **28** *Geog.* an imaginary circle of the earth or of the celestial sphere, as the equator or the equinoctial circle **29** *Hockey* the two wings and the center playing together **30** *Math. a)* the path of a moving point, thought of as having length but not breadth, whether straight or curved *b)* such a path when considered perfectly straight **31** *Mil. a)* a formation of ships, troops, etc. in which elements are abreast of each other *b)* the area or position in closest contact with the enemy during combat *c)* the troops in this area *d)* the officers in immediate command of fighting ships or combat troops ☆*e)* the combatant branches of the army as distinguished from the supporting branches and the staff **32** *Music* any of the long parallel marks forming the staff **33** *TV* a scanning line —***vt.*** **lined, lin'ing** **1** to mark with lines **2** to draw or trace with or as with lines **3** to bring or cause to come into a straight row or into conformity; bring into alignment: often with *up* **4** to form a line along *[*elms *line* the streets*]* **5** to place objects along the edge of *[line* the walk with flowers*]* ☆**6** *Baseball* to hit (a pitched ball) in a line drive —***vi.*** **1** to form a line: usually with *up* ☆**2** *Baseball* to hit a line drive —**all along the line** **1** everywhere **2** at every turn of events —**bring** (or **come** or **get**) **into line** to bring (or come or cause to come) into a straight row or into conformity; bring or come into alignment —**down the line** completely; entirely —**draw the** (or **a**) **line** to set a limit —☆**get a line on** [Colloq.] to find out about —**hard lines** [Brit. Slang] misfortune; bad luck —☆**hit the line** **1** *Football* to try to carry the ball through the opposing line **2** to try boldly or firmly to do something —**hold the line** to stand firm; not permit a breakthrough or retreat: often used figuratively —**in line** **1** in a straight row; in alignment **2** in agreement or conformity **3** behaving properly or as required —**in line for** being considered for —**in line of duty** in the performance of authorized or prescribed military duty —**lay** (or **put**) **it on the line** **1** to put up or pay money; pay up **2** to speak frankly and in detail **3** to stake (one's reputation, etc.) on something: usually with the object of the verb explicitly stated —**line out** ☆**1** *Baseball* to be put out by hitting a line drive that is caught by a fielder **2** to sing or utter forcefully, loudly, or emphatically *[*to *line out* a song*]* —**line up** **1** to form a line **2** to bring into a line **3** to organize effectively, secure a pledge of support from, etc. **4** to take a position (*against* a competitor or rival) —**on a line** in the same plane; level —**on line** in or into active use or production *[*the new plant came *on line* this year*]* —**out of line** **1** not in a straight line; not in alignment **2** not in agreement or conformity **3** impertinent, insubordinate, etc. —**read between the lines** to discover a hidden meaning or purpose in something written, said, or done —**lin'a·ble** or **line'a·ble** ***adj.***

line² (līn) ***vt.*** **lined, lin'ing** ⟦ME *lynen* < *lin,* long-fiber flax, linen cloth < OE, ult. < L *linum,* flax: from use of linen to line clothes⟧ **1** to put a layer or lining of a different material on the inside of **2** to be used as a lining in *[*cloth *lined* the trunk*]* **3** to fill; stuff: now chiefly in **line one's pockets,** to make money, esp. greedily or unethically

lin·e·age¹ (lin'ē ij) ***n.*** ⟦ME *linage* < OFr *lignage* < *ligne:* see LINE¹⟧ **1** direct descent from an ancestor **2** ancestry; family; stock **3** descendants from a common ancestor

line·age² (līn'ij) ***n.*** LINAGE

lin·e·al (lin'ē əl) ***adj.*** ⟦OFr *linéal* < LL *linealis* < L *linea:* see LINE¹⟧ **1** in the direct line of descent from an ancestor **2** hereditary **3** of or composed of lines; linear —**lin'e·al'i·ty** (-al'ə tē) ***n.*** —**lin'e·al·ly** ***adv.***

lin·e·a·ment (lin'ē ə mənt) ***n.*** ⟦ME *liniamente* < L *lineamentum* < *lineare,* to fashion to a straight line < *linea,* LINE¹⟧ **1** any of the features of the body, usually of the face, esp. with regard to its outline **2** a distinctive feature or characteristic **3** any extensive, linear surface feature on a planet, as a fault line, that indicates the

at, āte, cär; ten, ēve; is, īce; gō, hôrn, look, tōōl; oil, out; up, fur; ə *for unstressed vowels, as* a *in* ago, u *in* focus; ' *as in* Latin (lat''n); chin; she; zh *as in* azure (azh'ər); thin, *the;* ŋ *as in* ring (riŋ) *In etymologies:* * = unattested; < = derived from; > = from which ☆ = Americanism **See inside front and back covers**

a particular sentence. For instance, the computer would ignore "I *here* what you are saying." Also, if a word is so poorly spelled (for example, *dikshunary* for *dictionary*), the spell-checker may highlight the word for you, but it is unable to suggest any alternatives. These technical aids can improve your spelling and your confidence, but even with the most sophisticated computer, you still must carefully proofread your final draft.

To get the best use out of any dictionary, you must first be able to find the word you want and then be able to understand the information the dictionary is giving you.

■ *Finding the Word*

When you use a dictionary to look up a word in a book you are reading, you have no problem finding the word. However, when you are writing, you often use the dictionary to find words you have seen or heard but do not know how to spell. You can do two things: (1) get yourself a "bad speller's dictionary" listing many of the common misspellings in alphabetical order with the correct spelling after, and (2) learn the commonly confused letters and sounds.

The same sound can be produced by different combinations of letters. For instance, suppose that you are looking up the spelling of a word that means "a severe inflammation of the lungs" and sounds like *newmonya*. If you look under *n* in the dictionary, you won't find the word. But what other letter combinations also have the sound of *n*? *kn, gn,* and *pn.* Therefore, you should look under each of these combinations until you find the word you want: *pneu mo nia.*

Here are some of the most common sound combinations. You can use these to help you look up words in the dictionary.

COMMON SOUND COMBINATIONS		
ā (long *a*, says its own name)	*a*–consonant–silent *e* *ai* *au* *ay* *ea* *ei* *ey*	name laid gauge play steak veil grey
ē (long *e*, says its own name)	*e* *e*–consonant–silent *e* *ea* *ee* *ie* *(c) ei* *ey* *eo* *oe* *y*	she Pete team feed believe receive key people amoeba city

ī (long *i*, says its own name)	*i*–consonant–silent *e*	fire
	y	cry
	ie	tie
	ei	height
	ai	aisle
	igh	high
	uy	buy
ō (long *o*, says its own name)	*o*	no
	o–consonant–silent *e*	note
	oa	boat
	ow	flow
	oe	foe
	ough	dough
	eau	beau
o͞o	*oo*	cool
	ew	blew
	ue	clue
	eu	maneuver
	u–consonant–silent *e*	rule
	ui	suit
	o	move
	oe	canoe
ū (long *u*, says its own name)	*u*–consonant–silent *e*	mule
	ou	you
	ew	few
	eau	beauty
	eu	feud
	iew	view
	yu	yule
∂ (uh) schwa—used in unaccented syllables	*a*	above
	e	agent
	i	busily
	o	bottom
	u	circus
	ou	curious
k	*k*	kill
	c	car
	cc	account
	ch	character
	ck	back
	qu	liquor
s	*s*	see
	c	city
	ps	psychology
	sc	scene
sh	*sh*	shine
	ci	special
	sci	conscious
	ch	machine
	ce	ocean
	ti	nation

EXERCISE A

Using the previous sound lists and your own knowledge of letter combinations, find the correct spelling of each of the following words in a dictionary.

1. ath′ let
   a person trained in contests requiring physical strength, skill   _____

2. mə dal′ yən
   a large medal   _____

3. O lim′ pik gamz
   an ancient Greek festival of contests in athletics, poetry,
      and music   _____

4. cham′ pe ən
   winning or capable of winning first place   _____

5. dis kwal′ ə fi
   to declare ineligible   _____

6. jim nas′ tiks
   exercises that develop and train the body and the muscles   _____

7. tram′ pə len
   a sheet of strong canvas stretched tightly on a frame   _____

8. res′ l
   to struggle hand to hand with an opponent   _____

9. di kath′ lən
   an athletic contest in which each contestant takes part
      in ten events   _____

10. i kwes′ tre ən
    horseback riding   _____

■ *Spelling Variations*

Obviously, when your dictionary search has been successful, the spelling of the word is in front of you in dark type. Sometimes you will find the dictionary giving you more information than you expected: a word may be given with several spellings. For example, the sample dictionary page shows two spellings for a word meaning limp or tired out: *limpsy* and *limpsey*. Either spelling is correct. In most dictionaries, the first spelling given is the more commonly used.

EXERCISE B

What are the other accepted spellings of these words?

1. chiseled   _____

2. catalog   _____

3. theater   _____

4. judgment   _____

5. Parcheesi   _____

■ *Syllables*

When you find a word in a dictionary, it is usually broken up by dots. These dots show where the word may be divided when the whole word won't fit at the end of a line. For example, if you had to split the word *linchpin,* you could do it only between the *h* and the *p: linch-pin.* These divisions can be a help in learning to spell the word. If you separate words incorrectly, readers see them as misspelled words.

EXERCISE C
Where can you divide the following words? Show how you think each word should be divided. Then check yourself with a dictionary.

EXAMPLE:
California   *Cal i for ni a*

1. behavior   _____

2. commitment   _____

3. controlled   _____

4. recommend   _____

5. attitude   _____

■ *Parts of Speech*

The dictionary also tells you whether the word is a noun, a verb, an adjective, or some other part of speech. For example, the *n.* placed after the pronunciation of the word *linden* on the sample dictionary page means *linden* is a noun. Recognizing these abbreviations is useful because many words can play several parts. Finding the precise form of the word you are looking for often means checking for the abbreviations. The word *line* on the sample page, for instance, is used both as a noun *(n.)* and as a verb (*vt.* for verb transitive and *vi.* for verb intransitive). The definitions for each form are grouped after each abbreviation.

EXERCISE D
Using your own dictionary, give the full term represented by the following abbreviations.

EXAMPLE:
n.   *noun*

1. adj.   _____

2. prep.   _____

3. pron.   _____

4. interj.   _____

5. adv.   _____

EXERCISE E
List the parts of speech given in the dictionary for each of the following words.

<u>EXAMPLE:</u>
   line   *n., vt., vi., adj.*

1. round   _____

2. in   _____

3. clean   _____

4. model   _____

5. yesterday   _____

■ *Meanings*

Finding the meanings of words is the basic use of the dictionary. Most words have several meanings, all closely related, but with shades of difference. It is important to check all the meanings until you find the one that explains the word in the context you are reading. For instance, if you were looking for the meaning of *line* in the sentence "She came from a great line of champions," you would have to look under the meanings until you came to number 14: *the descendants of a common ancestor or of a particular breed.*

EXERCISE F
Look up the italicized word in each sentence and give the definition that best fits the context.

<u>EXAMPLE:</u>
   It was a *limp,* dog-eared copy about the *Summer Olympics in 1996.*

   flexible, as in the binding of some books _____

1. Kerri Strug wanted her coffee *black.*

_____

2. The Olympic committee finally got down to the *core* of the issue.

_____

3. She was part of the first *string* of gymnasts.

_____

4. The other athletes were in *hot* pursuit.

_____

5. Another country's challenge did not *draw* a reply.

_____

■ Usage Labels

Dictionaries also label certain meanings of words if they are specialized or particular to a certain dialect of English. For example, on the sample dictionary page, definition number 24 for *line*—as it would be used in the sentence "She handed him a *line* about her last job"—is labeled [Colloq.], meaning *colloquial* or informal. These labels may help you choose your words with greater precision. Words with these labels are often not appropriate for formal papers.

EXERCISE G

Using your own dictionary, find the meanings of the following terms. Write the definition in your own words.

1. Colloquial [Colloq.] _____

_____

2. Slang _____

_____

3. Archaic [Arch.] _____

_____

4. Obsolete [Obs.] _____

_____

5. Dialect [Dial.] _____

_____

EXERCISE H

Find the meaning given for the italicized words in the following sentences. Put the usage label accompanying that meaning in the blank.

EXAMPLE:

He had a smooth *line*. *colloquial*

1. Abdul had to *make tracks* before his coach caught him.   _____

2. The only way he could stop eating pizza was to go *cold turkey*.   _____

3. He was *slick* with his excuses on the telephone.   _____

4. Abdul desperately tried to imitate the old traditions by saying, "I have a *boon* to

   ask of you." (Archaic)   _____

5. If he continued eating junk food, he would be lucky to own a *croker sack*.

   (Dialect)   _____

■ *Word History*

Dictionaries also give the history of the word: they tell you what it meant in the past and what languages it came from. (You will find a section in the front of most dictionaries explaining the symbols used in the word histories.) For example, the sample dictionary page gives the history of *line* in brackets after the pronunciation. The word came from a merging of the Middle English *line* with the Old French *ligne*. Both these words came from the Latin *linea*, which meant "linen thread" and derived from *linum*, which meant "flax," the plant that gives us linen.

Learning the history of a word often makes the word easier to remember. Paying attention to word histories will gradually deepen your knowledge of the language you speak and write. Sometimes sharing the history of a word with your reader will add depth to your paper.

EXERCISE I

With the help of a dictionary, find the original meanings of these words.

EXAMPLE:
line   *linen thread*

1. sacrifice   _____

2. hazard   _____

3. judge   _____

4. marshal   _____

5. window   _____

WHAT'S IN THE DICTIONARY FOR A WRITER?

SPELLING

SYLLABICATION

PARTS OF SPEECH

MEANINGS

USAGE LABELS

WORD HISTORY

● Improving Your Spelling

If you are a poor speller, you may get very discouraged sometimes because you think you can't spell *anything*. But that's not the case. Most people have definite patterns to their misspelling. They miss the same words over and over, or they make the same kinds of mistakes.

The way to overcome this spelling problem is to recognize what words or what spelling patterns give you trouble by keeping a list of words that you misspell. When you get a paper back from your teacher, write down any words that are marked for spelling. In one column, put down the word the way you spelled it. In another column, write the correct spelling. When you have a dozen or so words, study your list to see if there are any patterns of spelling that regularly give you trouble. For instance, look at this list:

Incorrect Spelling	Correct Spelling
terrable	terrible
refussing	refusing
planed	planned
evidince	evidence
occured	occurred
hopping	hoping
returnible	returnable
dependibility	dependability
acceptence	acceptance
riden	ridden
terreble	terrible
ocurred	occurred

What spelling problems seem to give this student trouble? She misses the *i, e,* or *a* at the end of several words: return*a*ble, terr*i*ble, evid*e*nce, accept*a*nce, depend-*a*bility. She also isn't sure when to double the consonant: ri*dd*en, refu*s*ing, pla*nn*ed, ho*p*ing, o*c*ur*r*ed.

Here is another list. Can you spot any problem areas for this student?

Incorrectly Spelled	Correctly Spelled
aventure	adventure
strat	straight
almos	almost
moshun	motion
minature	miniature
piture	picture
suppose	supposed
Wensday	Wednesday
there	their
sucseed	succeed
recieve	receive

This student seems to spell by pronunciation. He leaves letters out because he doesn't hear those letters when he says the word: a*d*venture, straig*h*t, pi*ct*ure. Sometimes, he doesn't choose correctly between two possible spellings for the same sound: mo*ti*on, rec*ei*ve, th*ei*r.

If you're lucky, you will notice some patterns in the words you have trouble spelling, and then you can train yourself to watch out for those trouble areas or those specific words that always give you problems.

However, even if you don't discover a pattern, there are some ways you can improve your spelling.

TO IMPROVE YOUR SPELLING
1. KEEP A SPELLING LIST.
2. BREAK WORDS INTO SYLLABLES.
3. MEMORIZE THE FOUR SPELLING RULES.

■ Spelling Cards

First, make a 3 × 5 card for each word whose spelling gives you trouble. Tape these cards to your bathroom mirror or on the cover of a notebook or on the bulletin board next to your phone—anywhere that you will see them every day. Practice a few words as you brush your teeth, or wait for class to start, or talk on the phone. Just seeing the words correctly spelled will help them to stay in your memory, but spelling them out loud or copying them a few times will help even more. Every three weeks or so take down some old cards and put up some new ones.

■ Syllables

Second, get into the habit of breaking words down into syllables. The dictionary will show you the syllables in a word. Every word is a combination of vowel sounds (*a, e, i, o, u,* and sometimes *y*) and consonant sounds (all the other letters). Each syllable in a word contains one vowel sound and usually one or more consonant sounds. It is easier to spell a word if you break it into syllables and can hear more easily the separate sounds of each part of the word. The words below are divided into syllables:

> sep a rate
>
> Feb ru ar y
>
> ad ven ture
>
> min i a ture
>
> ter ri ble
>
> ac cept ance
>
> oc curred

Seeing and hearing the syllables of words can help you spot the part of the word that's giving you trouble. Many people, for example, have trouble remembering the first *a* in sep*a*rate. You can handle a trouble spot like this by thinking of some memory trick such as, "There's *a rat* in the middle of separate," or by making a card with *sep A rate* written on it and studying it for a few weeks until you have mastered that word, or by using a dictionary to check your spelling of that word whenever you use it.

Breaking a word into syllables can also help you see if there is a root part of the word to which some prefix or suffix has simply been added. In the box are some examples of words that are generally in the same family.

RELATED WORDS		
Prefix	**Root**	**Suffix**
pro	ceed	ing
ex	ceed	
suc	ceed	ed
pro	claim	
re	cla(i)m	ation
dis	claim	er
in	duc(t)	tion
pro	duc(t)	tiv ity
pro	duc(e)	er
con	duct	

Recognizing a familiar part in an unfamiliar word may help you to spell the unfamiliar word correctly.

Studying the syllables in a word can also help you overcome the problem of leaving out letters. You can train yourself to see and/or hear all the letters. For example, if you had made a study card for *Feb ru ar y,* you could probably spell the word easily by concentrating on the sound that is frequently lost in pronunciation: Feb *ru* ar y.

■ *Spelling Rules*

Third, there are some fairly reliable spelling rules. Memorizing these rules can cut down on the number of individual words whose spelling you have to memorize.

1. Use *i* before *e*
   Except after *c,*
   Or when sounded as *a,*
   As in *neigh*bor and *weigh.*

<u>EXAMPLES:</u>

re ceive	re lief
con ceive	be lieve
de ceive	be siege

Exceptions (No rule is perfect!)
leisure, neither, weird, height

2. Words ending in silent *e* usually drop the *e* before adding a vowel suffix. The *e* remains with a consonant suffix.

<u>EXAMPLES:</u>

hide	+	-ing	=	hiding
name	+	-ed	=	named
desire	+	-able	=	desirable
drive	+	-er	=	driver
name	+	-less	=	nameless
care	+	-ful	=	careful
sincere	+	-ly	=	sincerely
amaze	+	-ment	=	amazement

<u>EXCEPTIONS</u>

judge	+	-ment	=	judgment
argue	+	-ment	=	argument
true	+	-ly	=	truly
peace	+	-able	=	peaceable
courage	+	-ous	=	courageous

and other ⎰peace ... soft *c* and *g* ⎱courage ... words with *a, o* or *u* suffixes

3. In a word ending with consonant *-y*, change the *y* to *i* before adding any suffix that doesn't begin with *i*.

<u>EXAMPLES:</u>

worry	+	-ed	=	worried
worry	+	-ing	=	worrying
lonely	+	-ness	=	loneliness
try	+	-ed	=	tried
try	+	-ing	=	trying
study	+	-ous	=	studious
silly	+	-ness	=	silliness

4. Words of one syllable or accented on the last syllable that end in a vowel–consonant pattern double the final consonant before adding vowel suffixes. The doubled consonant keeps the vowel sound short.

<u>EXAMPLES:</u>

slip	+	-ed	=	slipped
plan	+	-ing	=	planning
occur	+	-ence	=	occurrence
hid	+	-en	=	hidden
jam	+	-ed	=	jammed
permit	+	-ing	=	permitting

EXERCISE J

SUFFIXES					
-ed	-ing	-ous	-able	-ible	-ness
-ance	-ence	-ment	-ly	-less	-full

To each word given below, add as many of the suffixes in the table as you can. What spelling rules can you use for each word? Check the dictionary for each.

<u>EXAMPLE:</u>

manage	+	-ed	=	managed	Rule 2
manage	+	-ing	=	managing	Rule 2
manage	+	-able	=	manageable	Rule 2 (Excep.)
manage	+	-ment	=	management	Rule 2

1. grace + _____ = _____ _____

2. happy + _____ = _____ _____

3. grieve + _____ = _____ _____

4. prefer + _____ = _____ _____

5. equip + _____ = _____ _____

6. commit + _____ = _____ _____

7. pity + _____ = _____ _____

8. fit + _____ = _____ _____

9. transfer + _____ = _____ _____

10. state + _____ = _____ _____

● **Easily Confused Words**

In some cases, what looks like a misspelling is really a confusion between two similar words. Look at the following list. If any of these pairs of words give you trouble, make study cards for them or try to find some memory trick to help you remember the difference between them. Note that the spell-check function on your computer cannot determine which word is correct in the context of the sentence.

1. ac CEPT   ex CEPT
   (to receive)   (to exclude)

   He accepted the award.
   No one except his mother came.

2. af FECT   ef FECT
   (to influence)   (a result; to bring about)

   Her life affected us all.
   The effect was tremendous.
   The doctor effected her recovery.

3. cite   site   sight
   (to summon or quote) (place)   (the power to see; something seen)

   She cited the line from her coach to prove her point.
   The site for the new gym is on the corner.
   The sight of the sprained ankle made me sick.

4. DES ert   des SERT
   (a hot, dry place)   (a sweet served after a meal)

   Training would be difficult in a desert.
   I rarely eat desserts.

5. here   hear
   (in this place)   (to sense with the ears)

   I have lived here for forty years.
   You hear with your ears.

6. it's   its
   (it is)   (belonging to it)

   It's a shame you didn't win.
   Our team has lost its standing.

7. new   knew
   (not old)   (past tense of *know*)

Her new routine got better results.
I knew him before he was famous.

8. passed   past
   (went by)   (a time before the present)

   I passed the goal several times.
   In the past, women were not allowed to enter the race.

9. PRIN ci pal   PRIN ci ple
   (most important; head   (a fundamental law)
       of a school)

   His principal reason for becoming a principal was to make more money.
   Religion gives us an ethical principle to guide our actions.

10. right   rite   write
    (just; correct; that which (a ceremony)   (to form letters)
        is due to anyone)

    You're right; it is your right to have an attorney present.
    Funeral rites help us deal with death.
    The sponsor could write a very effective proposal.

11. scene   seen
    (a sight; part of a play)   (observed)

    I have never seen such a beautiful scene.

12. their   there   they're
    (belonging to them)   (in that place)   (they are)

    Their uniforms all looked alike there.
    They're clean now.

13. two   too   to
    (2)   (also; excessive)   (toward; for)

    Too has too many *o*'s.
    Zoo too has too many *o*'s.
    The two words sound alike to many people.

14. your   you're
    (belonging to you)   (you are)

    You're very possessive of your belongings.

15. whose   who's
    (belonging to whom)   (who is)

    Who's to say whose way is best?

EXERCISE K
Choose the correct word for the blanks in each sentence below.

(two, too, to)   1. Zaina sent _____ men _____ prison

because they admired her _____ much.

(affect, effect)   2. Could she have such an _____ on them? She never

thought her beauty would _____ them in a bad way.

(here, hear)   3. Zaina could not _____ well, but the incident

happened right _____.

(new, knew)   4. Zak and Nga _____ she would pass by here on

her _____ motorcycle.

(scene, seen)   5. They had _____ how she made even this poor

area a beautiful _____.

(your, you're)   6. Trust me, _____ not going to believe

_____ ears.

(principal, principle) 7. They thought that the basic _____ of might makes

right would be the _____ issue influencing Zaina.

(their, they're, there) 8. _____ fight to the death _____

proved _____ as fragile as love itself.

(accept, except)   9. Everyone was able to _____ their deaths

_____ Zaina.

(its, it's)   10. _____ a pity that violence is _____
own reward.

EXERCISE L
Edit the following sentences by underlining any misspelled words. Using your dictionary as necessary, write the correct spelling of the underlined words on the line beneath each sentence.

1. Aleksandr recieved a call from the regional athletic committee.

_____

2. They informed him that he past the initial screening.

_____

3. He would be their riseing star in there list of candidates.

_____

4. Aleksandr did not know weather to be scarred or happy.

_____

5. He had never concieved that he would subject himself too such intense competition.

_____

6. His liesure time was so limited that he thought he would never find a wife.

_____

7. He loved swiming but never met anyone at the pool.

_____

8. He hung up the phone after decideing to chose the desireable alternative.

_____

9. He prepared to meet the committee at there condoninium.

_____

10. There expecting a champion on they're way to there first meet.

_____

EDITING PRACTICE:
Underline any misspelled words in the following paragraph. Then rewrite it on a separate sheet of paper, correcting any spelling errors. Use your dictionary to check yourself.

Its know surprise to me that you one the gold metal. After seeing what occured during the figir skatting competision, I new you wood win. Beleive me, I was so proud of you're preformance. Your rhythm and controll couldn't help but effect the judges. Their can be no arguement that youre the best in your catagory. The other too skaters don't posess half your lovlyness on the ice. I relize you had to work long hours to succede. So please except a personnel word of congradulations from me on this happyest of occassions. Its a privledge to know you and be your freind.

▶ PROBLEMS IN SENTENCE CONSTRUCTION

In addition to monitoring for spelling in the editing process, you should also be checking for errors in sentence construction that may confuse or distract your reader. Review the problems of sentence fragments, subject–verb agreement, pronoun reference, pronoun agreement, adjective and adverb forms, misplaced and dangling modifiers, and shifts in verb tense and point of view.

● Sentence Fragments

(See also page 91.)

A base sentence expresses a complete idea by showing a subject involved in some action set in a time frame and not introduced by a subordination signal. A fragment is an incomplete idea that has been punctuated as if it were a base sentence. In essence, a fragment disguises itself as a sentence. Have you ever heard the expression, "It looks like a duck, walks like a duck, but is not a duck"? A fragment looks like a sentence (it starts with a capital letter and finishes with an end mark of punctuation). A fragment acts like a sentence (it tries to convey important information). Why then are fragments not sentences?

Fragment Type #1

FRAGMENT	**Halted before entering the track.**
EDITED	**The runner halted before entering the track.**

This fragment type disguises itself as a sentence but has **no subject.**

Fragment Type #2

FRAGMENT	**The athlete in the cut–off jeans.**
EDITED	**The athlete in the cut–off jeans smirked.**

This fragment type disguises itself as a sentence but has **no verb.**

Fragment Type #3

A.

Fragment	When I finally reached the bathroom.
Edited	When I finally reached the bathroom, I cried.

B.

Fragment	Which was always acceptable for women.
Edited	This behavior, which was always acceptable for women, seemed inappropriate.

C.

Fragment	Dancing blindly to music by Sting.
Edited	Dancing blindly to music by Sting, we realized we had gone to school together.

D.

Fragment	Frightened by what could happen.
Edited	Frightened by what could happen, we said goodbye.

E.

Fragment	To get home safely.
Edited	To get home safely, I called a taxi.

This fragment type disguises as a sentence but has **no base sentence.** This type is particularly difficult to spot because it sometimes has a subject and a verb in the subordinate word group.

Exercise M

Edit the following groups of words so they are no longer fragments.

1. Experienced some difficult moments during the summer.

_____

2. The symbol with the five circles.

_____

3. Because he could never keep quiet.

_____

4. Who used to live down the street from us.

_____

5. Calling her to attention every minute.

_____

6. Driven crazy by the nagging.

_____

7. Were just being boys.

_____

8. The short man in the uniform of his country.

_____

9. That struck the ground before the tree.

_____

10. Fighting his way through the surf.

_____

11. To give money to street people.

_____

12. Secured the splinter with a pair of tweezers.

_____

13. Whose leg has been twisted since the accident.

_____

14. Born into a family of good-humored souls.

_____

15. To sit in the auditorium alone.

_____

16. Feeling ill all the way home on the plane.

_____

17. The best athlete from the area.

_____

18. Although they lost the last game of the tournament.

_____

19. Charmed by the sound of her voice.

_____

20. If I ever see her again.

_____

Fragments are often pieces of long sentences that accidentally get broken off. Attaching them to the base sentence, before or after, often offers a simple solution. Sometimes you will prefer rewriting the fragment so that it has its own subject and its own verb that shows time.

FRAGMENT	When I am near the stadium. I will visit Kerri.
EDITED	When I am near the stadium, I will visit Kerri.
EDITED	I am near the stadium. I will visit Kerri.
FRAGMENT	Smiling broadly, Bruce walking down the aisle.
EDITED	Smiling broadly, Bruce walked down the aisle.
EDITED	Bruce smiled broadly. He walked down the aisle.

EXERCISE N
Edit the following groups of words so that there are no sentence fragments.

1. In the beginning. Sport was a religious cult. A preparation for life.

_____

_____

2. People wanted to gain victory over foes. To influence the forces of nature. To promote fertility among crops and cattle.

_____

_____

3. A basic need, which caused primitive people to play games. Actually helped
    them relieve tension. Served as an outlet for harmful urges.

    _____

    _____

4. Another reason for the origin of sports. Defending oneself. Defending the
    tribe. Practice to escape danger.

    _____

    _____

5. In cold climates. Games provided exercise. Making the blood run through
    the veins. Keeping people warm.

    _____

    _____

6. Some sports came from a desire to survive. Some enemies were natural and
    some supernatural. Humans and beasts.

    _____

    _____

7. Beginning as fertility magic. Ensuring birth. Sport also celebrated the return
    of spring. Numerous examples in ancient records.

    _____

    _____

8. A tug of war used in Assam, India. One team forces of evil. Another the
    increase in nature.

    _____

    _____

9. Watched by huge crowds. Wrestling matches in southern Nigeria. Took the
    form of a religious ritual. To strengthen the growth of crops.

    _____

    _____

10. Thinking sport a gift from the gods. Primitive people associated sports with religion. Even the first Olympic games were played in honor of Zeus.

_____

_____

An excellent way to spot fragments in paragraphs and essays is to read each sentence in isolation. Try editing your next assignment by reading the last sentence by itself. Examine it as though you were doing a sentence exercise in this book. Then, read the next-to-last sentence, and so on back to the beginning.

● Subject–Verb Agreement

(See also pages 149–155.)

In order to avoid confusing your reader, you have to be sure that the subjects and verbs in your sentences match. A singular subject needs a singular verb, and a plural subject needs a plural verb.

Most of the time, agreement is no problem since the form of the verb is usually exactly the same whether it is singular or plural. Problems with agreement can occur only when the verb is in the present form or the has-or-have-plus-participle form. These verb forms have two endings, one with an *-s* (for *he, she,* or *it* subjects) and one without (for all other subjects).

Note: Many people think that words become plural by adding *s*. This statement is true for many nouns but not for verbs. In fact, the opposite is true for verbs because the singular verb forms for many *he, she,* or *it* subjects add *s*. (He jumps, she writes, it kicks.) However, the verb forms for plural subjects do not end in *s*. (They jump, they write, they kick.)

Look at it this way:

> Jane runs. *(singular)*
>
> Jane and Bill run. *(plural)*
>
> Jane *has* run. *(singular)*
>
> Jane and Bill *have* run. *(plural)*

When the subject is obviously singular or plural, and it occurs in its usual position at the beginning of the sentence, you should have no trouble using the correct singular or plural verb.

EXERCISE O

In each sentence below, determine whether the subject is singular or plural; then make the verb agree with the subject by choosing the appropriate present tense verb form.

EXAMPLES:

(develop)   Carl Lewis **has developed** a new system for focusing on the event.

(find)   Viewers **find** our sports coverage thorough.

(have)   1. Wilma Rudolph _____ twenty-one brothers and sisters.

(cause)   2. Scarlet fever and pneumonia _____ her left leg to be paralyzed.

(set)   3. As a high school basketball star, she _____ a single scoring record of 49 points.

(become)   4. At sixteen, Wilma Rudolph _____ a member of the winning 100-meter Olympic relay team.

(commend)   5. They _____ her for being the outstanding athletics champion of the Olympics in Rome.

(win)   6. No other American woman _____ three track gold medals in the Olympics.

(call)   7. Europeans _____ her *la gazelle noire,* the black gazelle.

(make)   8. Her autobiography, *Wilma,* _____ her story widely known.

(establish)   9. Herself a mother of four, she _____ the Wilma Rudolph Foundation to help youngsters both athletically and academically.

(spend)   10. She also _____ much of her time as a lecturer, talk-show host, author, and goodwill ambassador.

There are a few situations where you may have trouble recognizing the subject or recognizing whether it is singular or plural. These are the situations you need to watch out for in editing your writing.

1. Subjects joined by *and* are plural. However, singular subjects followed by *as well as, together with,* or *in addition to* do *not* become plural.

   Swimming *and* bicycling (plural)

   Swimming *as well as* bicycling (singular)

   The gymnast *and* her coach (plural)

   The gymnast *together with* her coach (singular)

   Tennis *and* soccer (plural)

   Tennis *in addition to* soccer (singular)

2. Subjects joined by *or* and *nor* are considered separately. The subject closer to the verb determines whether the verb should be singular or plural.

   Kerri Strug or her *teammates* (plural)

   Her teammates or *Kerri Strug* (singular)

   Her hometown nor the *big cities* (plural)

   The big cities nor her *hometown* (singular)

3. Prepositional phrases after the subject do not change the subject.

   The *son* of the Weissmullers (singular)

   Some *challenges* from the doctor (plural)

   A first-rate *swimmer* with many different strokes (singular)

   Sixty-seven swimming *records* to his credit (plural)

4. *Here* and *there* are not subjects. These words signal a delayed subject with which the verb must agree.

   Here comes the *batter* (singular)

   Here come the *batters* (plural)

   There is a *wealth* of information (singular)

   There are a dozen *records* to be broken (plural)

5. These subject pronouns are always singular:

another	everybody	no one
anybody	everyone	nothing
anyone	everything	one
anything	much	somebody
each	neither	someone
either	nobody	something

   Everything is wonderful (singular)

   Neither fights as well (singular)

   Anyone gets tired competing (singular)

6. These subject pronouns are always plural:

both	many
few	several

   Few claim victory (plural)

   Several agree (plural)

   Many know (plural)

   Both cry (plural)

7. These subject pronouns may be either singular or plural, depending on what is being discussed:

all	enough	none
any	most	some

None of the practice time remains (singular)

None of the practice times remain (plural)

All of his practice is focused (singular)

All of the players are focused (plural)

Some of the uniform has (singular)

Some of the teammates arrive (plural)

8. Some subjects, called *collectives,* may appear to be plural but are considered singular in most cases. Collective nouns are nouns like *team, herd, troop, audience, group,* and *jury,* in which a number of individuals are considered as one unit. These nouns require a plural verb only when the members of the unit act as individuals rather than as part of the unit. (This happens rarely.)

The jury disagree on the verdict *(plural)*

The jury agrees on the verdict *(singular)*

The herd stampedes across the prairie *(singular)*

The team have their uniforms cleaned *(plural)*

The audience cheers that scene *(singular)*

EXERCISE P

Edit the following sentences so that the verbs agree with the subjects. Cross out any incorrect forms; write correct forms above them.

1. Women has the most to do with changing social attitudes.

2. Then, they takes a real role in sports.

3. Local women, as well as other supporters, creates an atmosphere for Helen

   Wills Moody and Suzanne Lenglen to duel on the tennis court.

4. In addition, Gertrude Ederle swim the English Channel.

5. Many women from all areas of the country finds it possible to compete in

   sports that only males enjoyed.

6. The number of girls in sports in high schools or in colleges in the 1970s increase 600 percent.

7. During this same decade, the King vs. Riggs tennis match or the Boston Marathon show women becoming more important in sports.

8. One of the most dramatic growth sports are running.

9. Today women runs in marathons.

10. Sheila Young, together with other Olympic medalists in speed skating, have taken up the sport of cycling.

11. In 1975, a professional circuit for women surfers were initiated.

12. Title IX legislation or private foundations is attempts to get equal monies and facilities for female sports.

13. Does noncontact sports fulfill the traditional glamour function of female sports?

14. Either Debi Thomas or Chris Evert Lloyd receive both popularity and money.

15. Are there still suspicion of the female athlete?

16. Some of the bowling tours remains separate because Barbara Thorberg's 217 average would rank her third among all pro bowlers.

17. Most experts, along with a group of private individuals, has thrown out previous outlandish myths about the physical abilities of women.

18. Neither a woman nor any girls I know wants to miss out on choosing their own sports to reach their full biological potential.

19. All of the people in this community feels that research on women and sports is biased.

20. Young people, with their own value system, determines how sports will be played.

● Pronoun Reference

(See also pages 239–243.)

A pronoun is a word that stands for a noun. For example:

> **Mary Lou Retton bought a car, and she paid for it in cash.**

In this sentence, *she* stands for *Mary Lou,* and *it* stands for *car.*

UNCLEAR REFERENCE	**When Mary Lou saw her teammates in trouble with some muggers, she ran toward them.**

Does *them* mean *teammates* or *muggers?*

In editing this sentence, you might write:

EDITED	**When Mary Lou saw her teammates in trouble with some muggers, she ran toward her teammates.**

EDITED	**Mary Lou ran toward her teammates when she saw they were in trouble with some muggers.**

● Pronoun Agreement

(See also pages 233–238.)

If a pronoun refers to a specific person, place, or thing, it must match the noun that it refers to. A singular noun *(chair)* requires a singular pronoun *(it).* A plural noun *(chairs)* requires a plural pronoun *(they, them).* A feminine noun *(Rachel)* requires a feminine pronoun *(she, her).* A masculine noun *(George)* requires a masculine pronoun *(he, him).* Nouns of indefinite gender *(the producer, the owner)* can use masculine or feminine pronouns *(he, him, she, her).*

EXERCISE Q

Using the list of pronouns below, show which ones would match each of the following nouns or groups of nouns.

Singular	Plural
I, me	we, us
you	you
he, she, it, him, her	they, them

1. the son of a shepherd _____

2. Abebe Bikila _____

3. the Olympic marathon winner _____

 4. the first gold medal winners from Black Africa _____

 5. Bikila's appendix _____

 6. running barefoot through the streets of Rome _____

 7. Abebe Bikila and Emil Zatopek _____

 8. wearing shoes in Tokyo _____

 9. a break in his fibia _____

10. Abebe's mother _____

11. one of Emperor Selassie's bodyguards _____

12. patriotism and idealism _____

13. a paraplegic _____

14. his fans and I _____

15. sportswriter Jesse Robinson and you _____

16. a gang of discontents _____

17. the Olympic record _____

18. a trip to Ethiopia _____

19. a pair of outstanding athletes _____

20. Bikila and I _____

EXERCISE R

Edit the following sentences to correct any errors in the use of pronouns.

 1. Neither the media nor the racists favored his winning.

 2. Muhammad Ali gave Sonny Liston his round.

 3. No one wanted their ears to hear, "They all must fall / In the round I call."

 4. A fan from his old neighborhood and his trainer gave his support by shouting,

    "Float like a butterfly, / Sting like a bee."

5. Muhammad Ali converted to the Black Muslim faith. He followed their beliefs.

6. Liston's comeback hopes were dashed by his punch in the first round.

7. Muhammad Ali was convicted as a draft evader. They were looking for an excuse to strip him of his title.

8. He helped defend black dignity. They became a symbol of resistance throughout the world.

9. With his "rope-a-dope" technique, Ali beat George Foreman so he again was the heavyweight champion.

10. Many fans thought Leo Spinks or Joe Frazier could beat Ali, but he would not fight him again.

EXERCISE S

Rewrite the following paragraphs to correct any errors in subject–verb agreement or pronoun agreement.

1. Stock-car racing claim Richard Petty as the King Richard of the sport. He has recently retired from many years on the national circuit. Petty attributes their success to the ability to work as a team with the crew. The combination of driver, car, and crew produce the results. Richard's brother Maurice tended to the mechanical end of the sport. He was always grateful to him. Their father raced and so has Richard's son. In fact, Lee Petty won the first Daytona 500, and then the next year, Richard beat him. Richard Petty has won millions of dollars in prize money, but he has always felt if you relaxed, you would wind up in the hospital.

2. Billie Jean King fight hard for equality in sports. She or Margaret Smith have a record twenty Wimbledon titles. She also won the U.S. championship at Forest Hills several times. Tennis changed from being an amateur to a professional sport. It was an important moment, and she was in the forefront. Billie Jean focused on money as the key to change. They judge you on how much you have made. In the famous Riggs–King match, Billie Jean be carried in on his Egyptian litter and Bobby Riggs in a rickshaw. She gave him a live white pig because she claim he is a male chauvinist. She do not want tennis to be reserved for the rich, the white, and the males. All of these actions makes her a fascinating sports star.

● Adjective and Adverb Forms

■ *Adjectives*

(See also pages 105–112.)

You use adjectives to describe a subject or other noun more precisely. In editing, you should be sure you have used the correct form of the adjective.

The basic form of the adjective is called the simple form, but adjectives can take more than one form to show different degrees of the quality they describe. For instance, to show that one exercise is more difficult than another, you might say:

This exercise was *harder* than the first one.

Or, to show that one bicycle was more recently acquired than another, you might say:

My bike is *newer* than yours.

This form of the adjective is called the *comparative* because it is used to compare two people or objects. The word *than* appears after the comparative form.

There is also a *superlative* form of the adjective for use when you want to compare more than two people or objects. For example:

This exercise is the *hardest* one in the set.

or

My bike is the *newest* one in the rack.

Notice that the word *the* usually appears in front of the superlative form of the adjective.

Here is how you construct the comparative and superlative forms of adjectives.

ADJECTIVES OF ONE SYLLABLE

OR

ADJECTIVES OF TWO SYLLABLES
ENDING IN *-OW* OR *-Y*

⟩ ADD *-ER* OR *-EST*

Simple		Comparative		Superlative
tall	⟶	taller	⟶	tallest
*fit	⟶	fitter	⟶	fittest
long	⟶	longer	⟶	longest
*big	⟶	bigger	⟶	biggest

†funny   ——→   funnier   ——→   funniest

yellow   ——→   yellower   ——→   yellower

*Most adjectives that end in a single consonant double the consonant before adding -er or -est.

†Change the -y to -i before adding -er or -est.

OTHER ADJECTIVES OF TWO SYLLABLES

OR

ADJECTIVES OF THREE OR MORE SYLLABLES

USE MORE OR MOST

Simple		Comparative		Superlative
exciting	——→	more exciting	——→	most exciting
villainous	——→	more villainous	——→	most villainous
isolated	——→	more isolated	——→	most isolated
awful	——→	more awful	——→	most awful
remarkable	——→	more remarkable	——→	most remarkable

A few adjectives have unique comparative and superlative forms:

Simple		Comparative		Superlative
good	——→	better	——→	best
bad	——→	worse	——→	worst
little	——→	less	——→	least

EXERCISE T

For each sentence below, supply the correct form of the adjective: simple, comparative, or superlative.

(deep)   1. East Africa contains one of the _____ pockets of track talent in the world.

(good)   2. Its track stars have set the _____ world and Olympic records.

(exciting)   3. Ethiopia, Kenya, Tanzania, and Uganda have produced some of the _____ long-distance runners.

(strong)   4. The whole of Africa has generated _____ national pride than many other places.

(true)   5. Why is this _____ in Kenya?

(enthusiastic)   6. Kenya is the _____ nation in Africa today.

(devoted)   7. Keino inspired _____ Kenyans by his performances in the metric mile.

(good)   8. Kenya supplies _____ incentives for its athletes than other countries.

(high)   9. One reason East Africans have excelled is that they have run since

childhood in _____ altitudes than others.

(long, hard)   10. They work _____ and _____ than their counterparts.

EXERCISE U
Edit the following paragraphs for any errors in adjective form.

    1. Hank Aaron was one of the abler hitters on his team, the Milwaukee Brewers. He hit homers that were better than anyone's. But he was the most coolest player of them all. He had the air of a more calm businessman even during the more dramatic moments of a game. Hank Aaron's patience got him through the more rougher moments. His best and most gloriest moment was achieving the home run title everyone had assumed would always be Babe Ruth's.

    2. Vince Lombardi demanded the better from his football players. His excitingest opportunity came when he signed as head coach of the Green Bay Packers who had won only one game during the previous season. He made practice the most demanding than the games. He knew his players had to be physically and mentally tougher. The hero Lombardi said, "You're going to have to live with pain." In their first game, the now ferociously Green Bay Packers defeated their arch-rivals, the Chicago Bears. The most remarkablest statistic of his career is that Lombardi's Green Bay team went on to win five National League championships and the first two Super Bowls.

■ *Adverbs*

(See also pages 112–119.)

Like adjectives, adverbs may take different forms to show the degree of the quality involved. For instance, if you want to say that one athlete worked with more care than another, you could say:

> **Jennifer did the workout *more carefully* than Judi.**

If you want to say that Jennifer used more care than anyone else, you could say:

> **Jennifer did the workout the *most carefully* of anyone.**

IN GENERAL, *-LY* ADVERBS FORM THE COMPARATIVE AND SUPERLATIVE
BY USING *MORE* AND *MOST*.

Simple	Comparative	Superlative
commonly ⟶	more commonly ⟶	most commonly
slowly ⟶	more slowly ⟶	most slowly
deeply ⟶	more deeply ⟶	most deeply

A few adverbs use *-er* and *-est* to form the comparative and the superlative:

Simple	Comparative	Superlative
fast ⟶	faster ⟶	fastest
late ⟶	later ⟶	latest
near ⟶	nearer ⟶	nearest

Some adverbs have special forms for the comparative and superlative:

Simple	Comparative	Superlative
well ⟶	better ⟶	best
badly ⟶	worse ⟶	worst

EXERCISE V

In each sentence below, supply the appropriate form of the adverb: simple, comparative, or superlative.

(academically)   1. Debi Thomas achieves _____ than most young
                      women her age.

(easily)   2. Even with the demands of ice skating training, she was

                      _____ accepted to Harvard, Princeton, and Stanford
                      universities.

(devotedly)   3. The person who acted _____ was her mother who
                      drove Debi 150 miles a day for four years to practice skating.

(enthusiastically) 4. Her mother pays _____ for skating lessons than she
                      did before Debi had won so many awards.

(fast)   5. Debi Thomas has become famous _____ than some
                      other women athletes.

(frequently)   6. Other family members contribute _____ than many
                        fans might imagine.

(late)   7. Debi Thomas has become _____ sweetheart of the
                        media.

(deeply)   8. Her success has affected young skaters _____ than
                        other women's.

(suddenly)   9. Debi Thomas _____ became the first African
                        American to win a senior national championship and the first
                        African American to win a world championship.

(physically)   10. She is perhaps _____ powerful performer ever seen
                        in figure skating.

EXERCISE **W**
Edit the following paragraph for any errors in adverb form.

Figure skating requires more of the grace of a ballerina. However, like a long-distance runner, the skater effortlessliest must endure and must have more of the precision of a diamond cutter. The better figure skaters are the most athletically and artistically. Especially in the school figures, the skater must concentrate the best. Judges look for the most originalitiest and the bestest flawlessness.

■ *Confusion of Adjectives and Adverbs*

(See also pages 120–124.)

Many times, you can't tell whether a word is an adjective or an adverb just by looking at it. While it is true that many adverbs end in *-ly,* the word *early* can be an adjective as well as an adverb. And words like *better, fast,* and *worst* can also be either adjectives *or* adverbs.

When you are editing, you need to look at how the word is used in the sentence in order to choose between the adjective form and the adverb form. For instance, look at these two sentences:

> **Young athletes are** *independent.*
> **They respond** *independently.*

Independent in the first sentence describes *young athletes. Independent* functions as an adjective telling *what kind* of people the young athletes are. In the second sentence, *independently* tells *how* the action of responding took place.

Which of the following two sentences contains an adverb?

> **Erica ran quickly.**
> **She seemed quick.**

In the first sentence *quick* tells *how* she ran. *Quickly* is an adverb. *Quick*, in the second sentence, describes *she*. *Quick* is an adjective.

You also use adverbs to modify adjectives or other adverbs as the following examples show.

Jeff looked especially handsome.

Handsome describes Jeff; *handsome* is an adjective. *Especially* tells *how* handsome; *especially* is an adverb.

The paramedics arrived at the meet unbelievably quickly.

Quickly is an adverb telling *how* the paramedics arrived. *Unbelievably* is an adverb telling *how quickly* they arrived.

EXERCISE X
Supply the correct adjective or adverb form for each of the following sentences.

(proud)   1. "Pop" Warner's parents were being too _____.

(quiet)   2. He installed several innovative ideas _____.

(bad)   3. Some people thought his idea was _____ when he outfitted the Stanford team in pants of red rather than khaki.

(devastating)   4. "Pop" Warner's crouch start looked _____ the first night.

(strange)   5. His single and double wingback formations seemed _____.

(agile)   6. Jim Thorpe was his most _____ player.

(diligent)   7. Pop Warner tried _____ to find protective padding for his players' thighs and shoulders.

(small)   8. His teams were so _____ that he had only three substitutes.

(complete)   9. The players had to be _____ familiar with several positions and trained to kick.

(practical)   10. When the hunchback play became _____ , Warner used the disguise against Harvard.

(real)   11. The fans responded _____ enthusiastically.

(clear)   12. The play was a _____ violation of expectations.

(blatant)   13. Pop was dismissed from Carlisle because of his _____ use of profanity.

(skillful)   14. He went on to _____ coach many other winning teams.

(proud)   15. Today many small town teams still _____ boast a Pop
      Warner League.

EXERCISE Y
Edit the following paragraph for correct use of adjective and adverb forms.

   Brian arrived at the gym prompt at 5:30, feeling tiredly. He quick changed
clothes, putting on a workout suit that was fresh washed and a pair of new sneak-
ers. Then, he went upstairs and did a strenuous workout. Thursdays, he always
worked his chest and arms. He did several sets of bench presses, raising and low-
ering the bar careful with completely concentration. After several other chest exercises, he blasted his biceps with super sets of curls. These helped his growth
tremendous. Incredible, he had gone from a 16-inch to a 19-inch arm in just two
months of real intensely exercises. Finished, he took a warm shower and was on his
way home by 7:30. After his workout, he felt total well.

● Misplaced Modifiers

(See also pages 128–133.)

You choose modifiers to clarify or describe a particular word in a sentence. In
order to avoid confusing your reader, you should be sure that the modifier is as
close as possible to the word it describes.

MISPLACED	**Look for problems in every warm-up with stretching.**
EDITED	**Look for stretching problems in every warm-up.**
EDITED	**Look for problems with stretching in every warm-up.**
MISPLACED	**Covered with mud and tar, Scott Hamilton worked hard to clean his skates.**
EDITED	**Scott Hamilton worked hard to clean his skates, which were covered with mud and tar.**
EDITED	**Scott Hamilton's skates, covered with mud and tar, were difficult to clean.**

● Dangling Modifiers

(See also pages 134–136.)

Your reader will get very confused if your sentence has a modifier that has nothing
to describe.

DANGLING	**Some companies offer Olympic training sponsorships while working full-time.**

EDITED	**Some companies offer Olympic training sponsorships to *athletes* who are working full-time.**
EDITED	**Some companies offer athletes Olympic training sponsorships as well as full-time employment.**
DANGLING	**In order to be a champion, long years of training are necessary. (Who wants to be a champion?)**
EDITED	**If *someone* wants to be a champion, long years of training are necessary.**
EDITED	**In order to be a champion, a *person* needs long years of training.**

EXERCISE Z

Edit the following sentences so that all modifiers are clearly related to the words they describe.

1. Pete Rose was never alone baseball people noted.

   _____

2. He was always accompanied by his bat giving an interview on the field.

   _____

3. He was forever swinging the bat sitting at his locker after a game.

   _____

4. Always close enough for Rose to reach, he later leaned it against the wall of his office.

   _____

5. His black Mizuno bat no longer had a reason to be with him.

   _____

6. He seemed to have lost something special in his office in Riverfront Stadium or in Plant City, Florida.

   _____

7. He seemed to be forever looking for that bat losing popularity with the public.

   _____

8. To calm down before a game, the buckets of bubble gum and bags of sunflower seeds are loaded into the dugout.

_____

9. Changing the equipment of the game, skepticism and outrage emerge.

_____

10. Stitched in Haiti and rubbed in mud from the Delaware, Pete Rose tossed the ball to the pitcher.

_____

● Shifts in Verb Tense

(See also pages 243–247.)

You can confuse your reader if you set up a certain time frame in your sentence and then don't follow it. In editing, check your verbs for consistency.

SHIFT	Nancy Kerrigan *left* for the rink, but suddenly her car *breaks* down.
EDITED	Nancy Kerrigan *left* for the rink, but suddenly her car *broke* down.
SHIFT	The new Super Bowl advertising campaign *will cost* ten million dollars. However, it *was* worth the money.
EDITED	The new Super Bowl advertising campaign *will cost* ten million dollars. However, it *will be* worth the money.

● Shifts in Point of View

(See also pages 247–249.)

Your reader can easily become confused if you keep moving the focus from *I* to *you* to *he* in your sentences. In editing, make sure your sentences keep the same point of view.

SHIFT	*I* like going to sports events where *you* can see the athletes' faces.
EDITED	*I* like going to sports events where *I* can see the athletes' faces.
SHIFT	An *athlete* preparing for an event should realize *you* will be judged on *your* form and timing.
EDITED	An *athlete* preparing for an event should realize *she* will be judged on *her* form and timing.

EXERCISE AA
Edit the following sentences for shifts in verb tense or point of view.

1. Kareem Abdul-Jabbar has dominated every court he steps on since you are twelve years old and 6′8″.

   _____

2. Although he could have gone to any school, he chooses UCLA under Coach John Wooden.

   _____

3. He scored 31 points in his first game and you know they beat the varsity team.

   _____

4. In his first varsity game the next year, he will score 56 points.

   _____

5. A student like Kareem should know that your religion is a serious matter, so he became a Sunnite Muslim.

   _____

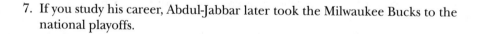

6. He is known for being an outstanding center and a fine man too.

   _____

7. If you study his career, Abdul-Jabbar later took the Milwaukee Bucks to the national playoffs.

   _____

8. A player like Abdul-Jabbar should realize you will be selected Rookie of the Year.

   _____

9. He has to wear shatterproof goggles because your eyes keep getting gouged in this no-contact sport.

   _____

10. He matches a record set by Wilt Chamberlain, the highest scorer in basketball history.

    _____

● Passive Verbs

(See also pages 82–86.)

A sentence can be written so that it emphasizes action being done *(active)* or action being received *(passive).*

ACTIVE	**Joshua ran the race.**
PASSIVE	**The race was run by Joshua.**

In most sentences, the active verb is more effective than the passive. Sentences with an active verb tend to be shorter and more direct. However, there are some times when you will want to use the passive verb. In editing, check any use of the passive verb to be sure it is appropriate.

Suppose, for instance, that you do not know who performed a certain action. You could write an active sentence such as:

Someone stole the sports equipment.

But that sentence would just emphasize your lack of knowledge. A passive sentence like

The sports equipment was stolen.

would probably be more effective since it puts emphasis on what you do know.

Or suppose that you know who performed an action, but you do not want your reader to know. For instance,

Bathing suits are not permitted in the Olympic village.

If you are the coordinator, this use of the passive may keep you from having to deal with complaints. However, readers may be suspicious of the passive that is used to conceal. Such use of the passive is frequent in bureaucratic and governmental writing where no one wants to assume responsibility for an action.

Finally, the passive verb can help you put emphasis on a certain idea. For instance, the sentence

The judges distributed the scores.

puts emphasis on the judges by making them the subject. The passive sentence

The scores were distributed by the judges.

puts emphasis on the scores by making them the subject. Which sentence you would use would depend on whether you were writing primarily about the judges or primarily about the scores.

EXERCISE BB

Rewrite each of the following sentences, changing active verbs to passive and passive verbs to active. In some sentences, you must supply a doer for the action. Be prepared to explain when you might choose one sentence or the other as more appropriate.

1. Basketball will be played by millions of people this year.

———————————————————————————

2. An indoor game was needed during the long winters between the football and baseball seasons.

———————————————————————————

3. James Naismith will design the game for the YMCA.

———————————————————————————

4. He had to move the ball with the hands rather than with a racket.

———————————————————————————

5. He gets the idea of a raised goal.

———————————————————————————

6. On the day the game was to be tested in 1891, peach baskets were used.

———————————————————————————

7. Each team will have nine players.

———————————————————————————

8. The YMCA network spread the game of basketball across the country.

———————————————————————————

9. Backboards are added in 1895.

———————————————————————————

10. The National Basketball League was composed of teams from Manhattan, Brooklyn, Philadelphia, and southern New Jersey.

———————————————————————————

EXERCISE CC

The following sentences contain a mix of all the problems discussed in this chapter. Edit them. Some sentences have more than one problem.

1. Jesse Owens break three world records in an hour.

---

2. Had sprained his back and was advised to withdraw from the meet.

---

3. Nazi Germany held the Berlin Olympics to glorify their Aryan ideal.

---

4. Anyone else would not have shown up for their event.

---

5. Afterwards, he said he had no pain during the event when it takes place.

---

6. He lost twenty pounds during the Berlin Olympics winning four gold medals.

---

7. The German audience loved him, but Hitler is not shaking his hand.

---

8. As an Olympic champion, endorsements were not in vogue.

---

9. Jesse Owens traveled the country to earn support even racing against a horse in Havana.

---

10. He would give himself a ten-yard disadvantage to make you think you could beat him.

---

11. Many people agree that because he was an African American he is not receiving some of the awards he should have.

12. Jesse Owens's story have a happy ending.

13. His optimism and energy make him the better survivor during the hard years.

14. In 1950, he was voted the most finest track star of the half-century.

15. In 1951, was honored in Germany as he jogged around the stadium as 75,000 Germans cheered.

EDITING PRACTICE:
Edit the following paragraphs to correct any problems in sentence construction that may confuse or distract a reader from the ideas being presented.

1. Spanish proverbs considering to be a whole person, a man must write a book, have a son, plant a tree, and fight a bull. People who are not familiar with the tradition view them with revulsion or enthusiasm. Bullfighting actually begins as a religious rite in which you worshipped the bull as a sacred beast. All over the world, the bull was viewed as a god. At times, even the bull's testicles was eaten and its flesh fed to boys. We can see today how bulls in advertising is equated with virility. Psychoanalysts have traced bullfighting to unconscious homosexuality and desires of patricide. As a cleansing of the soul, others have diagnosed bullfighting. People who watch them go home with a feeling of relief and even purification. People, like the matador, are trying to gain more better mastery over the beast within.

2. Babe Didrikson were firstly noticed when she was leading her team to the Amateur Athletic Union national basketball championship in the 1930s. Competing in the Olympics, six gold medals and four world records was awarded Ms. Didrikson. She was so good that her first try in the javelin throw breaks the world record by more than 11 feet. While many would have faded after her year of glory, you know Babe Didrikson would not. While barnstorming across America, running on a treadmill, starring as a pitcher for the Dodgers, even striking out Joe DiMaggio was just a few of her better unusual

sports activities. Didrikson's greater successes come on the amateur and profes-sional golf circuits. And later will receive the Associated Press Woman Athlete of the Year award six times.

▶ PUNCTUATION

(See also pages 164–181, 189–190, 202–205.)

Punctuation is an important way that you help your readers keep their focus on your main ideas. In editing, check to see that your punctuation clarifies rather than confuses.

DEFINITION OF A BASE SENTENCE

A GROUP OF WORDS THAT EXPRESSES A COMPLETE IDEA WITH
A **SUBJECT**
AND A **VERB** SHOWING PAST,   NOT INTRODUCED BY A
PRESENT, OR FUTURE TIME   **SUBORDINATION SIGNAL**

● Basic Sentence Patterns

Following is a list of the common sentence patterns and their punctuation. These will each be discussed individually.

1. Sentence.
   Sentence?
   Sentence!
2. Sentence; sentence.
3. Sentence; { however / moreover / nevertheless / therefore / thus } , sentence.
4. Sentence, { *but* / *or* / *yet* / *for* / *and* / *nor* / *so* } sentence.
5. Subordinate word group, BASE SENTENCE.
6. BASE SENTENCE subordinate word group.
7. BASE, subordinate word group, SENTENCE.

■ *Pattern 1*

A sentence by itself begins with a capital letter and ends with a period, a question mark, or an exclamation point. In all of the basic patterns, a question mark or an exclamation point could be substituted for the period.

> She can make it.
>
> Can she make it?
>
> She made it!

IMPORTANT: A subordinate word group (that is, any word group that does not fit the definition of a sentence) by itself should not be punctuated like a sentence. (See Chapter 5.)

> CONFUSING   **If he had been shorter.**
>
> CORRECTED   **She asked if he had been shorter.**
>
> CONFUSING   **Running swiftly.**
>
> CORRECTED   **Running swiftly, I caught up with the Yankees.**

■ *Pattern 2*

Two or more sentences joined without any coordination signal must be linked by a semicolon (;). Never use a comma in this pattern. (See Chapter 4.)

> **In one season, Lefty Gomez pitched twenty-six victories; Johnny Murphy was a competent relief pitcher.**
>
> ***Never:*** **In one season, Lefty Gomez pitched twenty-six victories, Johnny Murphy was a competent relief pitcher.**

■ *Pattern 3*

Two sentences joined by a linking adverb (*however, thus,* etc.) are punctuated with a semicolon placed after the first sentence and a comma placed after the adverb. This is simply a variation of pattern 2, except for the comma after the adverb. (See Chapter 4.)

> **Lefty Gomez served as manager for the Yankee farm team; in addition, he represented the Wilson Sporting Goods Company.**
>
> **Lefty Gomez had only a .147 batting average; however, he could always joke about his low average.**

■ *Pattern 4*

Two sentences joined with a coordination signal should be linked with a comma. An easy way to remember the coordination signals is by the first letters, which spell *boy fans: b*ut, *o*r, *y*et, *f*or, *a*nd, *n*or, *s*o. (See Chapter 4.)

> I'm throwing twice as hard, but the ball isn't going as fast.
>
> Lefty was called the Singular Señor, for he was of Spanish descent.

■ *Pattern 5*

When a sentence starts with a subordinate word group, a comma is a useful way of marking the end of the subordinate word group and the beginning of the base sentence. The marker helps signal the reader that the central idea in the sentence is coming. (See Chapter 5.)

> If Lefty were called by his given name, we would have heard shouts of "Vernon, Vernon."
>
> Even though Babe Ruth was king, Lefty was loved as the light-hearted lefthander.

■ *Pattern 6*

On the other hand, no punctuation is required when the subordinate word group follows the base sentence since the subordination signal by itself tells the reader the base sentence is finished. (See Chapter 5.)

> Lefty was elected to the Baseball Hall of Fame when he was sixty-three.
>
> Gomez outpitched the great Dizzy Dean while Murphy gave his customary help to win the game.

■ *Pattern 7*

When a subordinate word group interrupts the flow of the sentence, you should set it off with commas. (See Chapter 5.)

> Lefty Gomez, who was one of the slickest pitchers in the big leagues, was nearly flawless in the World Series.
>
> Lefty, without taking himself too seriously, said his success came from "clean living and a fast outfield."

EXERCISE DD

Edit the following sentences for correct punctuation. Use the list of sentence patterns to help identify the appropriate pattern, and write the number of the pattern in the space provided.

EXAMPLE:

___*4*___ Is Scotland where golf evolved, or is it the United States?

_____ 1. Since the grazing sheep in Scotland were the first golf architects the early players chose the best patches of turf.

_____ 2. The early golf courses in America were laid out but the courses were on land selected by players.

_____ 3. American golf architects have tried to imitate the Scottish links, because they want to preserve the traditions of the game.

_____ 4. The golf courses may be designed to be tough however golf equipment has made the game easier to play.

_____ 5. The famous St. Andrew's Club moved from cow pasture to cherry orchard it took two days to lay out the new course.

_____ 6. Tom Bendelow once he immigrated to the United States made his living by helping locals stake out golf course designs.

_____ 7. Macdonald laid out the first eighteen-hole course in the United States but Herbert Leeds laid out probably the best turn-of-the-century course in America.

_____ 8. Myopia's course has a dogleg fourth hole moreover holes such as this one have kept the course interesting for players right to the present.

_____ 9. As new designers emerged they tried to keep in mind the design philosophy that a poorly played shot should be a lost shot.

_____ 10. Macdonald's National in Southampton a course very carefully conceived remains a wonder for the student of golf architecture.

● Comma Splices and Run-on Sentences

If you fail to show with your punctuation where one idea ends and another begins, you run a great risk of confusing your reader. Sentences are the basic units of thought in writing, so sentences must be clearly marked.

COMMA SPLICE	**Olympic swimmers are often given their first lesson by one of their parents, the babies learn to paddle under water.**
RUN-ON	**Olympic swimmers are often given their first lesson by one of their parents the babies learn to paddle under water.**
EDITED	**Olympic swimmers are often given their first lesson by one of their parents. The babies learn to paddle under water.**
EDITED	**Olympic swimmers are often given their first lesson by one of their parents, and the babies learn to paddle under water.**
EDITED	**Olympic swimmers are often given their first lesson by one of their parents; the babies learn to paddle under water.**
COMMA SPLICE	**A seven-year-old child is the easiest to teach, some swimming instructors advise starting from birth.**
RUN-ON	**A seven-year-old child is the easiest to teach some swimming instructors advise starting from birth.**

EDITED	**A seven-year-old child is the easiest to teach. Some swimming instructors advise starting from birth.**
EDITED	**A seven-year-old child is the easiest to teach, but some swimming instructors advise starting from birth.**
EDITED	**A seven-year-old child is the easiest to teach; some swimming instructors advise starting from birth.**

EXERCISE EE

Edit the following sentences so that one sentence is correctly separated from another.

1. Florence Chadwick was recognized as a backstroke swimmer but she never got beyond second in the national championship.
2. Florence could swim at good speed for miles and miles she could not confine her talents to a small pool of water.
3. Coaches called the ambitious girl a misfit and they washed their hands of her.
4. Winners never quit, quitters never win.
5. She practiced every day in the rough ocean near her home in San Diego, she started winning long-distance races against men.
6. For years she had been working and saving money for the biggest swimming challenge, the English Channel crossing, she felt she was ready.
7. In a boat beside her, her father cheered her on he crouched and fed her from time to time.
8. Thirteen hours later, Florence Chadwick stepped out of the icy waters, she had become famous.
9. In 1952, she broke another long-standing record she swam the harsh Catalina channel in eighteen hours.
10. Florence Chadwick has been called the Queen of the World's Waterways, she conquered the English Channel, the Bosporus, and the Dardanelles.

● Commas

The basic function of the comma is to separate. As you can see from the sentence patterns shown in this chapter, commas may separate two or more equally important ideas, or they may separate a more important idea from a less important one used as an introduction or an interrupter.

■ *Commas with Coordinate Ideas*

A series of coordinate (equally important) adjectives should be separated by commas:

> **Walter Camp was short, young, and tough.**
>
> **This determined, imaginative man became the "father of American football."**

You can tell that adjectives are coordinate if you can reverse their order:

> **In 1876, Walter Camp was an ambitious, hard-working, and honest student at Yale.**

In 1876, Walter Camp was an honest, hard-working, and ambitious student at Yale.

In a sentence where you cannot reverse the order, no commas are used:

Four tall players / tall four players

Tall and *four* are not really coordinate adjectives here. They do not modify the same word. *Tall* modifies *players,* but *four* modifies *tall players.*

Commas are used only where the adjectives are coordinate. Here are other examples of commas with a series of coordinate ideas:

coordinate subjects
Rugby, football, and soccer combined to make the game of the day.

coordinate verbs
Walter Camp *imagined, designed, and implemented* revolutionary ideas for football.

coordinate complements
He gave the game *a complete new set of rules, the scrimmage method, and team signals.*
The Father of American Football handed down the scoring

coordinate modifiers
system *for touchdowns, field goals, and some penalties.*

coordinate sentences
Camp became the champion of football, for he had to fight to save the game from college administrators who thought it was a waste of time.

Although the comma before the *and* in a series is sometimes omitted, that comma can make a significant difference in the meaning of a sentence.

Cook ordered a green sweater, a case of champagne, a car with leather upholstery, and a radio.

Without the last comma, it is not clear whether Cook ordered a car and a radio separately, or a car with a radio in it.

Exercise FF
Edit the following sentences to make the coordination of parts clear to the reader.

1. Oarsmen football players and golfers were the idols at the turn of the twentieth century.
2. Rowing victories were featured in newspapers on the radio and over backyard fences.

3. Earning a living as a bricklayer rowing single sculls with a passion dreaming of winning the championship, John B. Kelly stayed focused on his goal.
4. Achieving scoring and repeating, Kelly gained a reputation of outstanding oarsman and Olympic champion.
5. His reputation soared flourished but vanished when the most hallowed race in Henley-on-Thames rejected him because he was a mere bricklayer.
6. Kelly waited patiently suffered disappointment and expressed anger.
7. Kelly the American champion oarsman could do little about the rejection the degradation the insult.
8. He went to Antwerp Paris and London.
9. Kelly's son John Jr. was trained taught and inspired by his father.
10. He brought his father vengeance when he won the Diamond Single Sculls the Championship Single Sculls and the Quarter-Mile Single Sculls.

■ *Commas with Subordinate Ideas*

Subordinate ideas need to be separated from the main idea in two situations. The first is when the subordinate idea precedes the main idea.

> *Ms. Oakley,* your fans are waiting.
>
> *Back in the last century,* someone showed a rifle to Annie Oakley.
>
> *Fascinated by the weapon,* she insisted on being shown how to use it.
>
> *Lifting the gun to her shoulder,* Annie fired the weapon.
>
> *To become an expert shot,* she practiced in the woods.
>
> *When Annie brought home so much quail that her father was able to start a thriving trade,* she was actually supporting her whole family.

The second situation calling for a comma is when the subordinate idea interrupts the main idea.

> I think, *my friend,* that Annie had earned enough to pay off the mortgage on the family farm.
>
> Word about Annie, *"Little Sure Shot,"* spread throughout the country.
>
> Buffalo Bill Cody, *despite hearing about the young girl's abilities,* had to see for himself.
>
> Her demonstration, *however,* astonished him.
>
> Ten minutes later, Buffalo Bill Cody, *humbled but excited,* offered Annie Oakley a contract.
>
> The audiences, *filled with excitement,* marveled at her feats with a rifle.
>
> Her favorite one, *if you want my opinion,* was hitting pennies tossed into the air.

In both situations, you use the commas to be sure that your reader is aware of what is the most important idea in your sentence—the base sentence. In a case where you begin with the base sentence and follow it with a less important idea, it is not usually necessary to separate the ideas with a comma.

> **Annie Oakley had someone toss 5,000 pennies in the air *as she proceeded to hit 4,777 of them.***
>
> **Annie defeated a male challenger *who asked her to marry him on the spot!***

Note that sometimes a subordinate idea in the middle of a sentence is *not* an interrupter; it is an important part of the main idea. For instance:

> **Any girl *who had such a keen eye* was bound to have movies made about her.**

Here the idea *who had such a keen eye* is necessary to the meaning of the sentence and should not be cut off from the main idea by commas.

USES OF THE COMMA

To separate coordinate ideas:
> **Annie Oakley fired at the Kaiser's cigarette, but she did not hurt his moustache at all.**
> **Annie was a remarkable shooter, an incredible legend, and a stunning symbol.**

To separate subordinate ideas from the base sentence:
> **A native of Cincinnati, Annie Oakley was known to all the world as "Little Sure Shot."**
> **Annie Oakley, a native of Cincinnati, was known to all the world as "Little Sure Shot."**

EXERCISE GG
Edit the following sentences, using commas to keep the reader's attention focused on the main idea.

1. By the time Willie Shoemaker reached his tenth birthday he was faced with a sad fact.
2. Although he was the eldest of five boys in his family he would always be the smallest of the lot.
3. "I've just not grown like the others" said Willie.
4. Willie who was always thin and tiny weighed barely 90 pounds when he entered high school.
5. Despite his small size and weight Willie managed to be a star in boxing and wrestling in high school competitions.

6. He believed kind reader that no matter what he did he would remain small.
7. Marking time until he grew up he finally made a bold decision.
8. Once he left school he went to work as an exercise boy at the Bay Meadows Racetrack.
9. Shoemaker only sixteen at the time decided he was going to become a jockey.
10. His first year as a jockey which established him solidly in his new career netted him $40,000.
11. Nicknamed "Silent Shoe" Willie kept to himself and acted as if nothing unusual had happened.
12. By winning 485 races in 1953 the pint-sized jockey established an all-time record.
13. "The Shoe" who continued to star in the headlines became the first jockey in history to win more than two million dollars in racing purses during one year.
14. When he misjudged the finish line, he actually won the Kentucky Derby but lost the race.
15. Becoming a turf immortal, Willie Shoemaker became a giant in horse-racing history.

EXERCISE HH
Edit the following sentences for appropriate use of commas.

1. After the Civil War the three new sports were baseball bicycling and lawn tennis.
2. Baseball the spectator sport was a man's game.
3. The bicycle-built-for-two moved women out into the sunshine and tennis kept them there.
4. By the time golf took hold in the 1890s women were ready to play.
5. A precedent which was set in Scotland was known as the Ladies' Green at St. Andrew's.
6. At the Shinnecock Hills Golf Club in New York the wives of the members convinced their husbands to create a nine-hole course for ladies only.
7. In places where the men could not be persuaded to share women created their own courses.
8. In Morristown New Jersey a group of female golfers organized a club built a seven-hole course and opened it for play in 1894.
9. The Brookline Country Club offered a restaurant bedrooms bowling alley lawn tennis a racing track and now a golf course.
10. Enthusiasm for golf grew crowding set in and women were frequently forced to make room.
11. The men who had financed the first women's golf club took the club back voted in an all-male slate of officers and offered a woman an "honorary presidency."
12. The only club that was not confiscated by men was the Women's National in New York.
13. Women golfers handicapped in their early efforts by their male counterparts were hampered also by fashions.
14. In spite of adversity the hardiest of women golfers kept on playing.

15. Robert Cox of Scotland donated a graceful thistle-topped silver loving cup the trophy that is still in competition.
16. Margaret Fox became a medalist a co-medalist and three times a semifinalist.
17. For some reason women's golf grew and prospered in Philadelphia as nowhere else.
18. Pansy Griscom was another of the early champions; she had a long career in golf drove a Red Cross ambulance in World War I and in fact was probably the first woman in Philadelphia to own and drive an automobile.
19. During World War I when all USGA championships were suspended an exhibition match to benefit the Red Cross was witnessed by a tall athletic fifteen-year-old girl.
20. This girl Glenna Collett had been a swimmer a diver and a baseball player on her brother's team and she would later become America's first great female golfer.

EDITING PRACTICE:
Edit the following letter to correct any errors in spelling, sentence structure, or punctuation.

Dear Freind,

The Special Olympics an organization which provides atheletic comitition for the mentally retarded continue to develope expand and improve it's programs. Approximately 10,000 atheleets in our state now participating in some phase of this program.

We are currantly involved in planing for our Winter Games in January. Because of last years overwhelming sucess, 130 special athletes have been invited to particapate this year.

As with any activity of this nature the winter program involve considerable expence. A partisapents lodging meals equipment and transportation requires an allocation of $175.

The Special Olympics Comittee would like to invite your group to except the challinge of supporting our program. Your contribution to help our Special Olympians reaching the finish line.

The sucess of our programs have been so large dependant on the involvement of individual's and community groups and it is only threw these cooperative efforts that we have been able to grow.

Thank you for your consederation of this request.

◀ *Acknowledgments* ▶

Corel GALLERY. © Corel Corporation, 1994. All rights reserved. Pages 3, 34 right, 65, 69, 70, 90, 95, 102, 107, 110, 122, 143, 159, 167, 178, 190, 207, 211, 212, 236, 241, 275, 282, 292, 298, 343, 355, 366.

© DeskGallery, Zedcor, Inc. All rights reserved. Pages 54, 74, 129, 151, 162, 219, 315.

Metro ImageBase, © 1988–1992 Metro Creative Graphics, Inc. All rights reserved. Pages 183, 203, 288, 309, 319, 324, 337, 351, 404, 407, 414.

LifeART Images. Copyright © 1989–1997 by TechPool Studios, Cleveland, OH. All rights reserved. Pages 43, 128, 227, 305.

Courtesy of Tech Graphics. Pages 16, 50, 173, 418.

Courtesy of Gary Moore. Pages 19, 20, 28, 34 left, 135, 195, 214, 245, 255, 271, 278, 352.

Page 375. Reprinted with permission of Macmillan USA, a Simon & Schuster Macmillan Company, from *Webster's New World College Dictionary,* Third Ed., Copyright © 1996 by Simon & Schuster Inc.

◀ *Index* ▶